100 BULLETS: D I R T Y

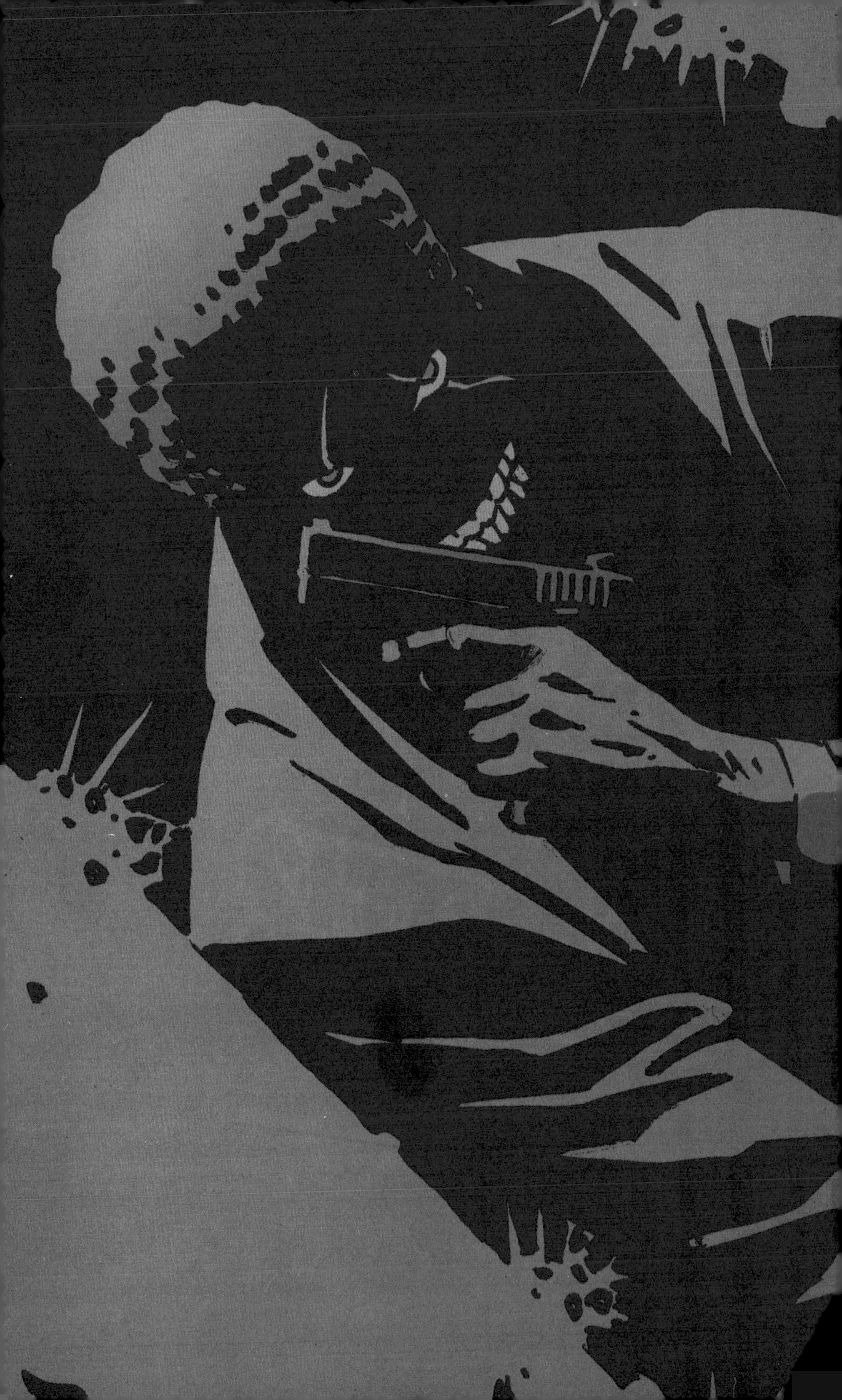

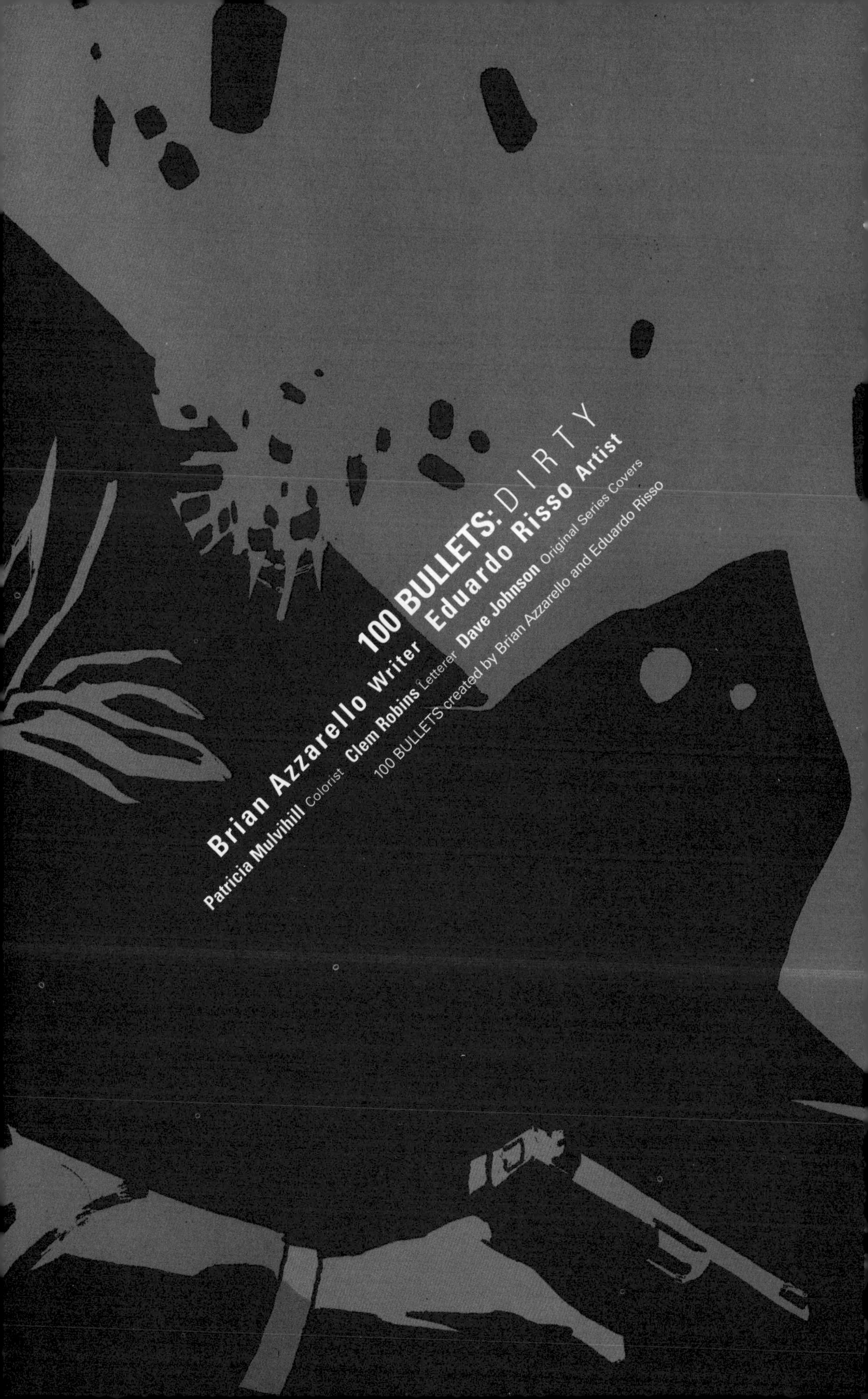

100 BULLETS: DIRTY

Brian Azzarello Writer
Eduardo Risso Artist

Patricia Mulvihill Colorist Clem Robins Letterer Dave Johnson Original Series Covers

100 BULLETS created by Brian Azzarello and Eduardo Risso

Karen Berger Senior VP-Executive Editor **Will Dennis** Editor-original series **Casey Seijas** Assistant Editor-original series
Scott Nybakken Editor-collected edition **Robbin Brosterman** Senior Art Director **Louis Prandi** Art Director **Paul Levitz** President & Publisher
Georg Brewer VP-Design & DC Direct Creative **Richard Bruning** Senior VP-Creative Director **Patrick Caldon** Executive VP-Finance & Operations
Chris Caramalis VP-Finance **John Cunningham** VP-Marketing **Terri Cunningham** VP-Managing Editor **Alison Gill** VP-Manufacturing
Hank Kanalz VP-General Manager, WildStorm **Jim Lee** Editorial Director-WildStorm **Paula Lowitt** Senior VP-Business & Legal Affairs
MaryEllen McLaughlin VP-Advertising & Custom Publishing **John Nee** Senior VP-Business Development **Gregory Noveck** Senior VP-Creative Affairs
Sue Pohja VP-Book Trade Sales **Steve Rotterdam** Senior VP-Sales & Marketing **Cheryl Rubin** Senior VP-Brand Management
Jeff Trojan VP-Business Development, DC Direct **Bob Wayne** VP-Sales

Cover illustration by **Dave Johnson** and **Eduardo Risso**.
Special thanks to **Eduardo A. Santillan Marcus** for his translating assistance.

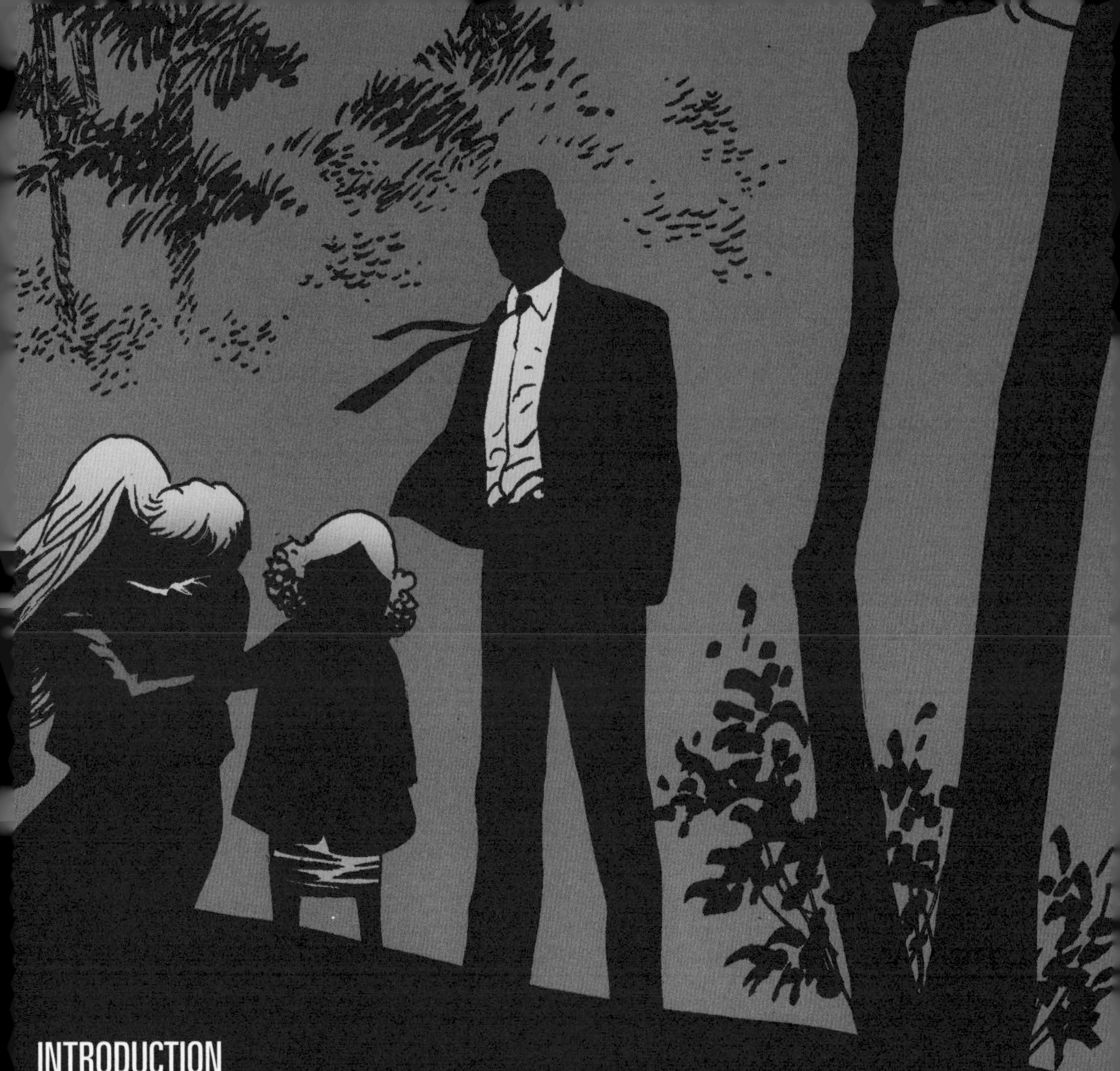

INTRODUCTION

Write an introduction... Yes, of course! Why not? It's an excellent opportunity, and I never did anything like this before (plus, we are so close to the end)... But I'm an artist! I have nothing to do with writing. Well, how hard can it be?

Looking back, it wasn't easy for me to move from the pleasures of reading comics to the pleasures of making them. The idea seemed so simple when I was a boy, but the many stumbling blocks that I encountered along the way forced me to recognize its cruel reality. The one thing that helped me to overcome these obstacles was the confidence that my early years in school and my first work experiences had brought me.

The main thing I learned in school was that I don't like to study, but since I *had* to, I also learned to manage my time well. My first couple of jobs, in turn, helped make it clear to me which profession I should choose. I began working at an early age helping my father in a garage, and in high school I split my time between studying, hard work and friends. Nowadays, I remember the experience with gratitude, not only because it taught me to value self-sufficiency but also because it showed me that work and play can be balanced so that neither has to suffer — given the energy of youth and the right priorities, of course.

Those jobs where I had to share space and time with a lot of people were the ones that pushed me towards comics. One day I realized that being part of a company — any company — meant that regardless of the fact that we were all pursuing a common goal, there was always going to be a sword hanging over me, and my head could be the one to roll if things went wrong. That was the day it became clear to me that I had to put all my energy into doing what I really loved.

Time has demonstrated to me that I made the right decision.

My chosen profession has given me more than I ever could have hoped for — especially the opportunity to continue living like Peter Pan, which is how I feel when I start to draw a story. I'm one of those readers who immediately gets sucked into characters' lives, and I try to keep that mindset when I'm creating as well. In addition to paying attention to the nuts and bolts of drawing, I also run everything past my inner Peter Pan to make sure all the elements are working properly to make the work engrossing. It's my small personal madness.

¡Caramba! I wasn't even paying attention, but here I am writing away!

A lot of people have told me that I should write my own stories. Many artists do this, of course, but illustrating your own words isn't a guarantee of quality. I suppose that anyone can write, but people who can do it *well* are definitely a minority. With 100 BULLETS, I have had the luck to work with someone who writes not just *well*, but is without a doubt one of the *best*.

If you're going to try to create a story that takes years to unfold, you have to give it something more than simple action and clever dialogue. It needs to have an outstanding plot — something that Brian Azzarello has certainly brought to 100 BULLETS. Of course, this isn't the only virtue that defines a good scriptwriter. He or she also has to know how to handle the timing of a story, a key element that is often overlooked but which I regard with the highest importance. The ability to choose the perfect moment to cut off the action or switch scenes is something that few writers have mastered, and Brian is definitely among them.

Besides his abilities as a writer, however, I have to call attention to another quality of Brian's which is also fairly uncommon: his generosity. There aren't many people who would give a collaborator so much latitude with their creation, especially on such a monumental work. But believe it or not, such generosity does exist, and Brian is a shining example of it.

All of us who have worked on 100 BULLETS have been given the space to flourish, and the result is that every aspect of the book displays its own distinctive quality — particularly the covers, as crafted by Dave Johnson. It might have been simpler if I had drawn them myself, but believe me, I could never have made so many covers that stood out on the shelves the way Dave did. He works with another quality that profoundly moves me: intelligence. He thinks before doing. That gives us something powerful enough to make the title instantly recognizable at a glance among hundreds of other comic books. It's sublime!

Coloring is another thing that's easy to overlook, but when the right colors are in the right place they can help a lot to sell the drama. It takes much more than just having access to a computer and its millions of available hues, though. Colors can provide the perfect finishing touch to a work, but placing them without a good eye and a solid design sense can generate a visual mirage that detracts from the drawing instead of enhancing it. Fortunately, Patricia Mulvihill has an abundance of chromatic talent, and her work has imbued the series with a distinctive aura of grace and elegance.

Clem, my unknown friend, I must finally admit here that I had never before paid attention to the fonts used in comics. What an oversight! Thank you for teaching me that lettering is a fundamental part of a comic book, one that works side by side with narration, composition and all of the other elements of this unique storytelling medium.

We all make a great team — and whether this is just pure luck, or the result of a careful plan constructed by the editors who trusted in us as professionals and gave us the freedom to do whatever we felt was needed to improve the series chapter by chapter, is an open question. My money is on the latter, my friends.

Life has taught me that luck can be around any corner, but if you turn the wrong way it will find someone else. With 100 BULLETS, I managed to turn the right way. Thanks Axel, Will, Casey, Karen — and thanks to you, our readers.

— Eduardo Risso
June 2008

A native of Leones, Argentina, Eduardo Risso began drawing professionally in 1981 with the magazine strips "Julio Cesar" and "El Angel." In 1986 he began an association with writer Carlos Trillo that continues to this day — their collaborations include the titles Fulù, Simon: An American Tale, J.C. Benedict, Chicanos and Borderline. After breaking into American comics in 1997, Risso first worked with writer Brian Azzarello on the 1998 Vertigo miniseries JONNY DOUBLE, which led directly to their partnership on 100 BULLETS as well as the DC graphic novel BATMAN: BROKEN CITY. Risso's work on 100 BULLETS has earned him three Eisner Awards, two Harvey Awards and the Yellow Kid Award.

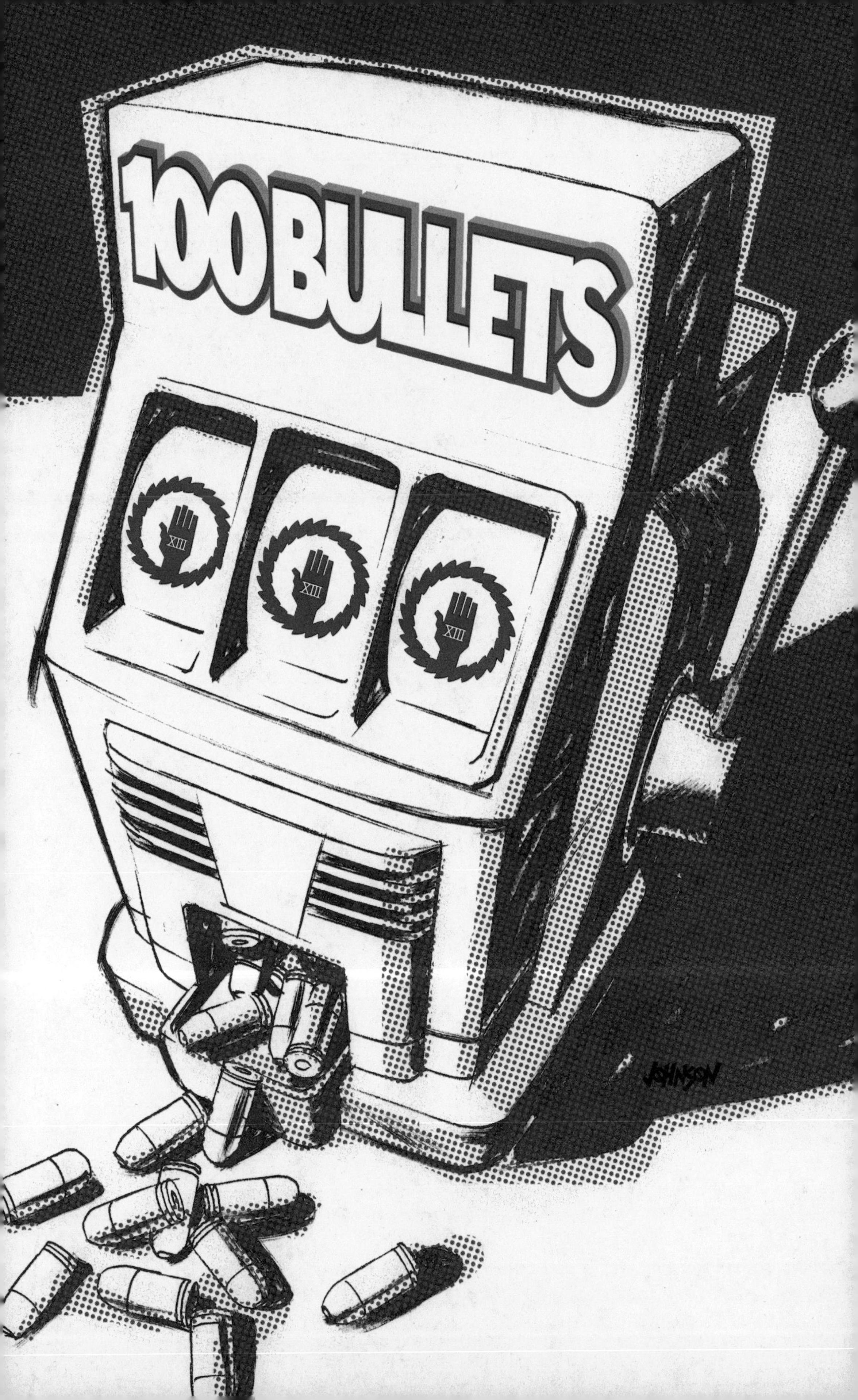
100 BULLETS
XIII
XIII
XIII
JOHNSON

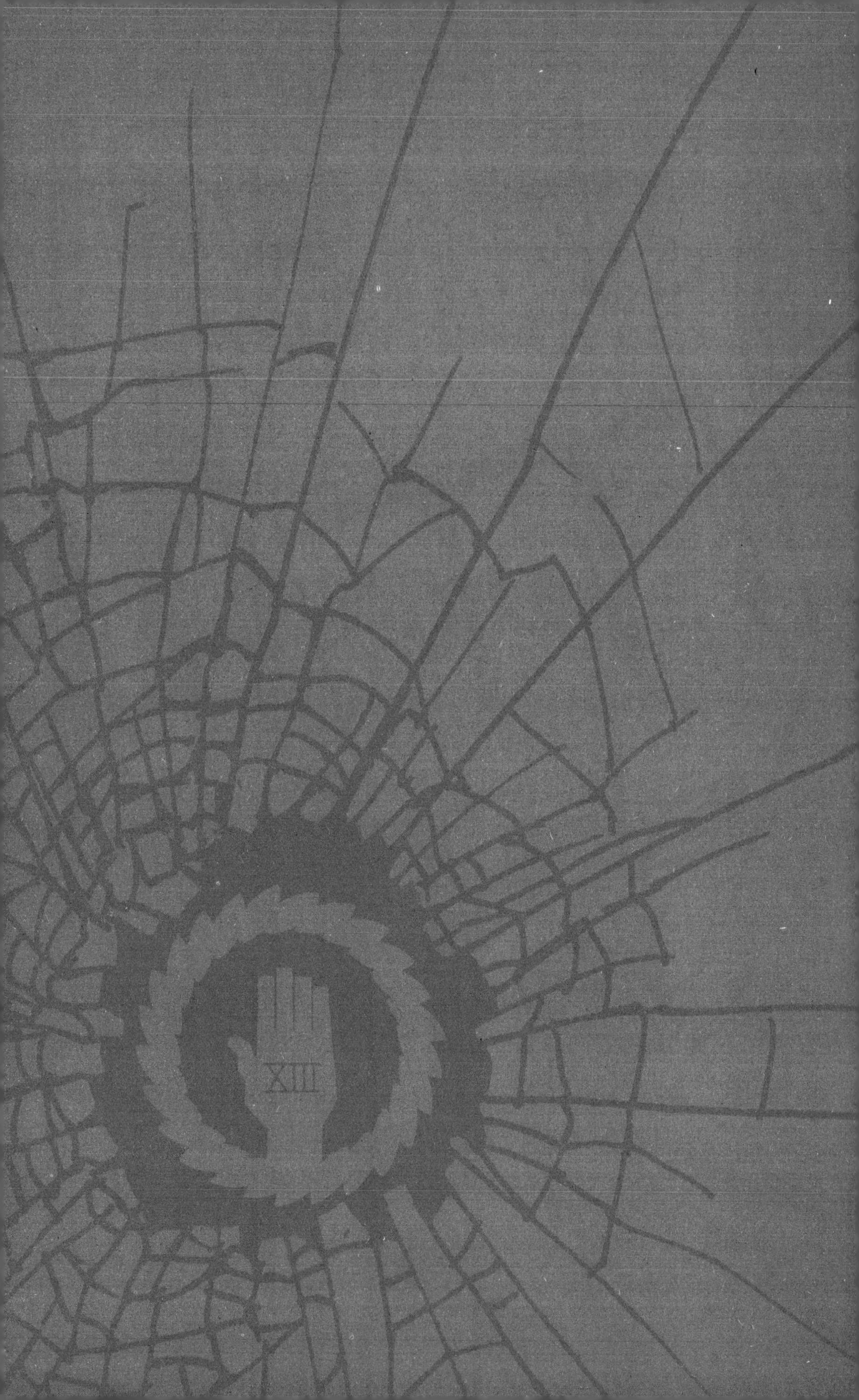
XIII

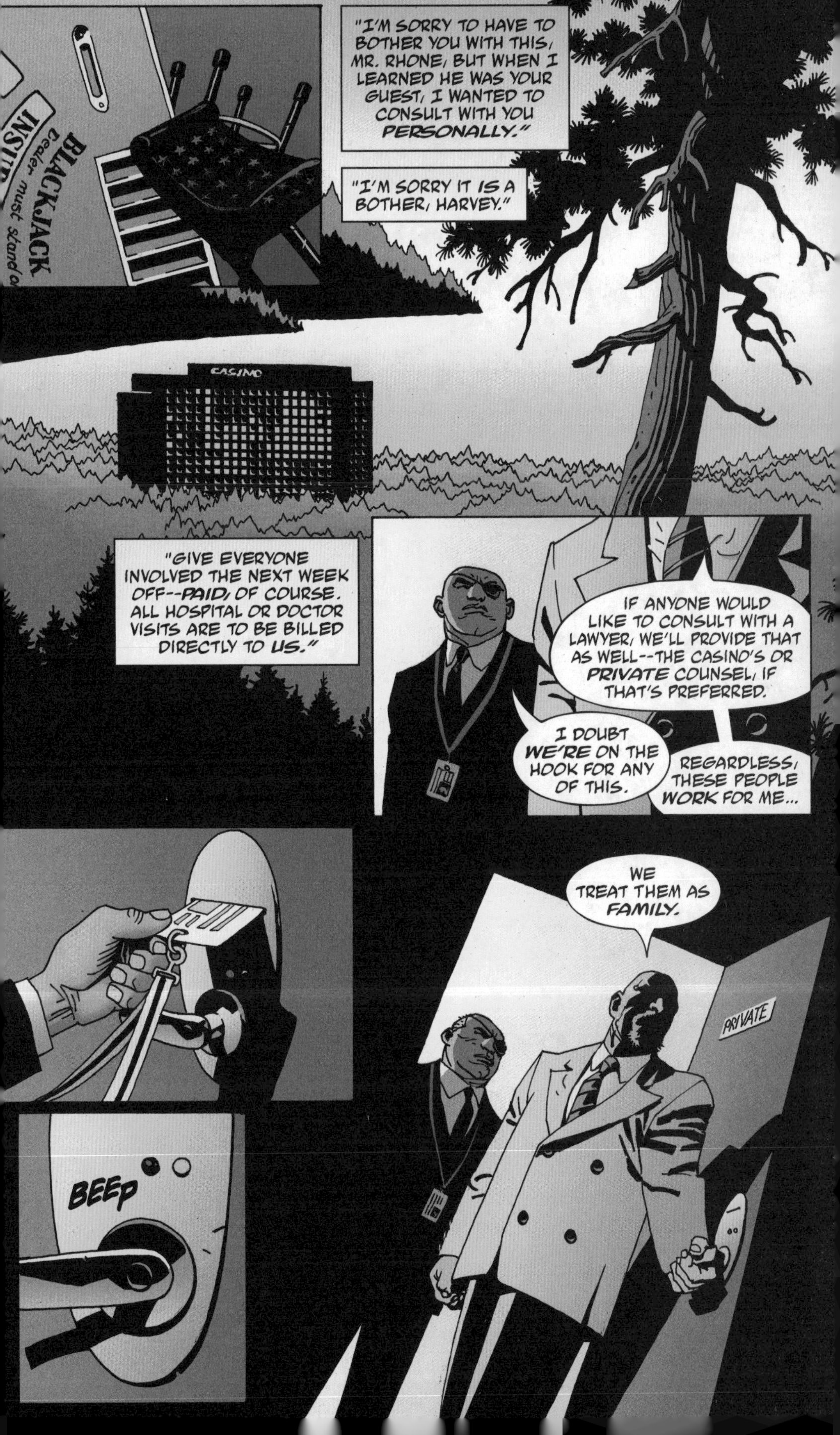
BLACKJACK
"I'M SORRY TO HAVE TO BOTHER YOU WITH THIS, MR. RHONE, BUT WHEN I LEARNED HE WAS YOUR GUEST, I WANTED TO CONSULT WITH YOU PERSONALLY."
"I'M SORRY IT IS A BOTHER, HARVEY."
CASINO
"GIVE EVERYONE INVOLVED THE NEXT WEEK OFF--PAID, OF COURSE. ALL HOSPITAL OR DOCTOR VISITS ARE TO BE BILLED DIRECTLY TO US."
IF ANYONE WOULD LIKE TO CONSULT WITH A LAWYER, WE'LL PROVIDE THAT AS WELL--THE CASINO'S OR PRIVATE COUNSEL, IF THAT'S PREFERRED.
I DOUBT WE'RE ON THE HOOK FOR ANY OF THIS.
REGARDLESS, THESE PEOPLE WORK FOR ME...
BEEP
WE TREAT THEM AS FAMILY.
PRIVATE

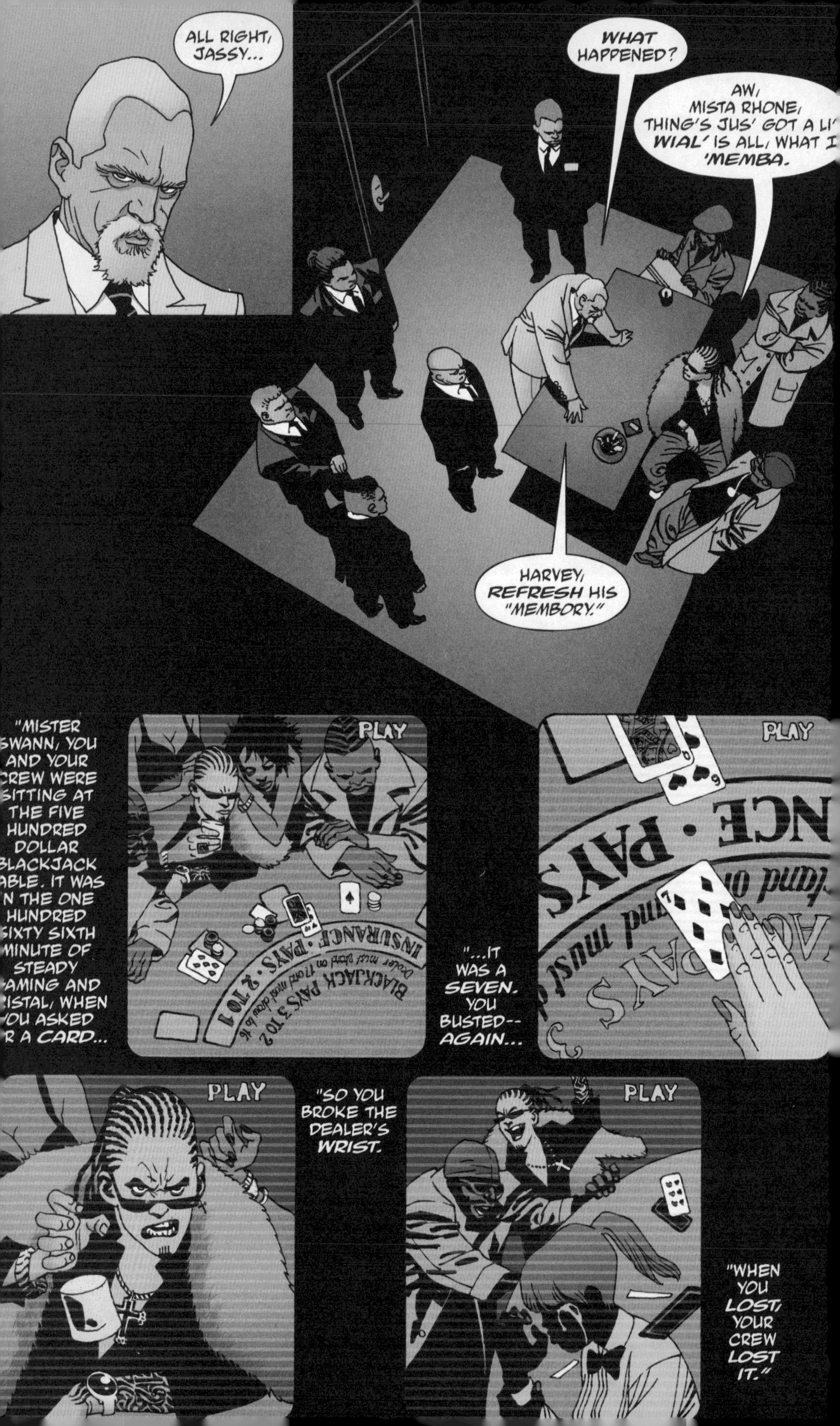
ALL RIGHT, JASSY...
WHAT HAPPENED?
AW, MISTA RHONE, THING'S JUS' GOT A LI' WIAL' IS ALL, WHAT I 'MEMBA.
HARVEY, REFRESH HIS "MEMBORY."
"MISTER SWANN, YOU AND YOUR CREW WERE SITTING AT THE FIVE HUNDRED DOLLAR BLACKJACK ABLE. IT WAS N THE ONE HUNDRED SIXTY SIXTH MINUTE OF STEADY AMING AND RISTAL, WHEN OU ASKED R A CARD...
PLAY
"...IT WAS A SEVEN. YOU BUSTED-- AGAIN...
PLAY
PLAY
"SO YOU BROKE THE DEALER'S WRIST.
PLAY
"WHEN YOU LOST, YOUR CREW LOST IT."

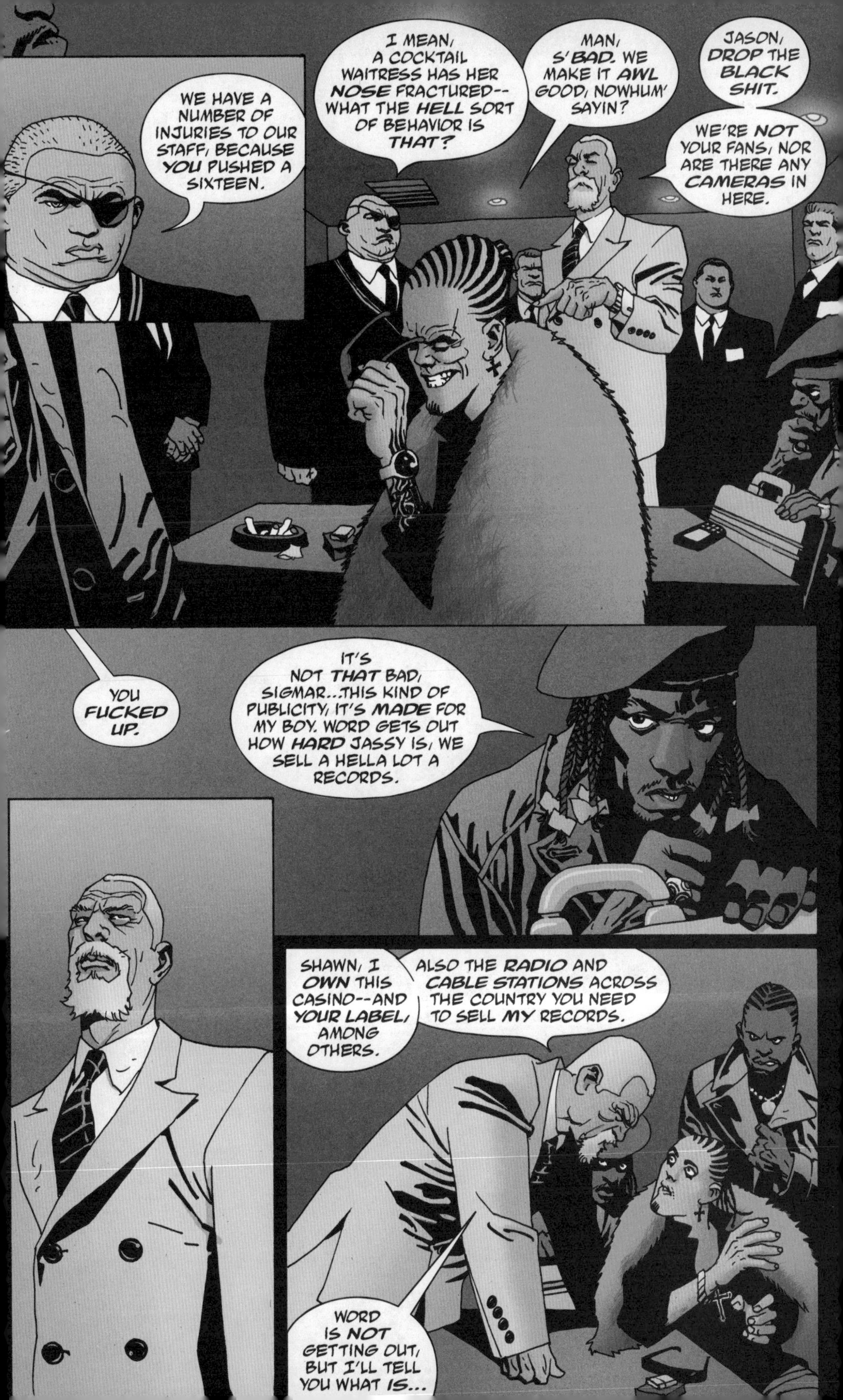

WE HAVE A NUMBER OF INJURIES TO OUR STAFF, BECAUSE YOU PUSHED A SIXTEEN.
I MEAN, A COCKTAIL WAITRESS HAS HER NOSE FRACTURED-- WHAT THE HELL SORT OF BEHAVIOR IS THAT?
MAN, S' BAD. WE MAKE IT AWL GOOD, NOWHUM' SAYIN?
JASON, DROP THE BLACK SHIT.
WE'RE NOT YOUR FANS, NOR ARE THERE ANY CAMERAS IN HERE.
YOU FUCKED UP.
IT'S NOT THAT BAD, SIGMAR...THIS KIND OF PUBLICITY, IT'S MADE FOR MY BOY. WORD GETS OUT HOW HARD JASSY IS, WE SELL A HELLA LOT A RECORDS.
SHAWN, I OWN THIS CASINO--AND YOUR LABEL, AMONG OTHERS.
ALSO THE RADIO AND CABLE STATIONS ACROSS THE COUNTRY YOU NEED TO SELL MY RECORDS.
WORD IS NOT GETTING OUT, BUT I'LL TELL YOU WHAT IS...

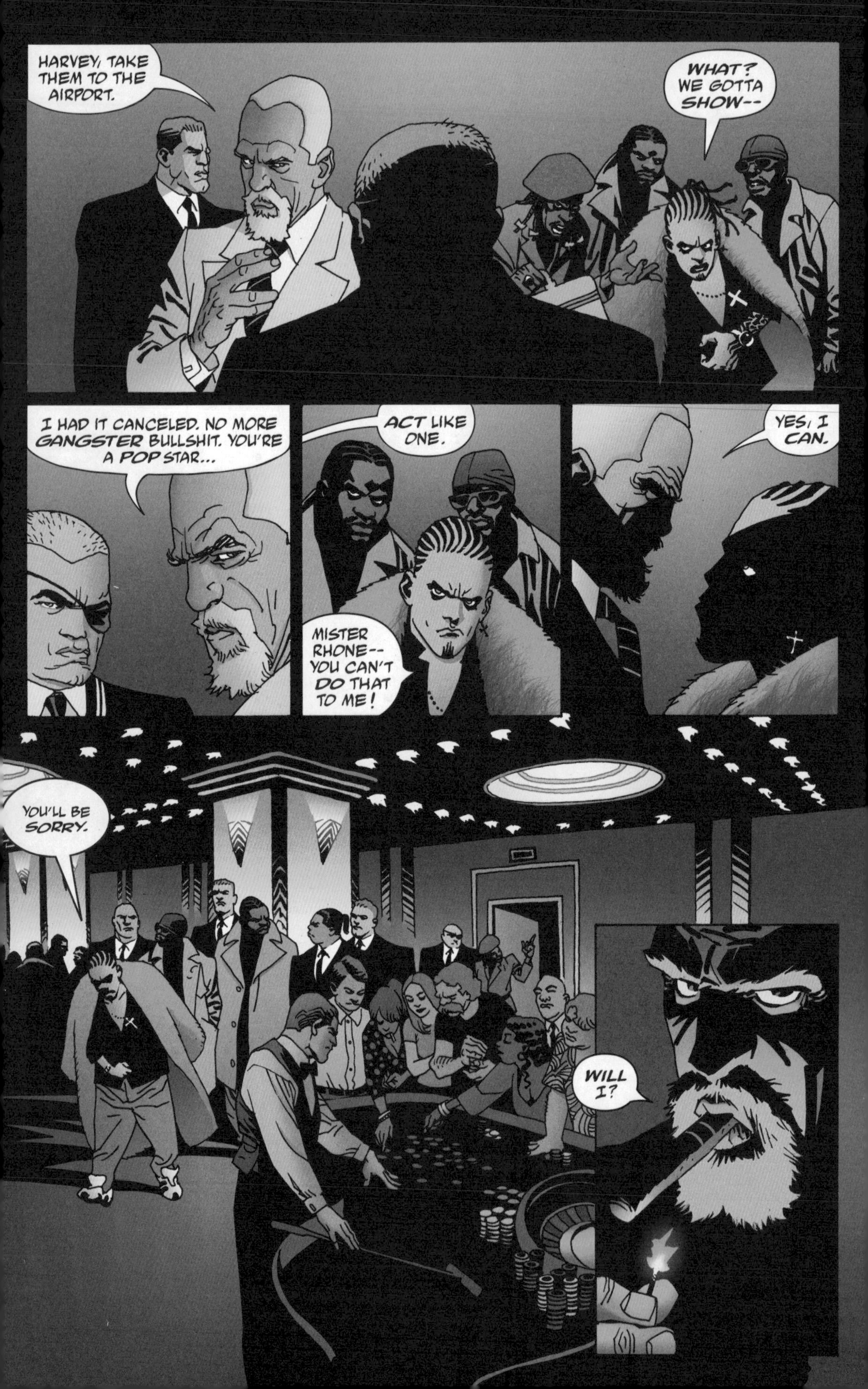
HARVEY, TAKE THEM TO THE AIRPORT.
WHAT? WE GOTTA SHOW--
I HAD IT CANCELED. NO MORE GANGSTER BULLSHIT. YOU'RE A POP STAR...
ACT LIKE ONE.
MISTER RHONE-- YOU CAN'T DO THAT TO ME!
YES, I CAN.
YOU'LL BE SORRY.
WILL I?

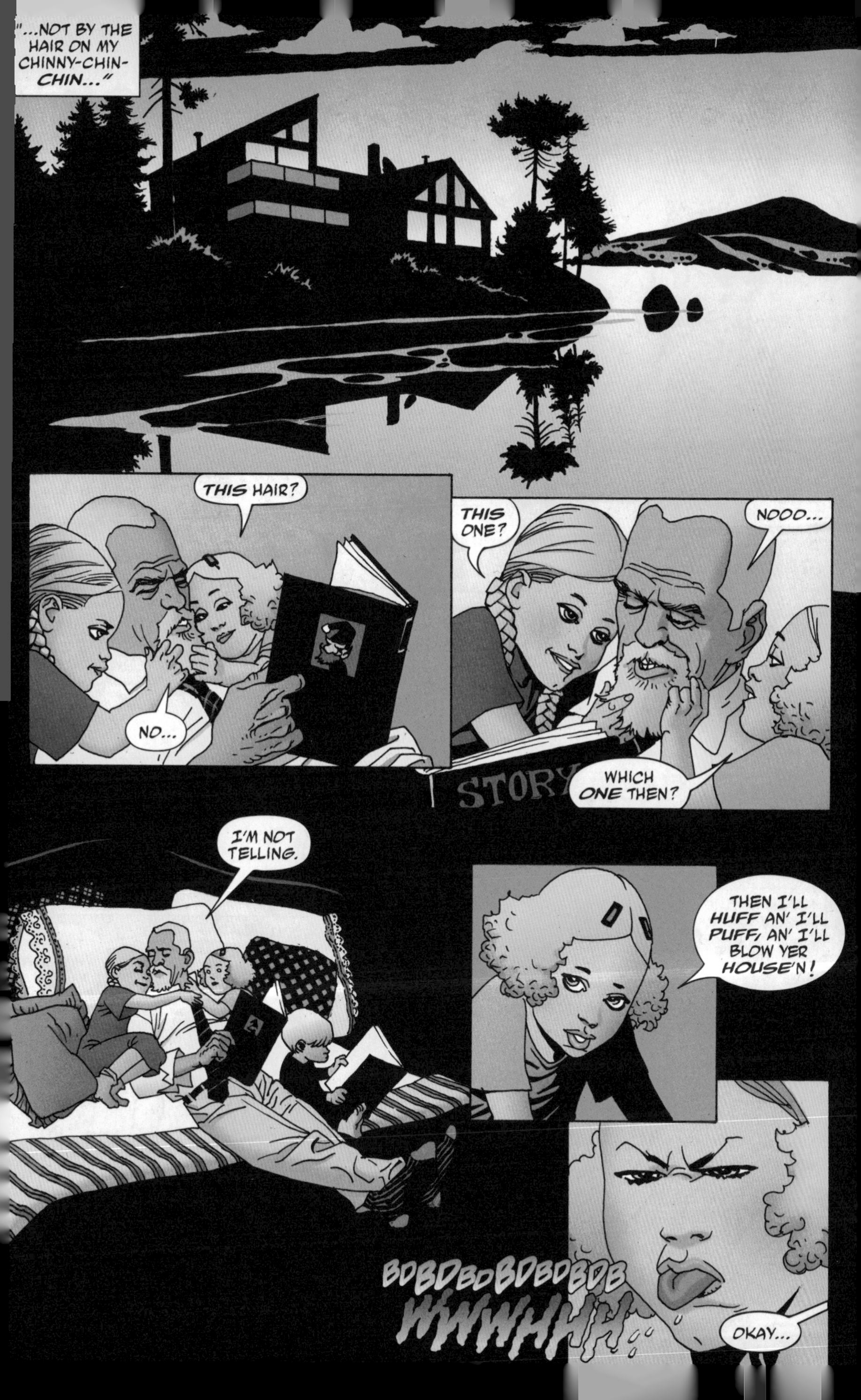
"...NOT BY THE HAIR ON MY CHINNY-CHIN-CHIN..."
THIS HAIR?
NO...
THIS ONE?
NOOO...
STORY
WHICH ONE THEN?
I'M NOT TELLING.
THEN I'LL HUFF AN' I'LL PUFF, AN' I'LL BLOW YER HOUSE'N!
BDBDBDBDBDBDB
WWWHHH
OKAY...

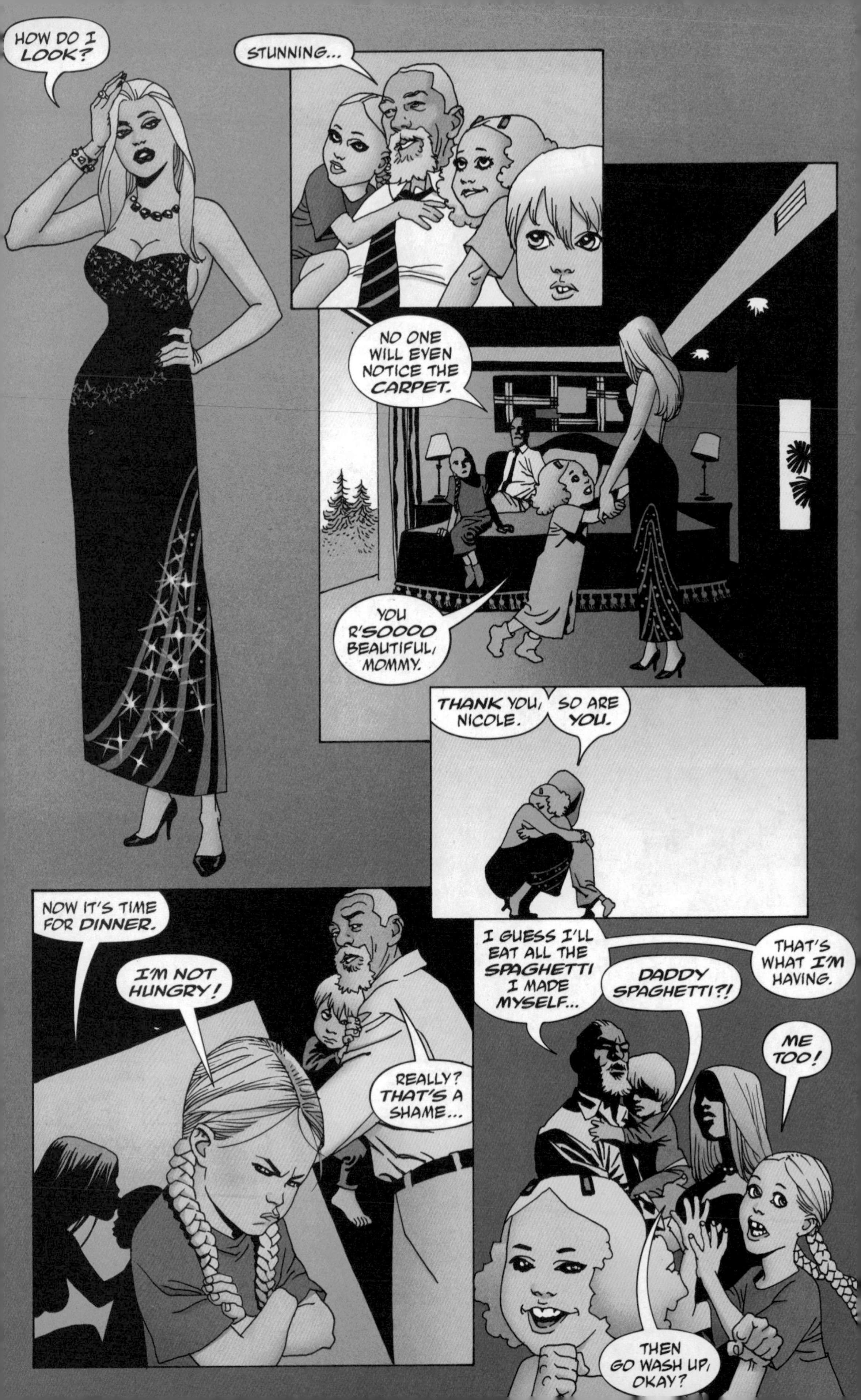
HOW DO I LOOK?
STUNNING...
NO ONE WILL EVEN NOTICE THE CARPET.
YOU R'SOOOO BEAUTIFUL, MOMMY.
THANK YOU, NICOLE.
SO ARE YOU.
NOW IT'S TIME FOR DINNER.
I'M NOT HUNGRY!
REALLY? THAT'S A SHAME...
I GUESS I'LL EAT ALL THE SPAGHETTI I MADE MYSELF...
DADDY SPAGHETTI?!
THAT'S WHAT I'M HAVING.
ME TOO!
THEN GO WASH UP, OKAY?

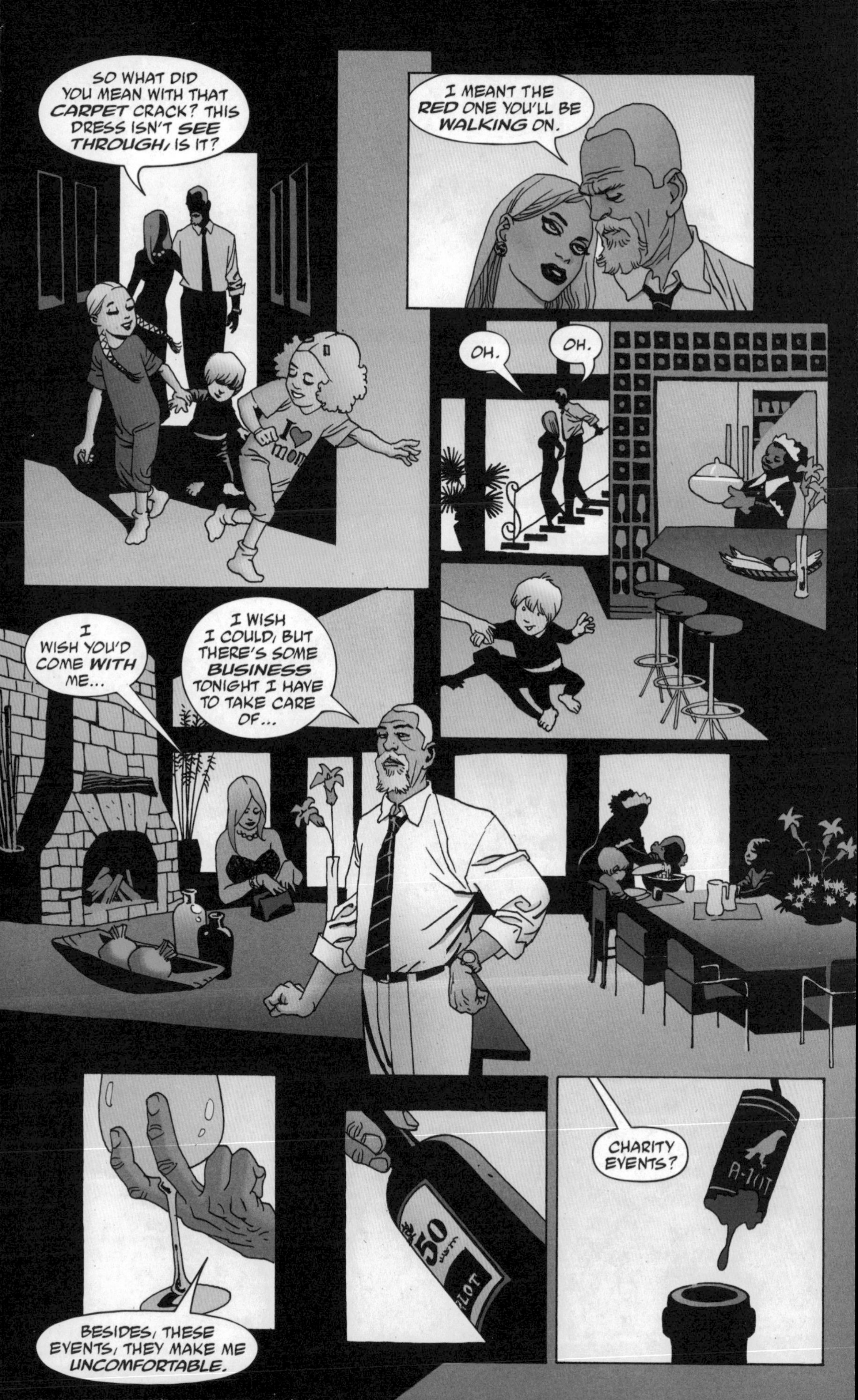

SO WHAT DID YOU MEAN WITH THAT CARPET CRACK? THIS DRESS ISN'T SEE THROUGH, IS IT?
I MEANT THE RED ONE YOU'LL BE WALKING ON.
OH.
OH.
I WISH YOU'D COME WITH ME...
I WISH I COULD, BUT THERE'S SOME BUSINESS TONIGHT I HAVE TO TAKE CARE OF...
BESIDES, THESE EVENTS, THEY MAKE ME UNCOMFORTABLE.
CHARITY EVENTS?

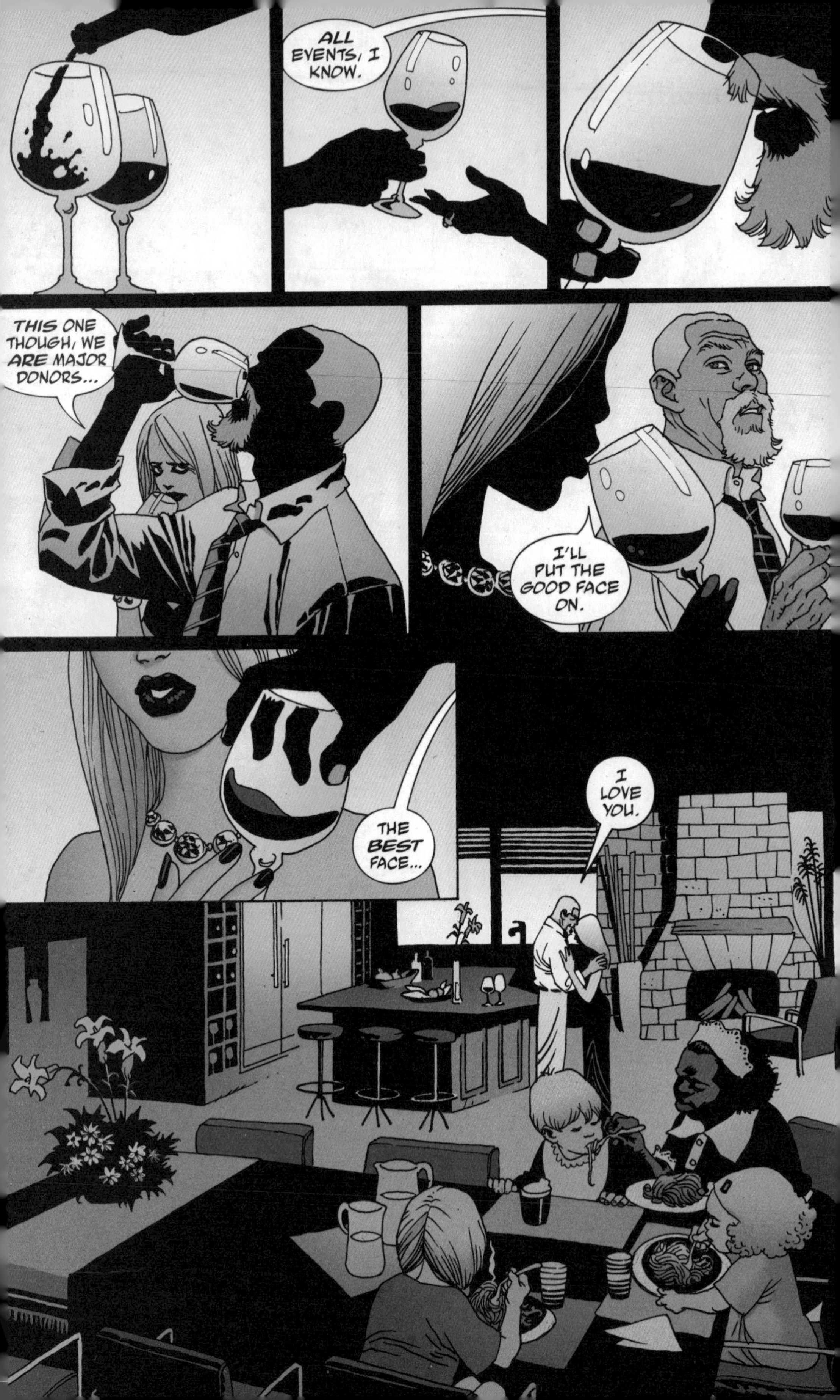
ALL EVENTS, I KNOW.
THIS ONE THOUGH, WE ARE MAJOR DONORS...
I'LL PUT THE GOOD FACE ON.
THE BEST FACE...
I LOVE YOU.

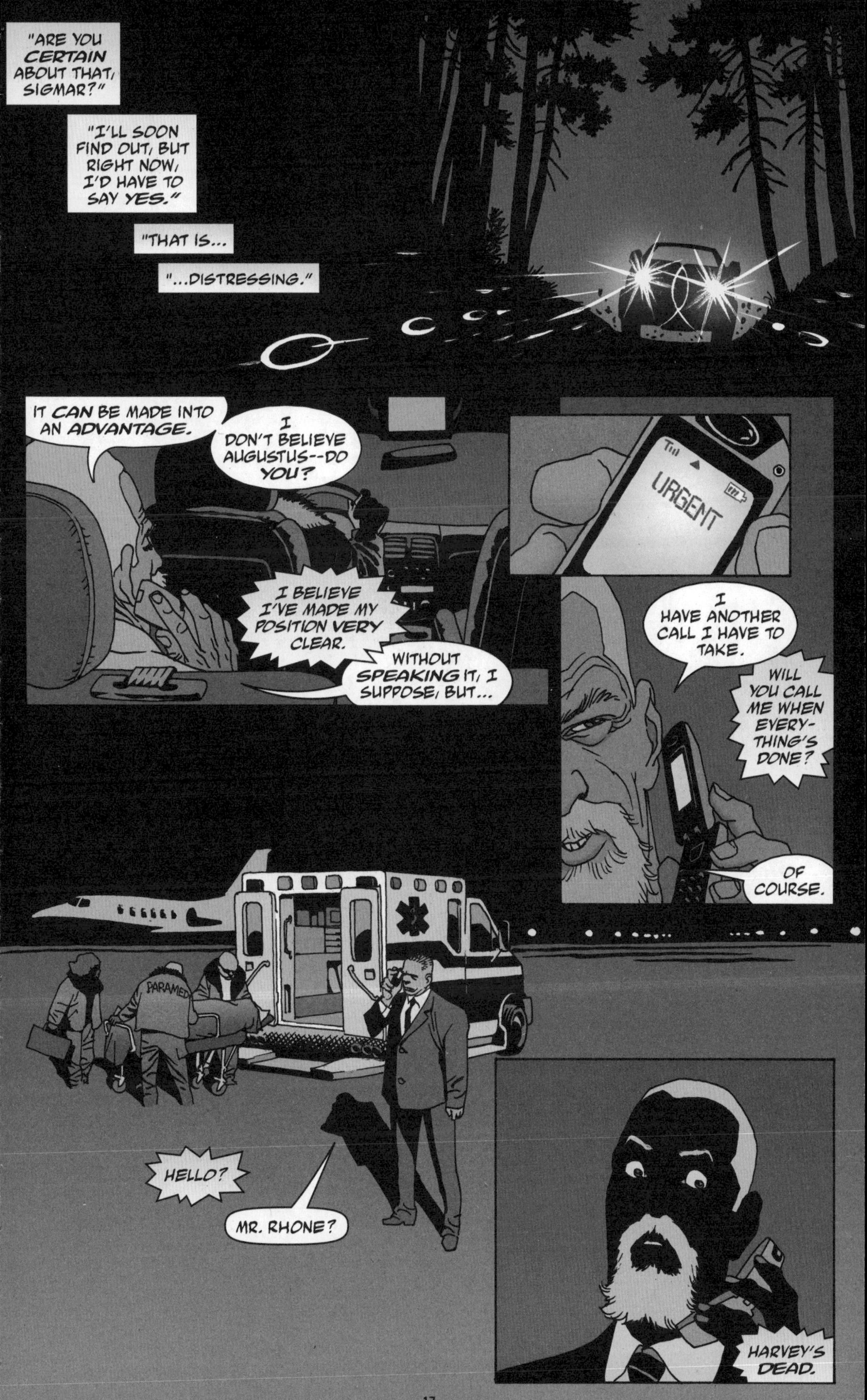
"ARE YOU CERTAIN ABOUT THAT, SIGMAR?"
"I'LL SOON FIND OUT, BUT RIGHT NOW, I'D HAVE TO SAY YES."
"THAT IS...
"...DISTRESSING."
IT CAN BE MADE INTO AN ADVANTAGE.
I DON'T BELIEVE AUGUSTUS--DO YOU?
I BELIEVE I'VE MADE MY POSITION VERY CLEAR.
WITHOUT SPEAKING IT, I SUPPOSE, BUT...
URGENT
I HAVE ANOTHER CALL I HAVE TO TAKE.
WILL YOU CALL ME WHEN EVERYTHING'S DONE?
OF COURSE.
PARAMED
HELLO?
MR. RHONE?
HARVEY'S DEAD.

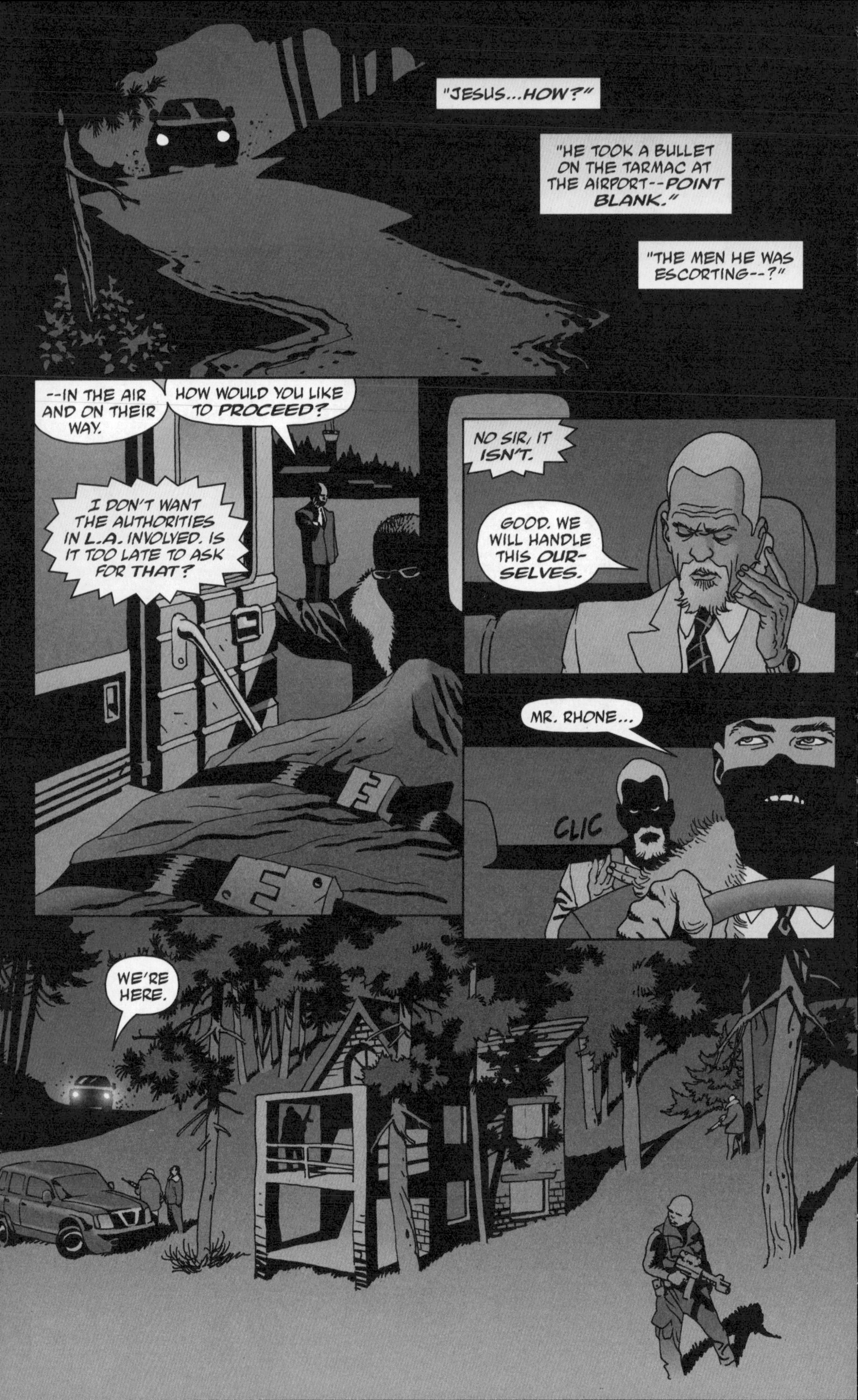
"JESUS...HOW?"
"HE TOOK A BULLET ON THE TARMAC AT THE AIRPORT--POINT BLANK."
"THE MEN HE WAS ESCORTING--?"
--IN THE AIR AND ON THEIR WAY.
HOW WOULD YOU LIKE TO PROCEED?
I DON'T WANT THE AUTHORITIES IN L.A. INVOLVED. IS IT TOO LATE TO ASK FOR THAT?
NO SIR, IT ISN'T.
GOOD. WE WILL HANDLE THIS OURSELVES.
MR. RHONE...
CLIC
WE'RE HERE.

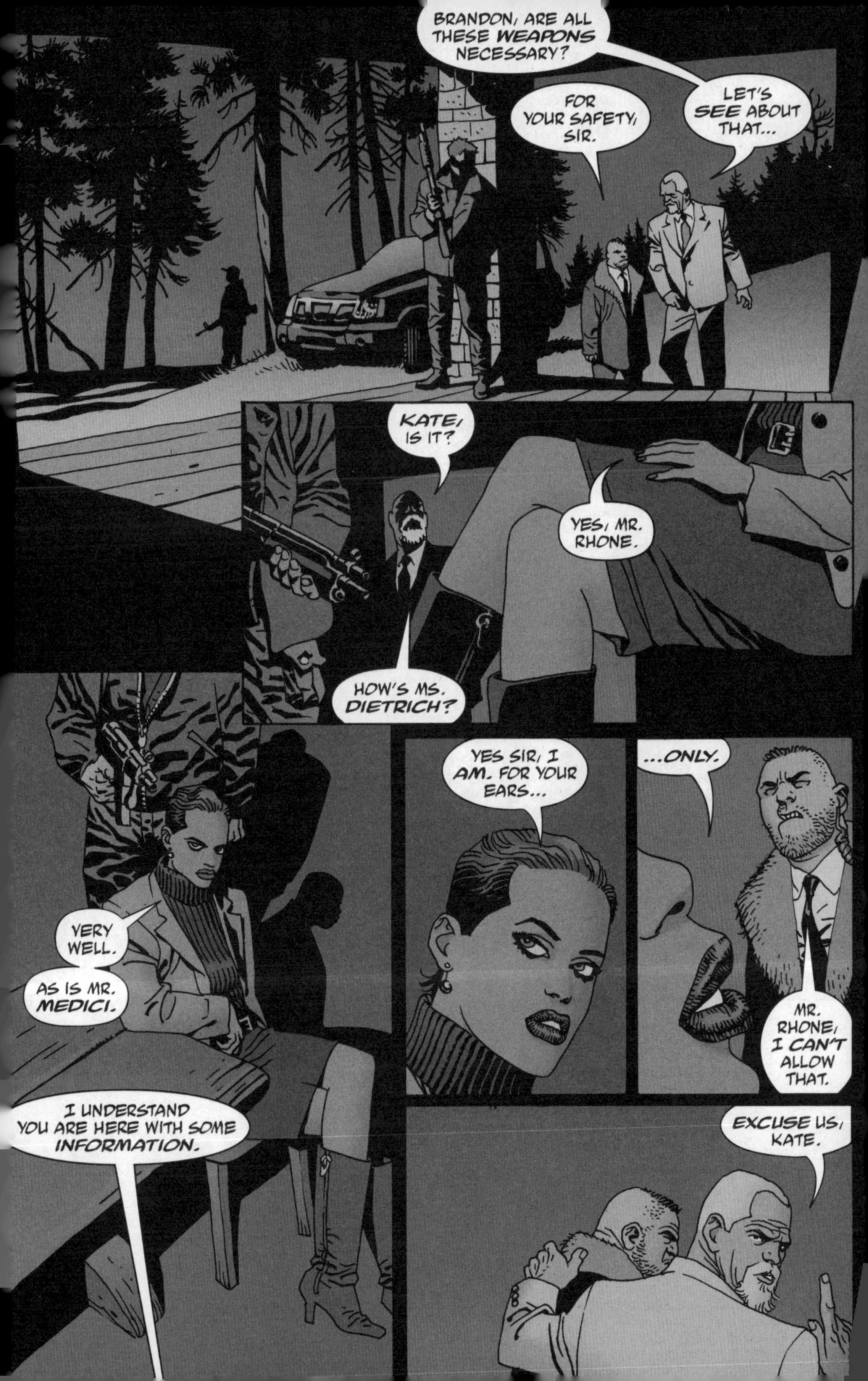
BRANDON, ARE ALL THESE WEAPONS NECESSARY?
FOR YOUR SAFETY, SIR.
LET'S SEE ABOUT THAT...
KATE, IS IT?
YES, MR. RHONE.
HOW'S MS. DIETRICH?
VERY WELL.
AS IS MR. MEDICI.
I UNDERSTAND YOU ARE HERE WITH SOME INFORMATION.
YES SIR, I AM. FOR YOUR EARS...
...ONLY.
MR. RHONE, I CAN'T ALLOW THAT.
EXCUSE US, KATE.

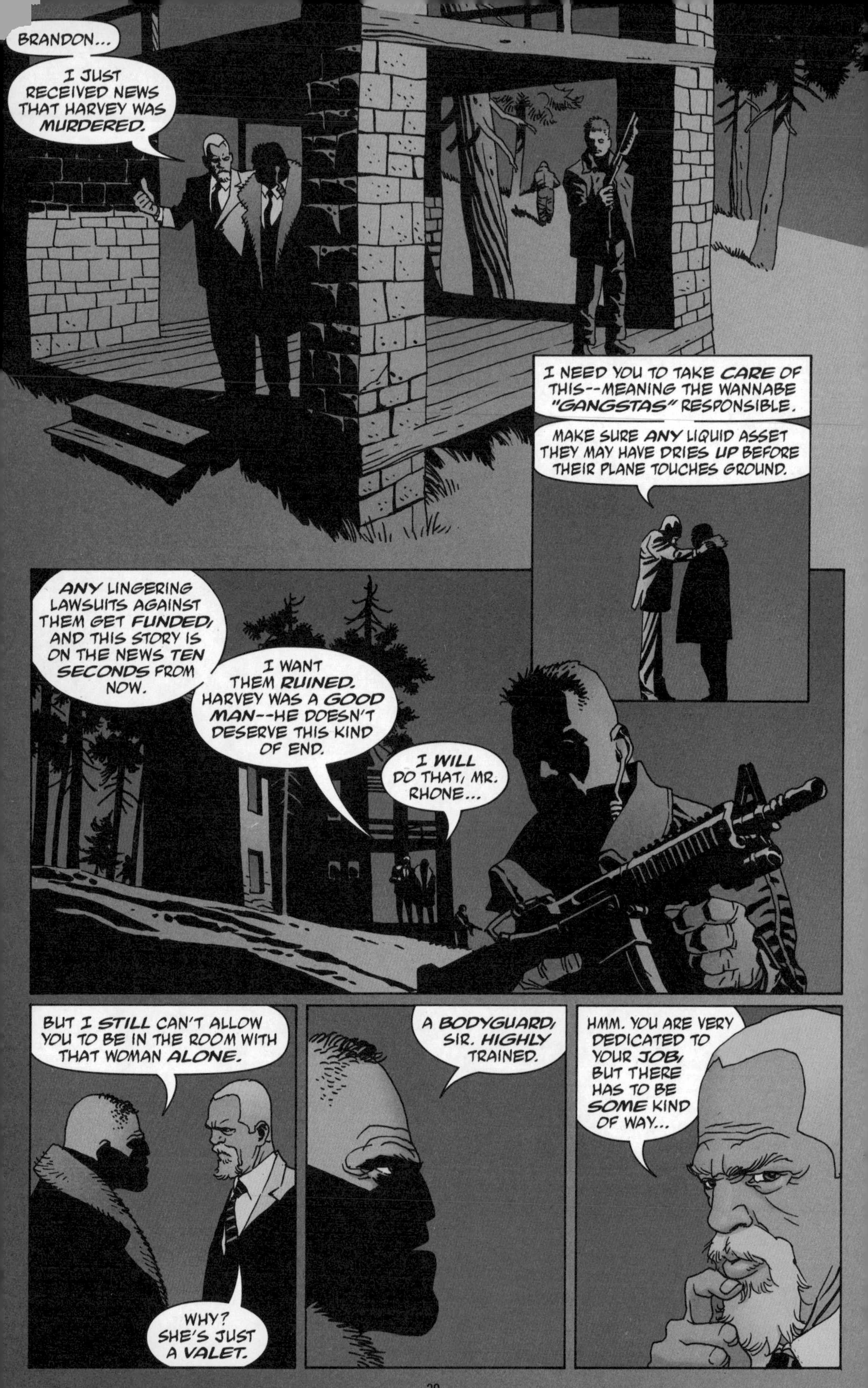
BRANDON...
I JUST RECEIVED NEWS THAT HARVEY WAS MURDERED.
I NEED YOU TO TAKE CARE OF THIS--MEANING THE WANNABE "GANGSTAS" RESPONSIBLE.
MAKE SURE ANY LIQUID ASSET THEY MAY HAVE DRIES UP BEFORE THEIR PLANE TOUCHES GROUND.
ANY LINGERING LAWSUITS AGAINST THEM GET FUNDED, AND THIS STORY IS ON THE NEWS TEN SECONDS FROM NOW.
I WANT THEM RUINED. HARVEY WAS A GOOD MAN--HE DOESN'T DESERVE THIS KIND OF END.
I WILL DO THAT, MR. RHONE...
BUT I STILL CAN'T ALLOW YOU TO BE IN THE ROOM WITH THAT WOMAN ALONE.
WHY? SHE'S JUST A VALET.
A BODYGUARD, SIR. HIGHLY TRAINED.
HMM. YOU ARE VERY DEDICATED TO YOUR JOB, BUT THERE HAS TO BE SOME KIND OF WAY...

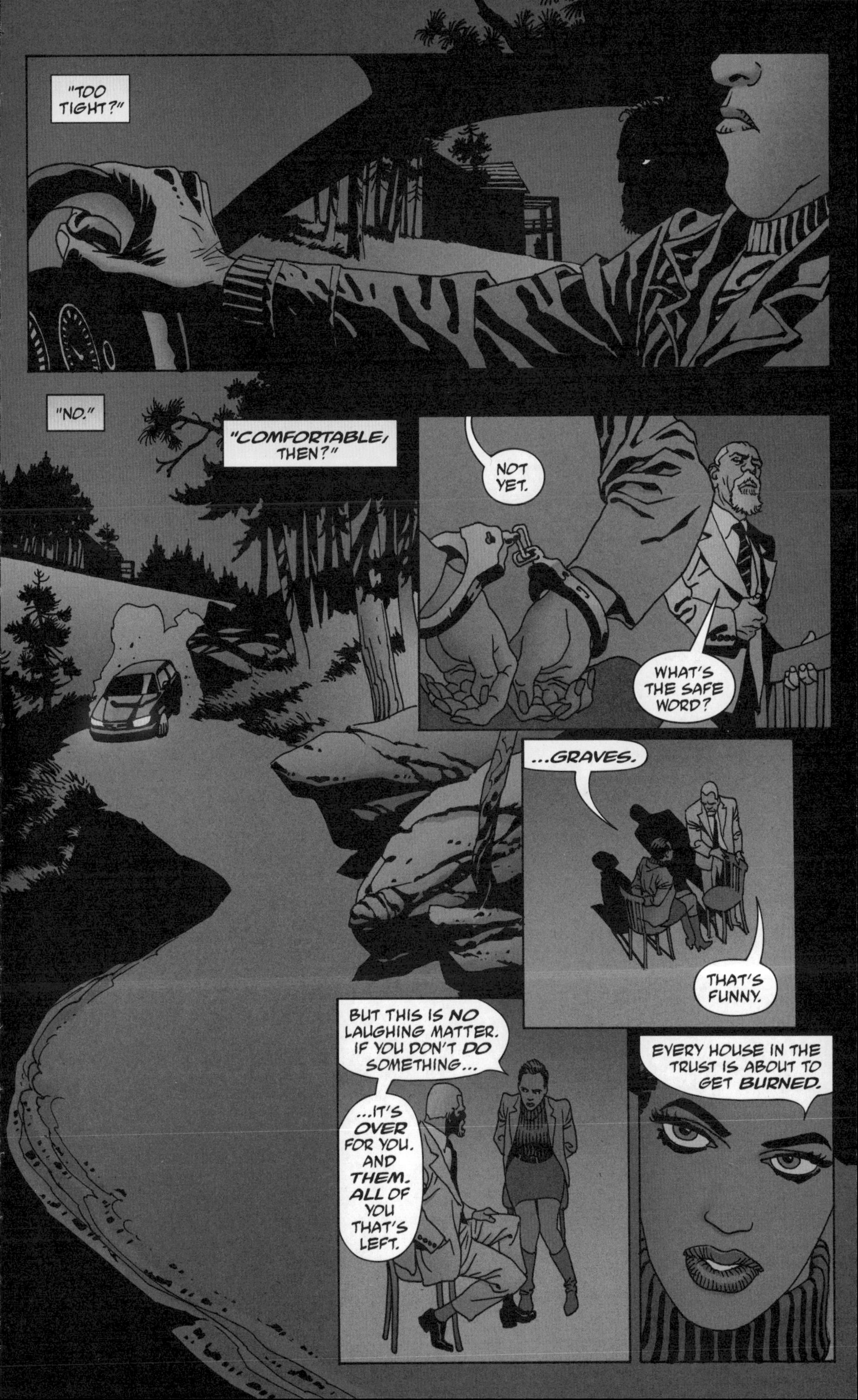
"TOO TIGHT?"
"NO."
"COMFORTABLE, THEN?"
NOT YET.
WHAT'S THE SAFE WORD?
...GRAVES.
THAT'S FUNNY.
BUT THIS IS NO LAUGHING MATTER. IF YOU DON'T DO SOMETHING...
...IT'S OVER FOR YOU. AND THEM. ALL OF YOU THAT'S LEFT.
EVERY HOUSE IN THE TRUST IS ABOUT TO GET BURNED.

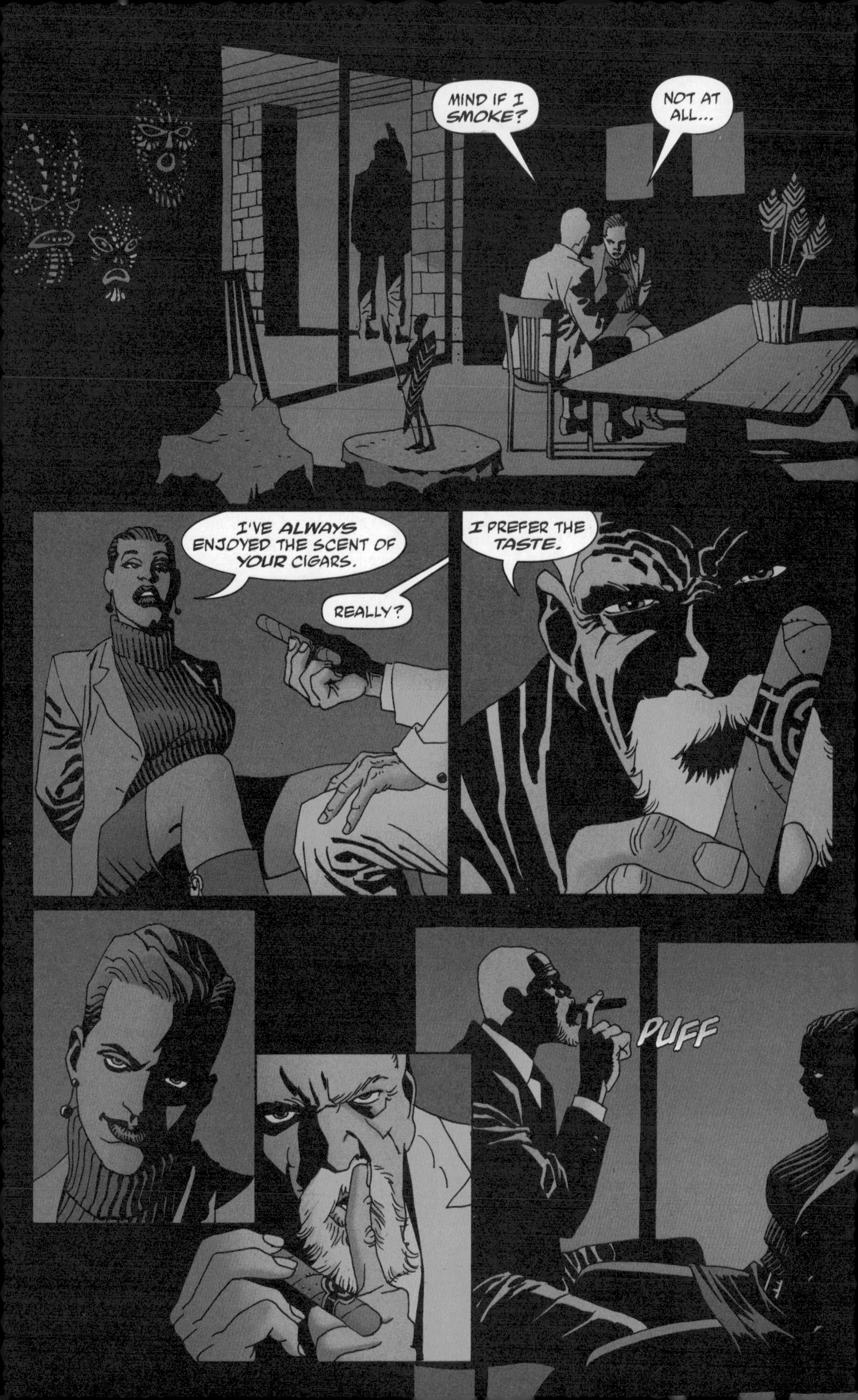
MIND IF I SMOKE?
NOT AT ALL...
I'VE ALWAYS ENJOYED THE SCENT OF YOUR CIGARS.
REALLY?
I PREFER THE TASTE.
PUFF

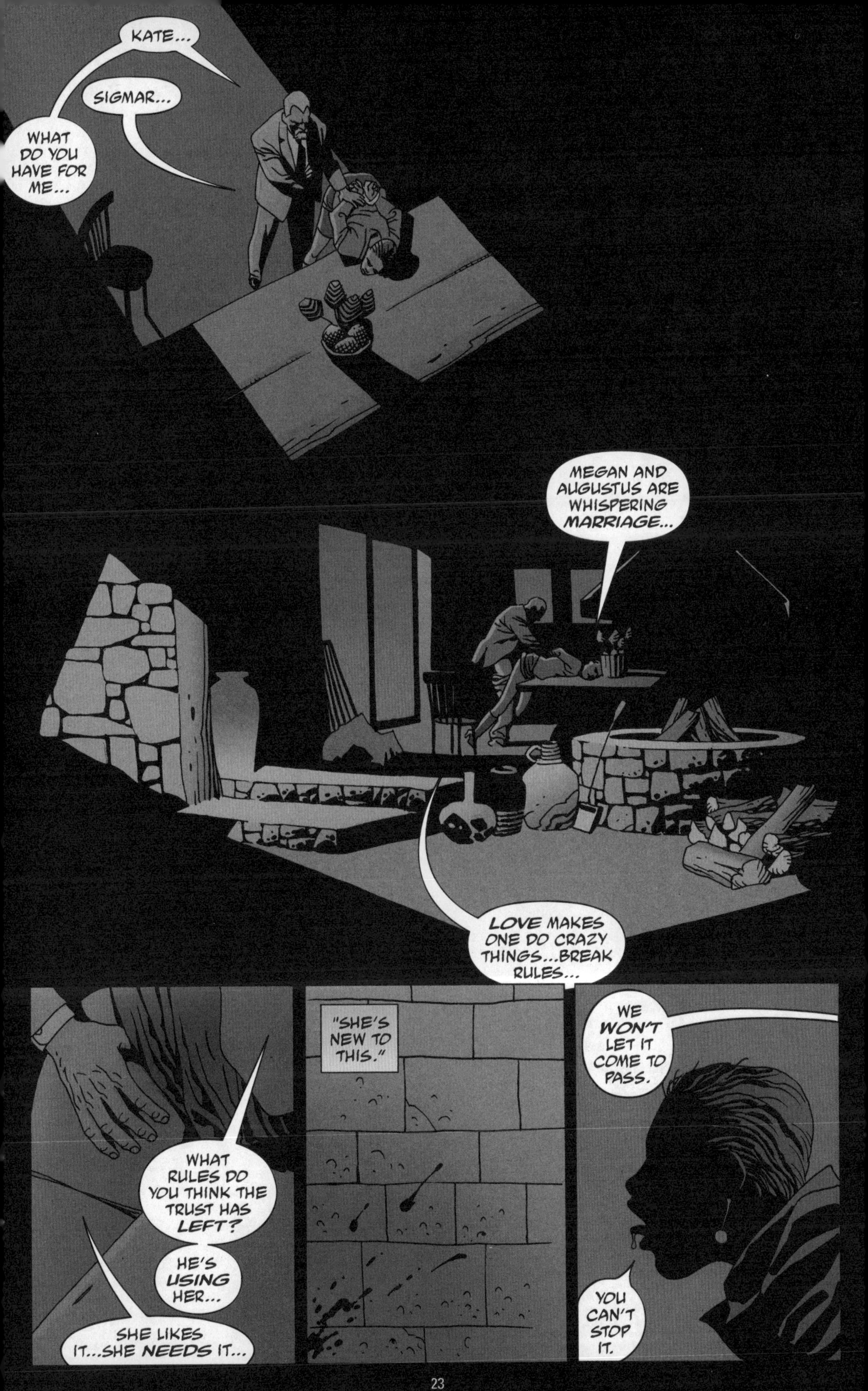
KATE...
SIGMAR...
WHAT DO YOU HAVE FOR ME...
MEGAN AND AUGUSTUS ARE WHISPERING MARRIAGE...
LOVE MAKES ONE DO CRAZY THINGS...BREAK RULES...
WHAT RULES DO YOU THINK THE TRUST HAS LEFT?
HE'S USING HER...
SHE LIKES IT...SHE NEEDS IT...
"SHE'S NEW TO THIS."
WE WON'T LET IT COME TO PASS.
YOU CAN'T STOP IT.

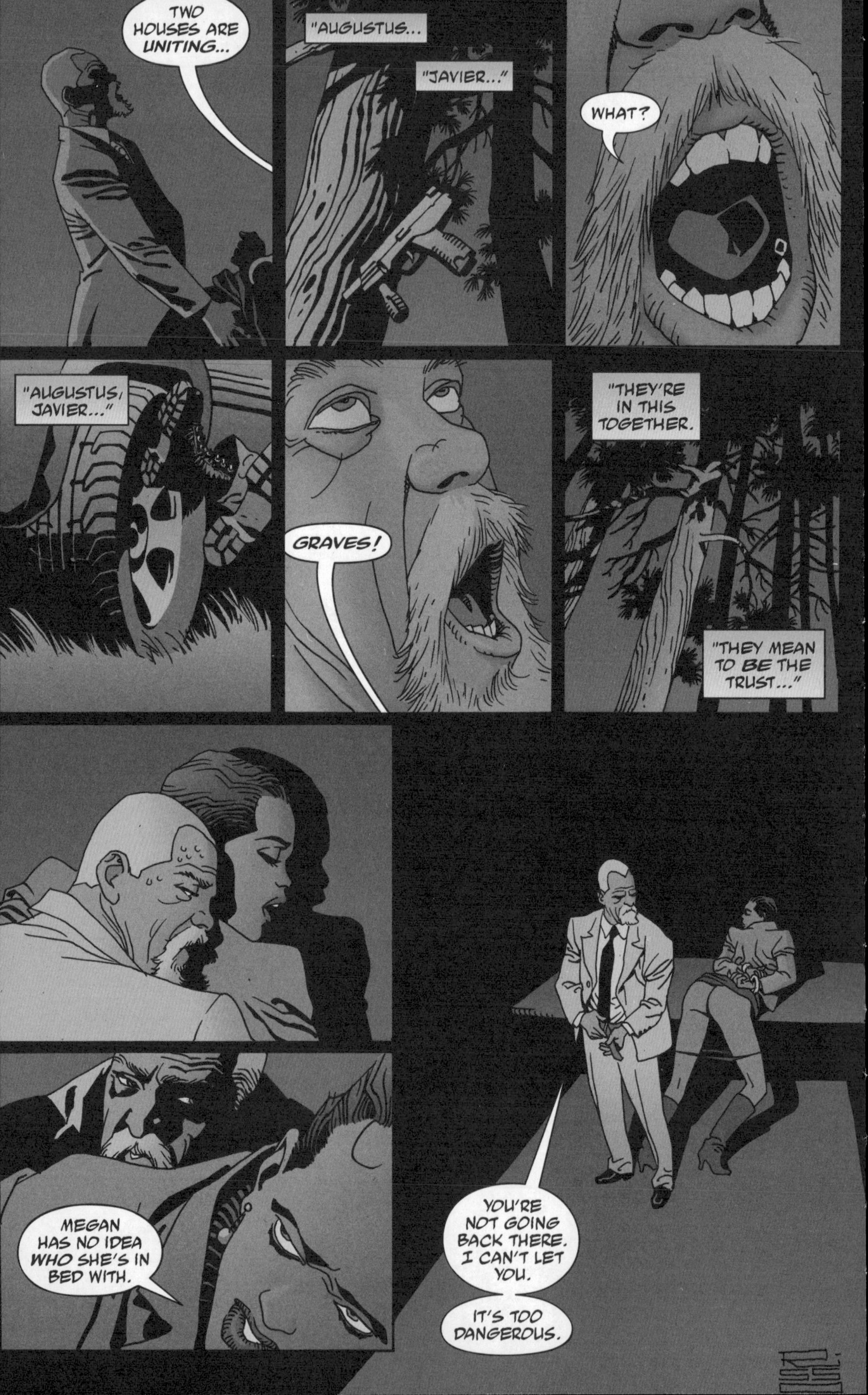
TWO HOUSES ARE UNITING...
"AUGUSTUS...
"JAVIER..."
WHAT?
"AUGUSTUS, JAVIER..."
GRAVES!
"THEY'RE IN THIS TOGETHER.
"THEY MEAN TO BE THE TRUST..."
MEGAN HAS NO IDEA WHO SHE'S IN BED WITH.
YOU'RE NOT GOING BACK THERE. I CAN'T LET YOU.
IT'S TOO DANGEROUS.

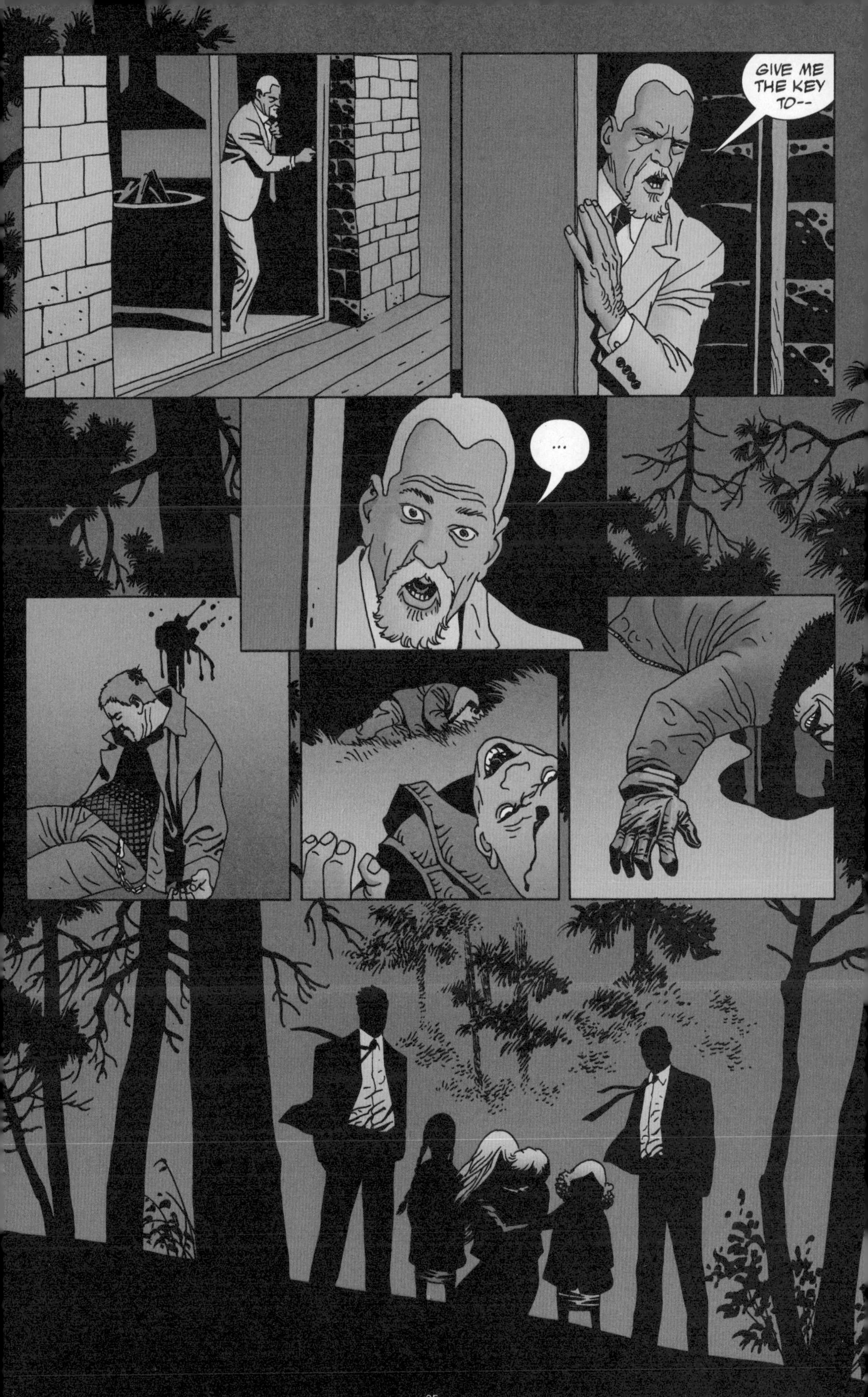
GIVE ME THE KEY TO--
...

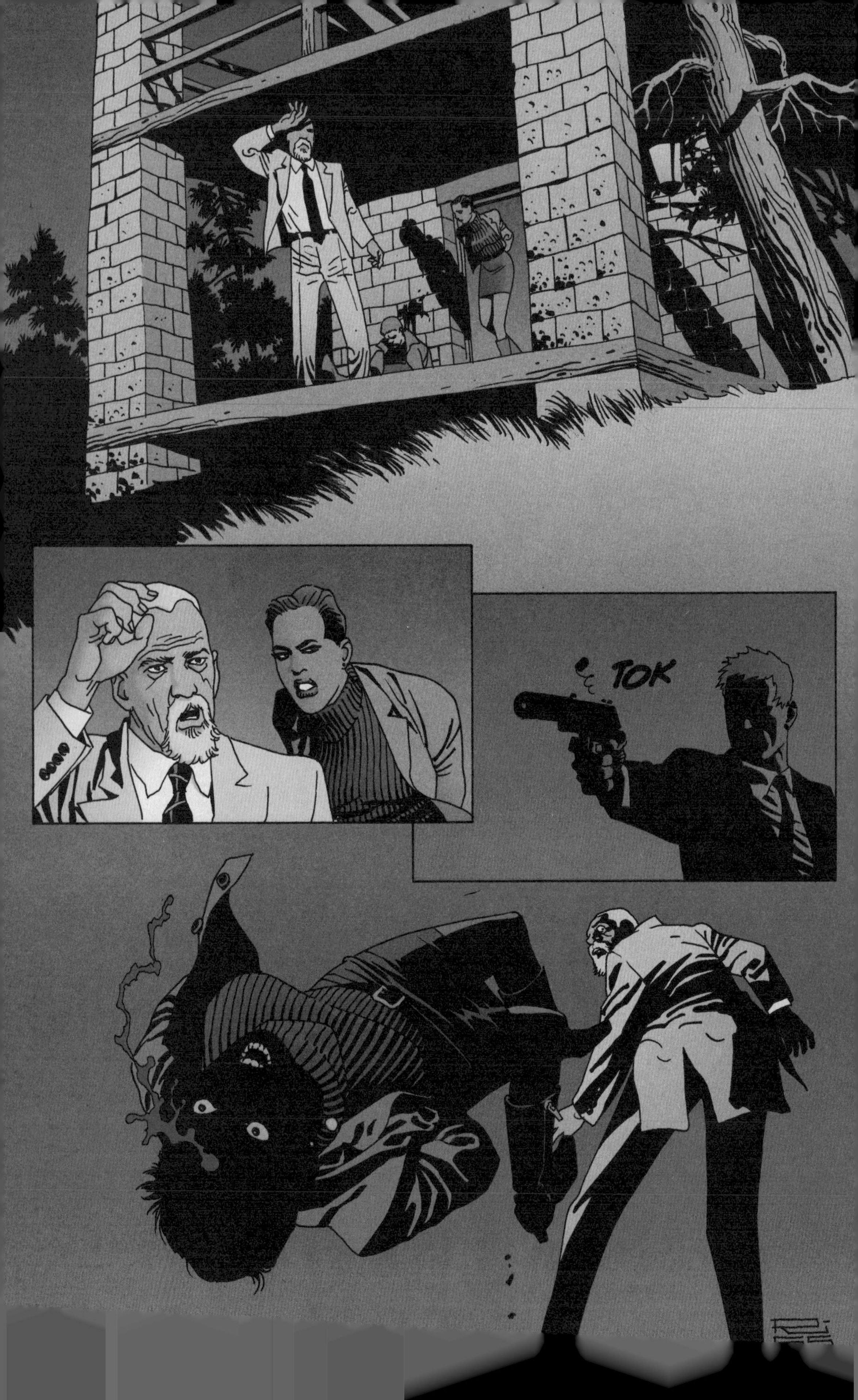
TOK

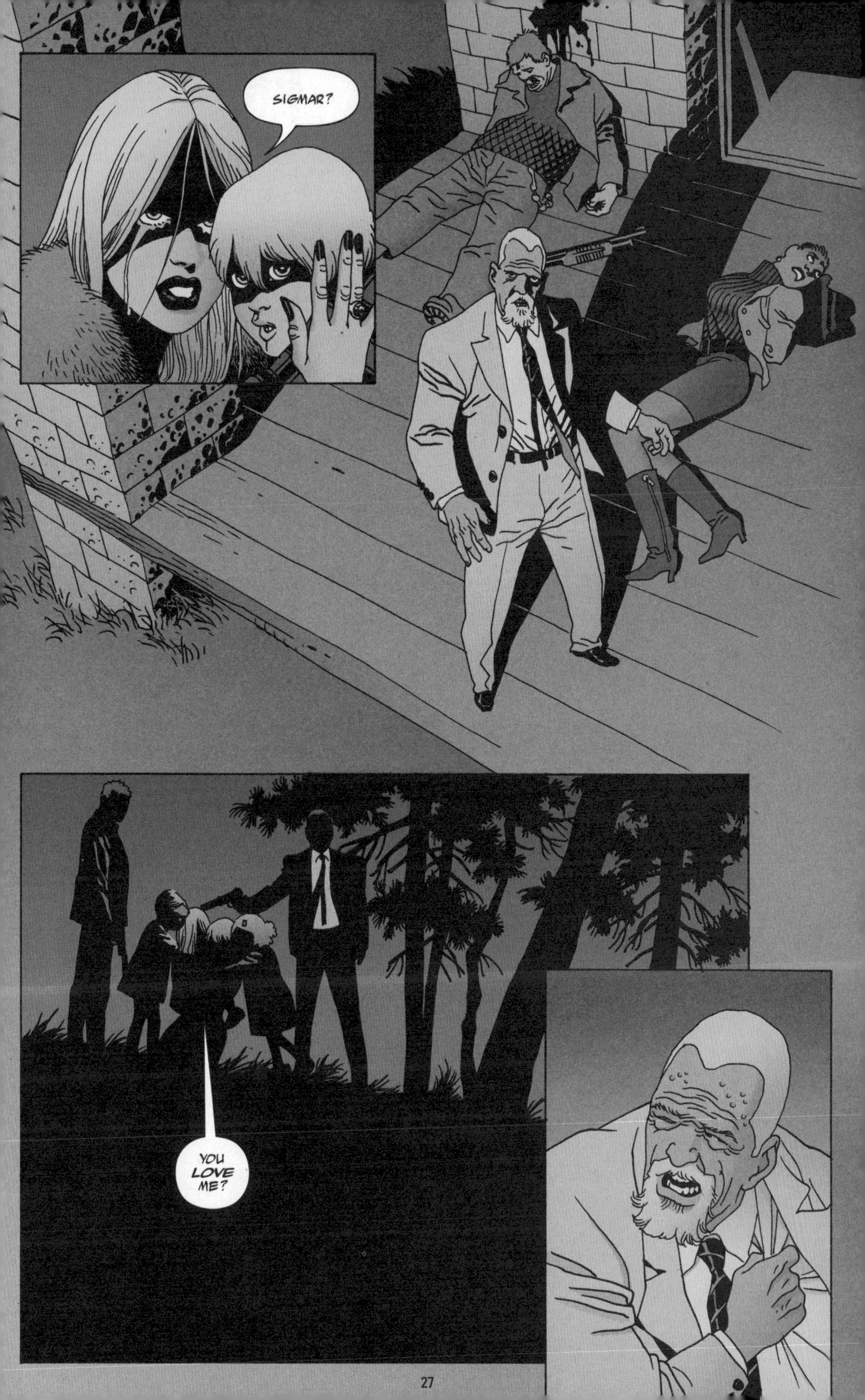
SIGMAR?
YOU LOVE ME?

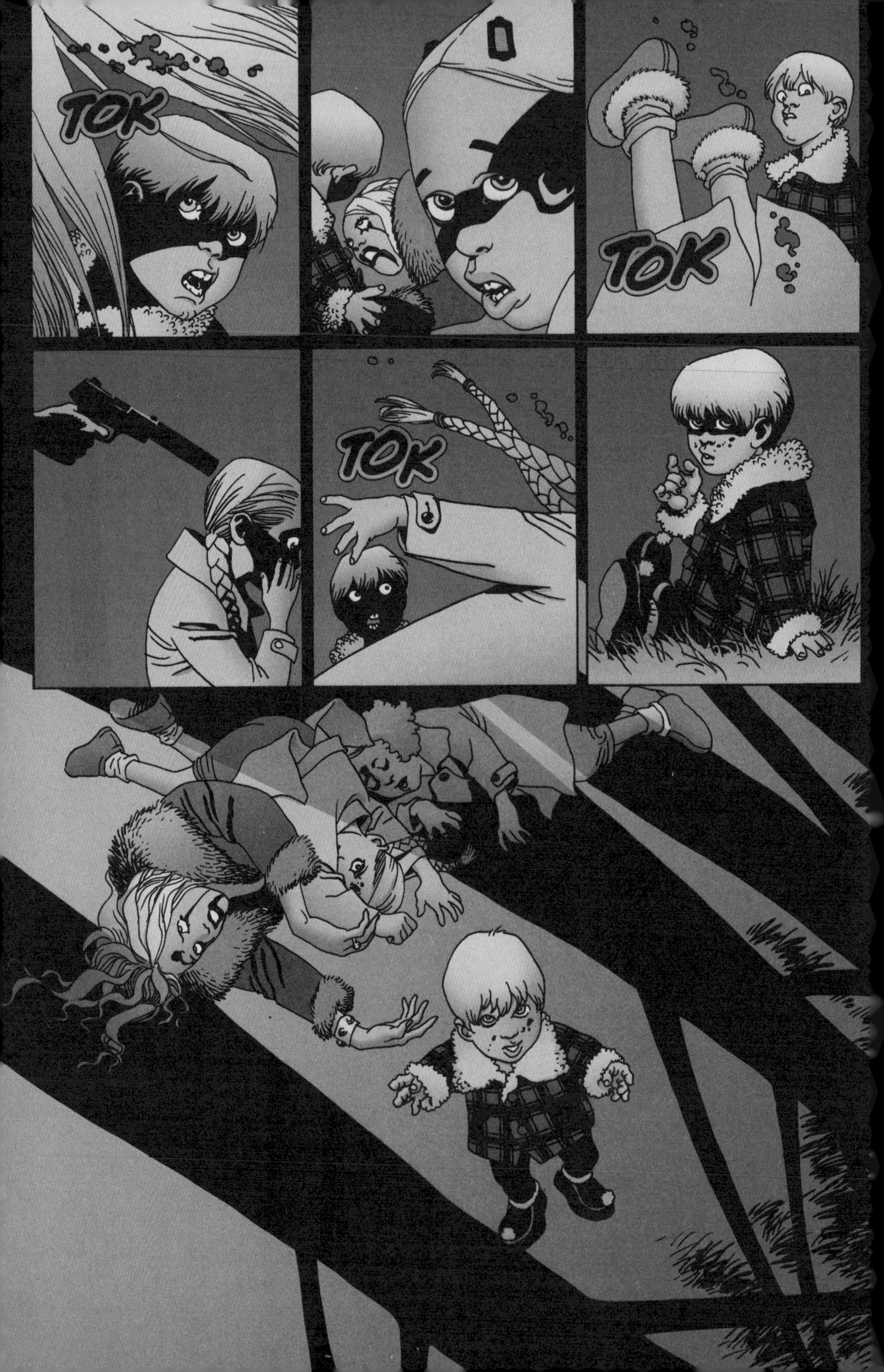
TOK
TOK
TOK

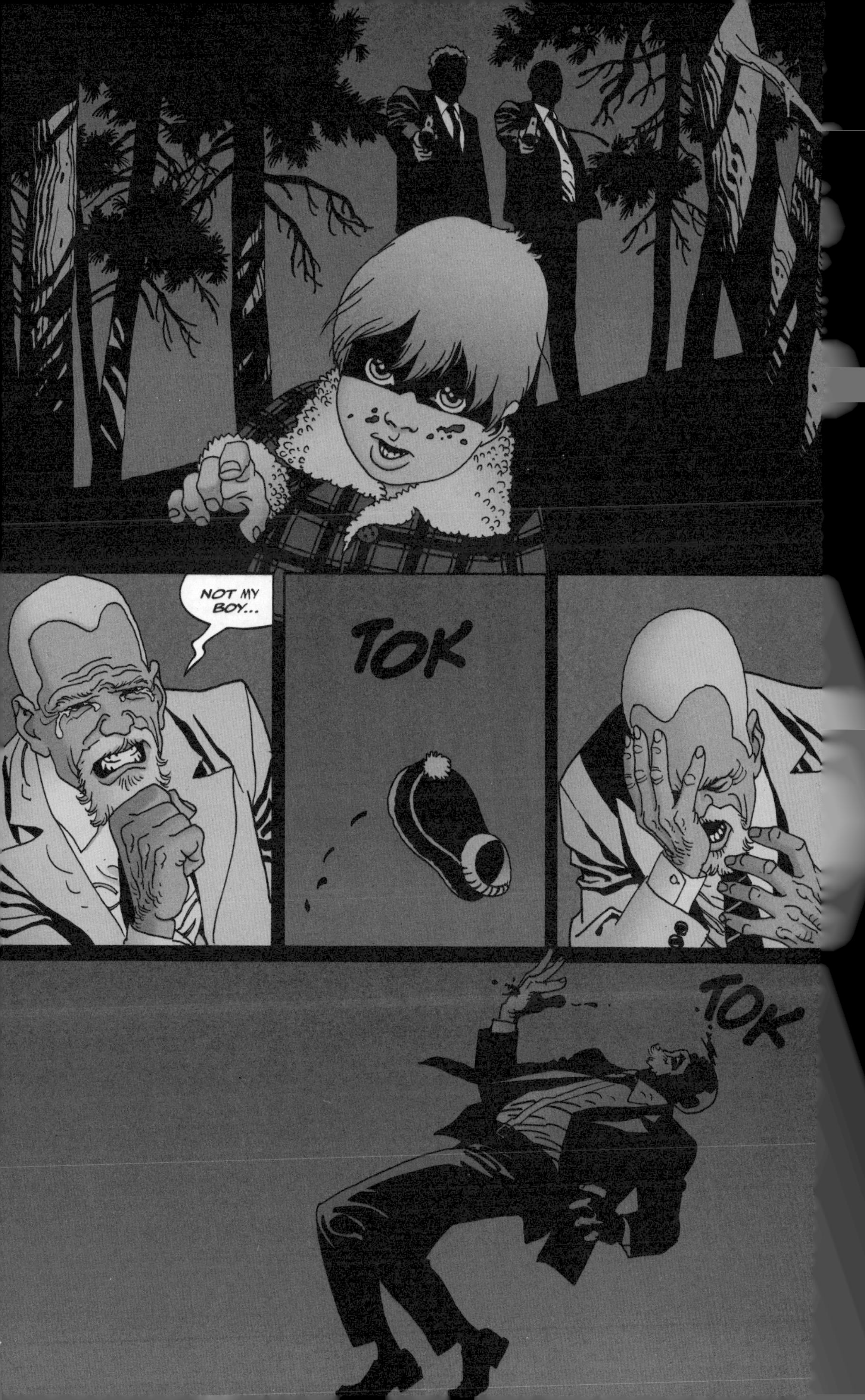
NOT MY BOY...
TOK
TOK

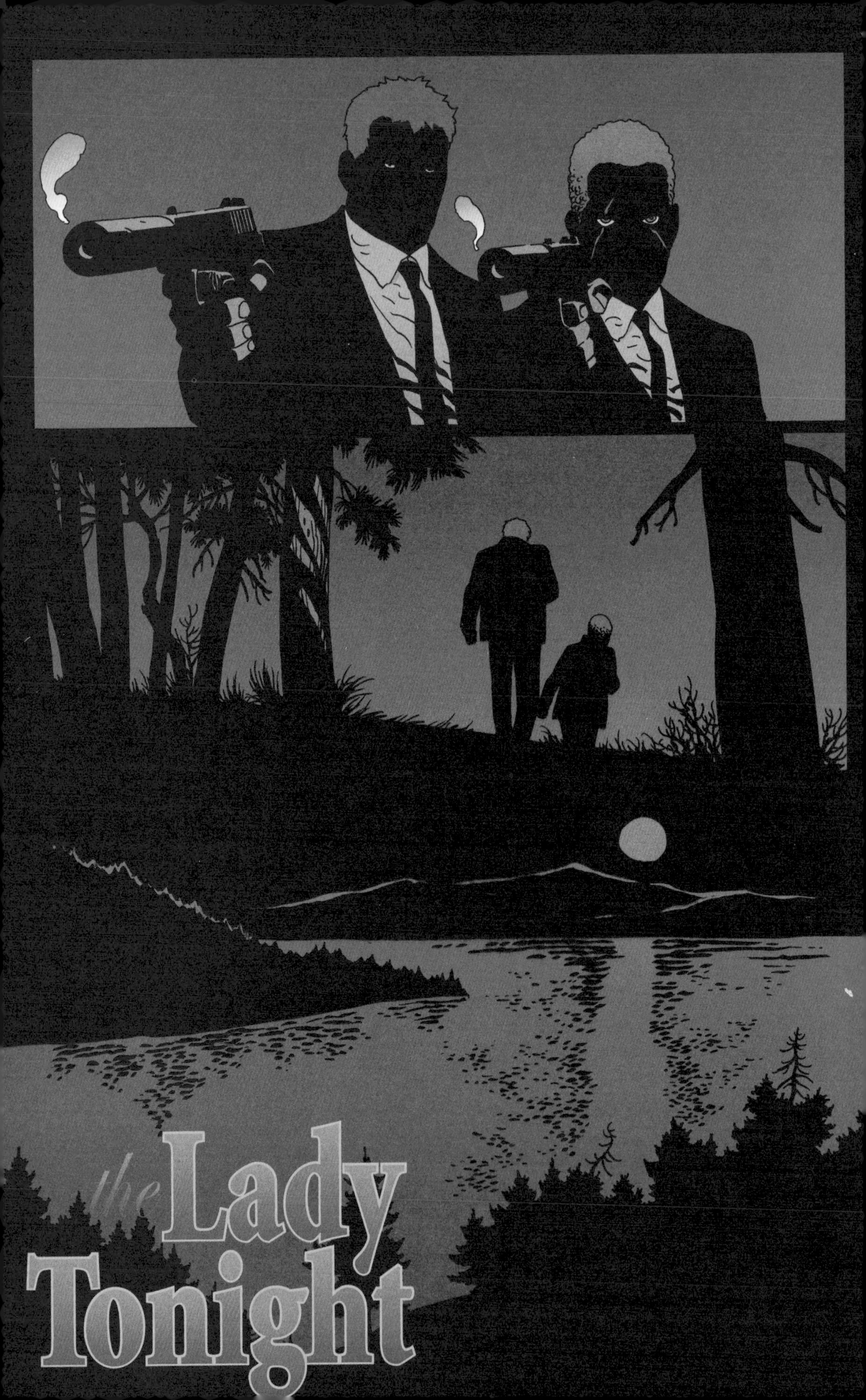
the Lady
Tonight

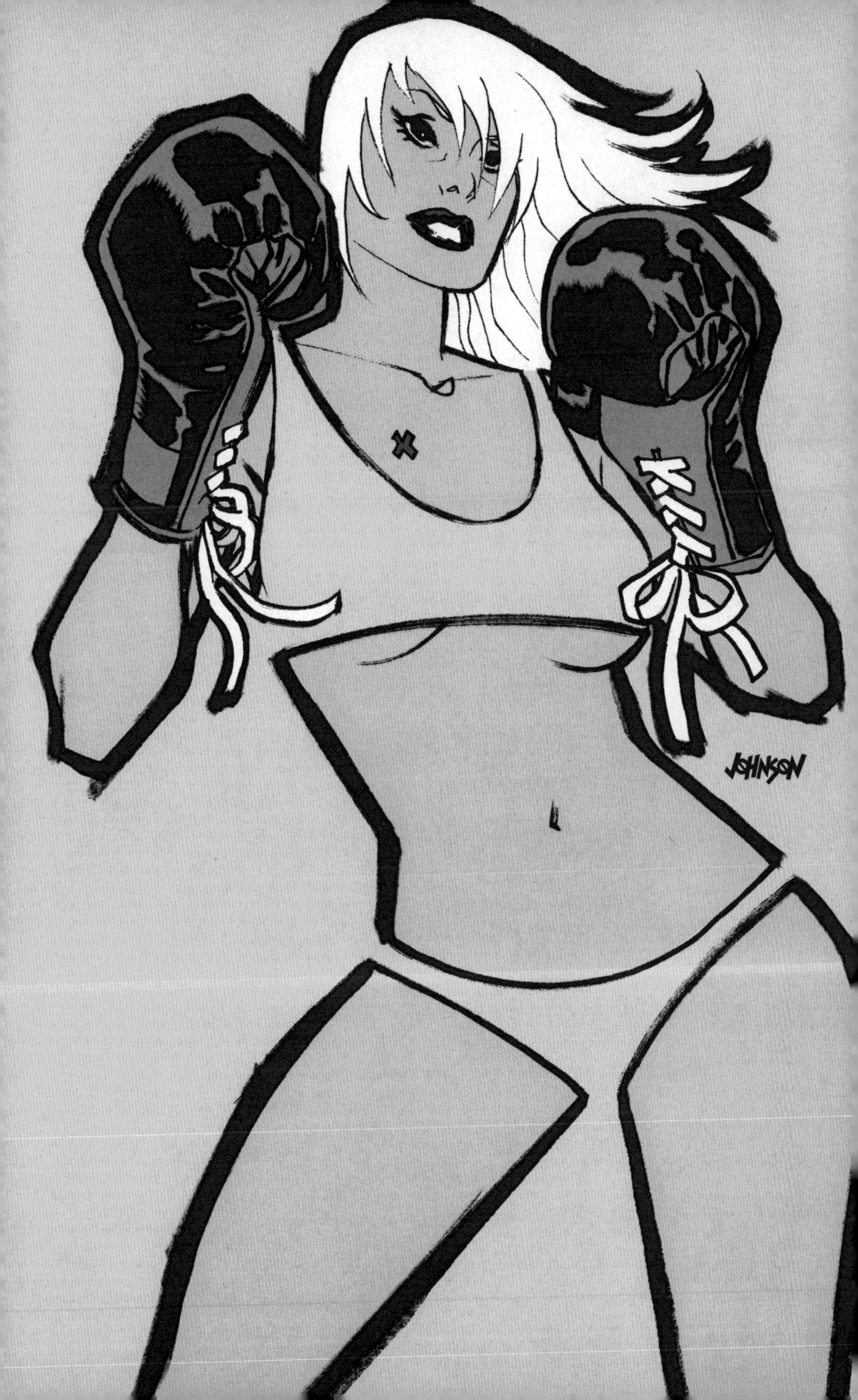
JOHNSON

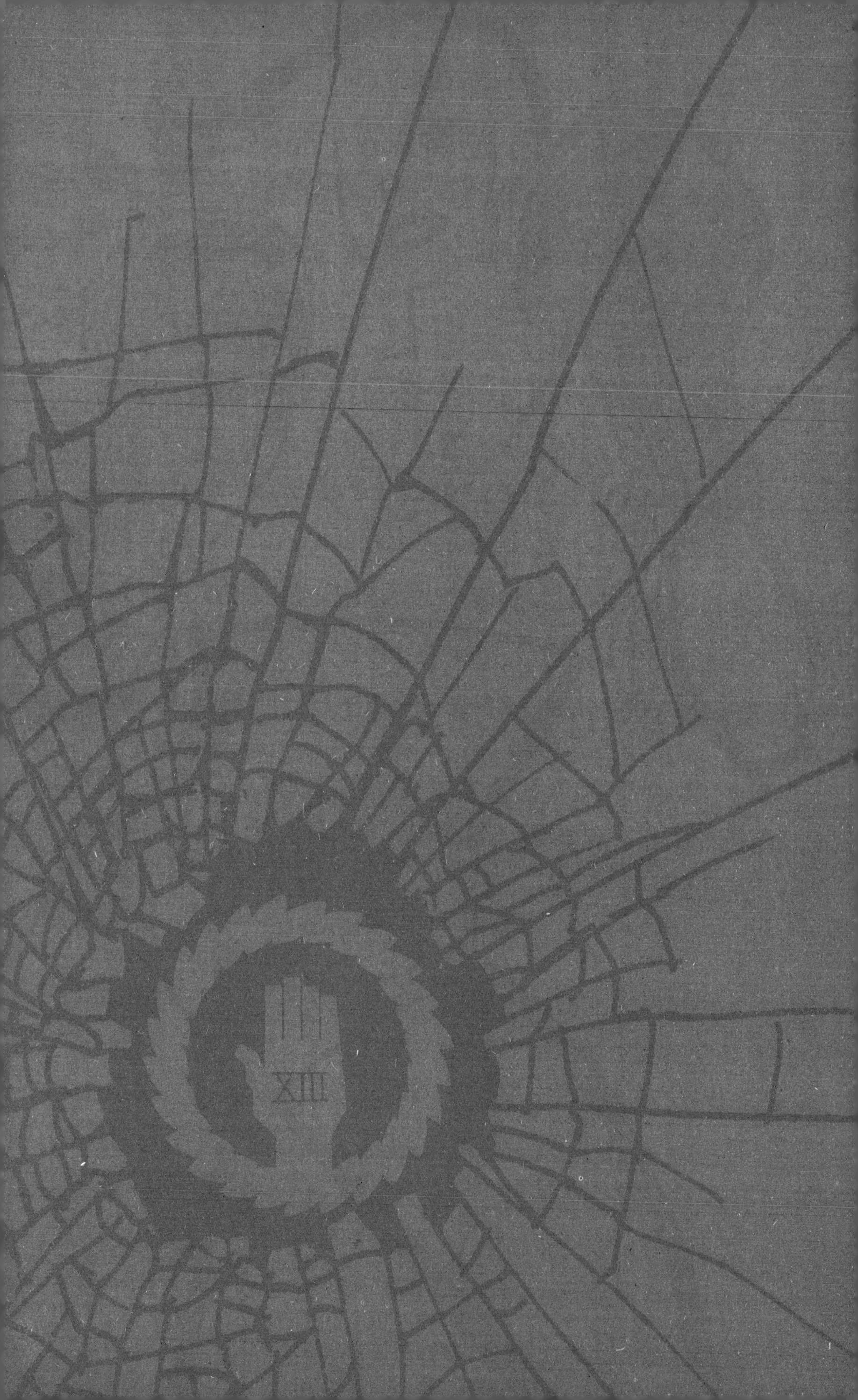
XIII

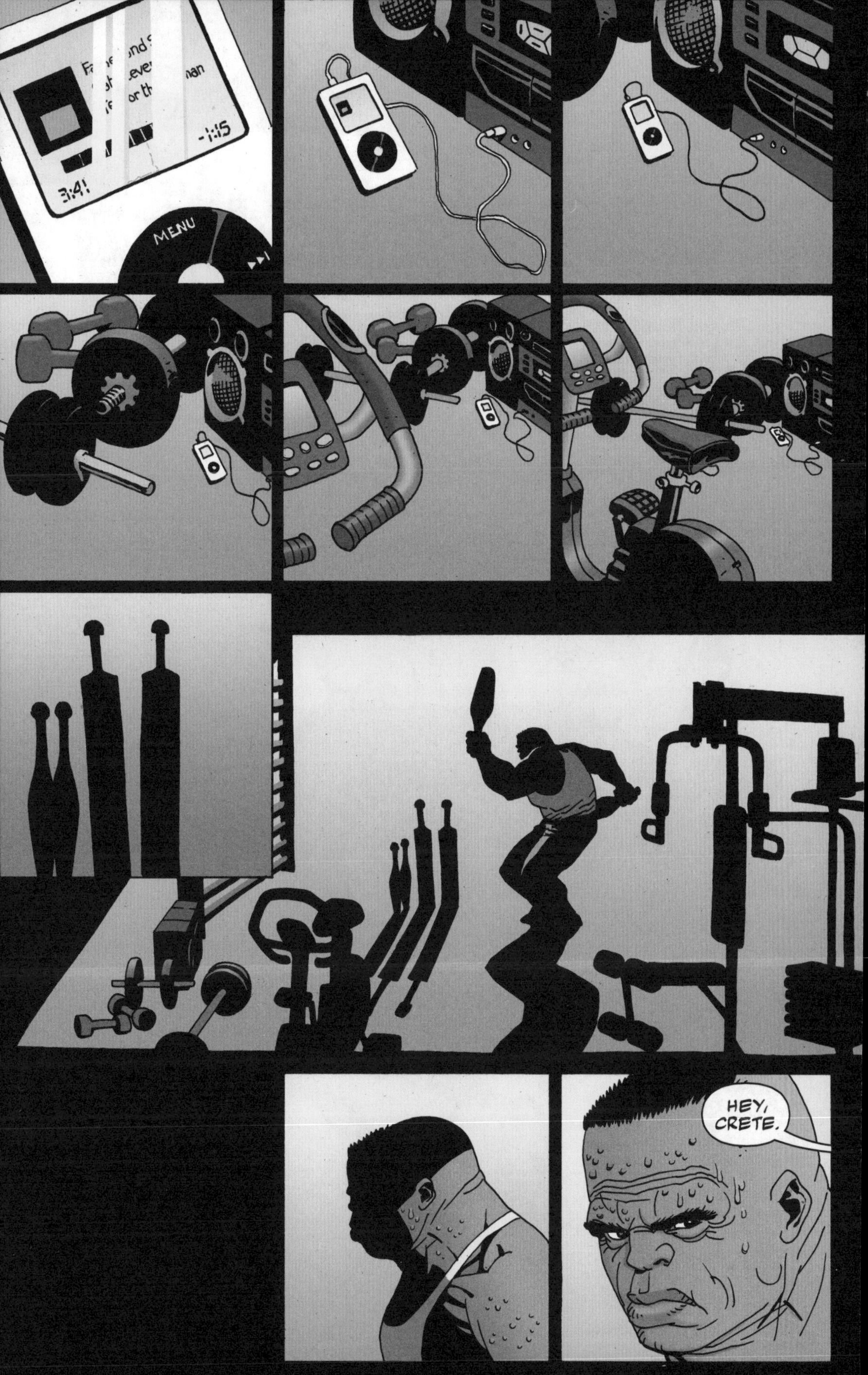
-1:15
3:41
MENU
HEY, CRETE.

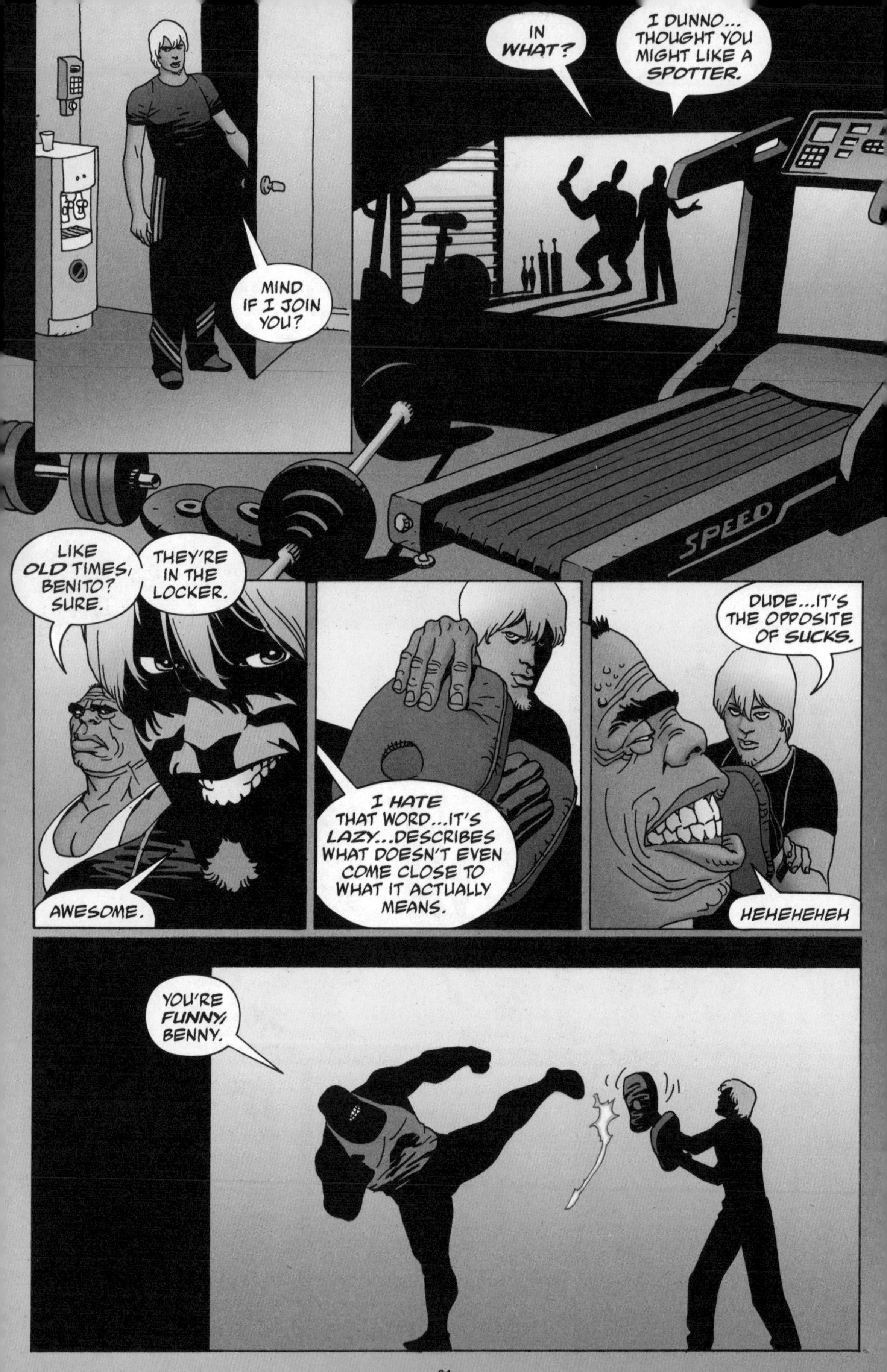
MIND IF I JOIN YOU?
IN WHAT?
I DUNNO... THOUGHT YOU MIGHT LIKE A SPOTTER.
SPEED
LIKE OLD TIMES, BENITO? SURE.
THEY'RE IN THE LOCKER.
AWESOME.
I HATE THAT WORD...IT'S LAZY...DESCRIBES WHAT DOESN'T EVEN COME CLOSE TO WHAT IT ACTUALLY MEANS.
DUDE...IT'S THE OPPOSITE OF SUCKS.
HEHEHEHEH
YOU'RE FUNNY, BENNY.

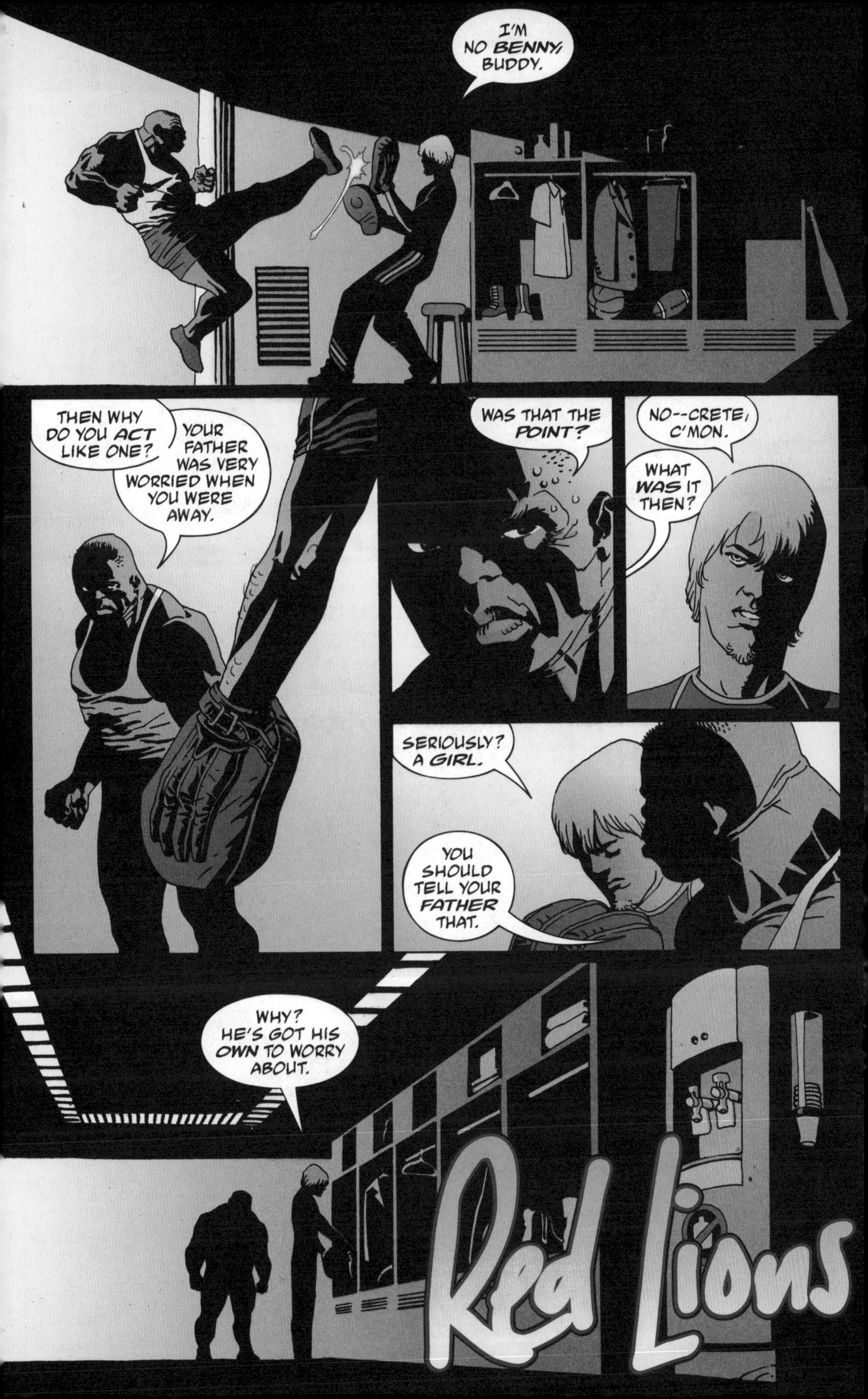
I'M NO BENNY, BUDDY.
THEN WHY DO YOU ACT LIKE ONE?
YOUR FATHER WAS VERY WORRIED WHEN YOU WERE AWAY.
WAS THAT THE POINT?
NO--CRETE, C'MON.
WHAT WAS IT THEN?
SERIOUSLY? A GIRL.
YOU SHOULD TELL YOUR FATHER THAT.
WHY? HE'S GOT HIS OWN TO WORRY ABOUT.
Red Lions

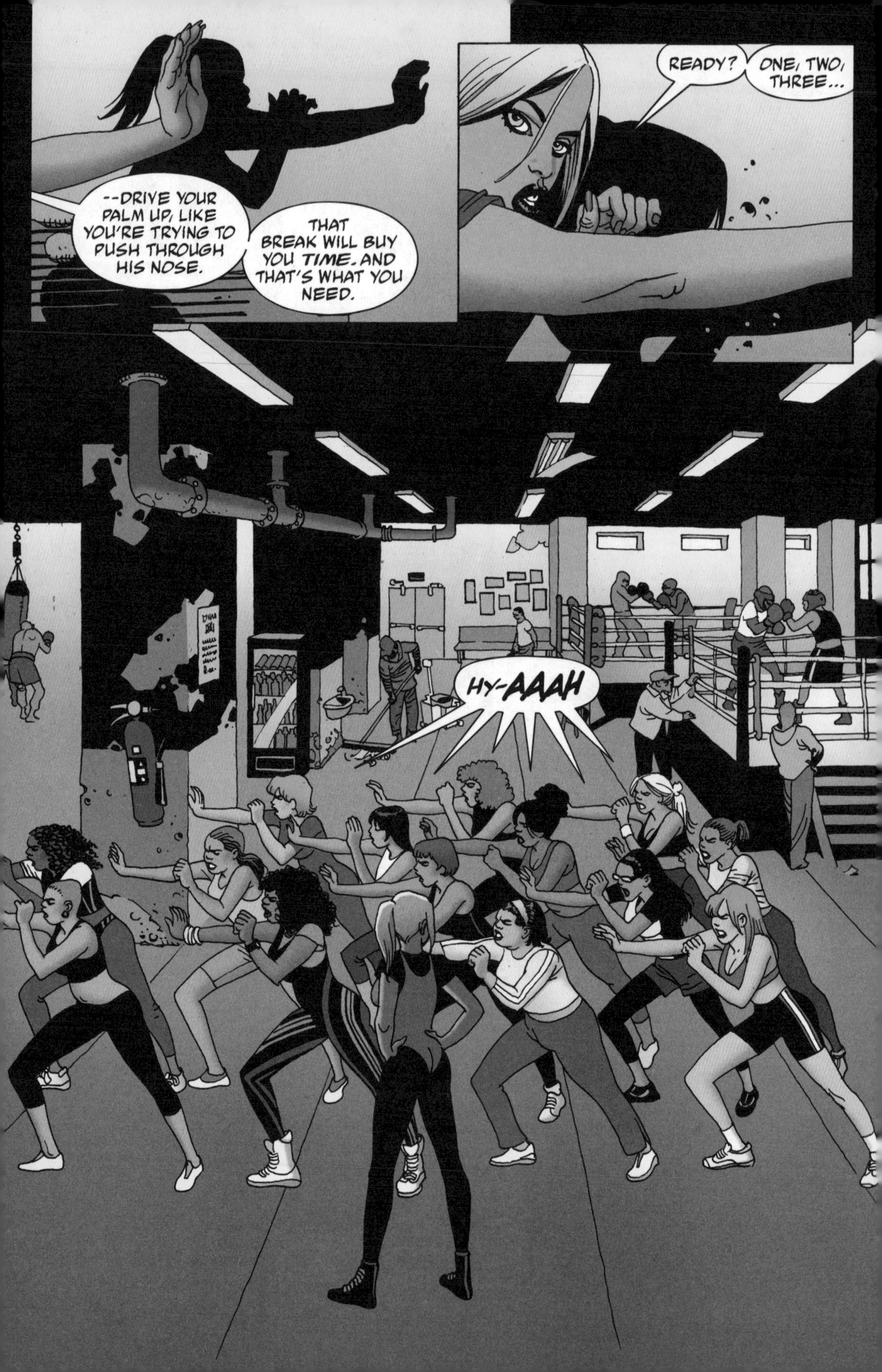
--DRIVE YOUR PALM UP, LIKE YOU'RE TRYING TO PUSH THROUGH HIS NOSE.
THAT BREAK WILL BUY YOU TIME. AND THAT'S WHAT YOU NEED.
READY?
ONE, TWO, THREE...
HY-AAAH

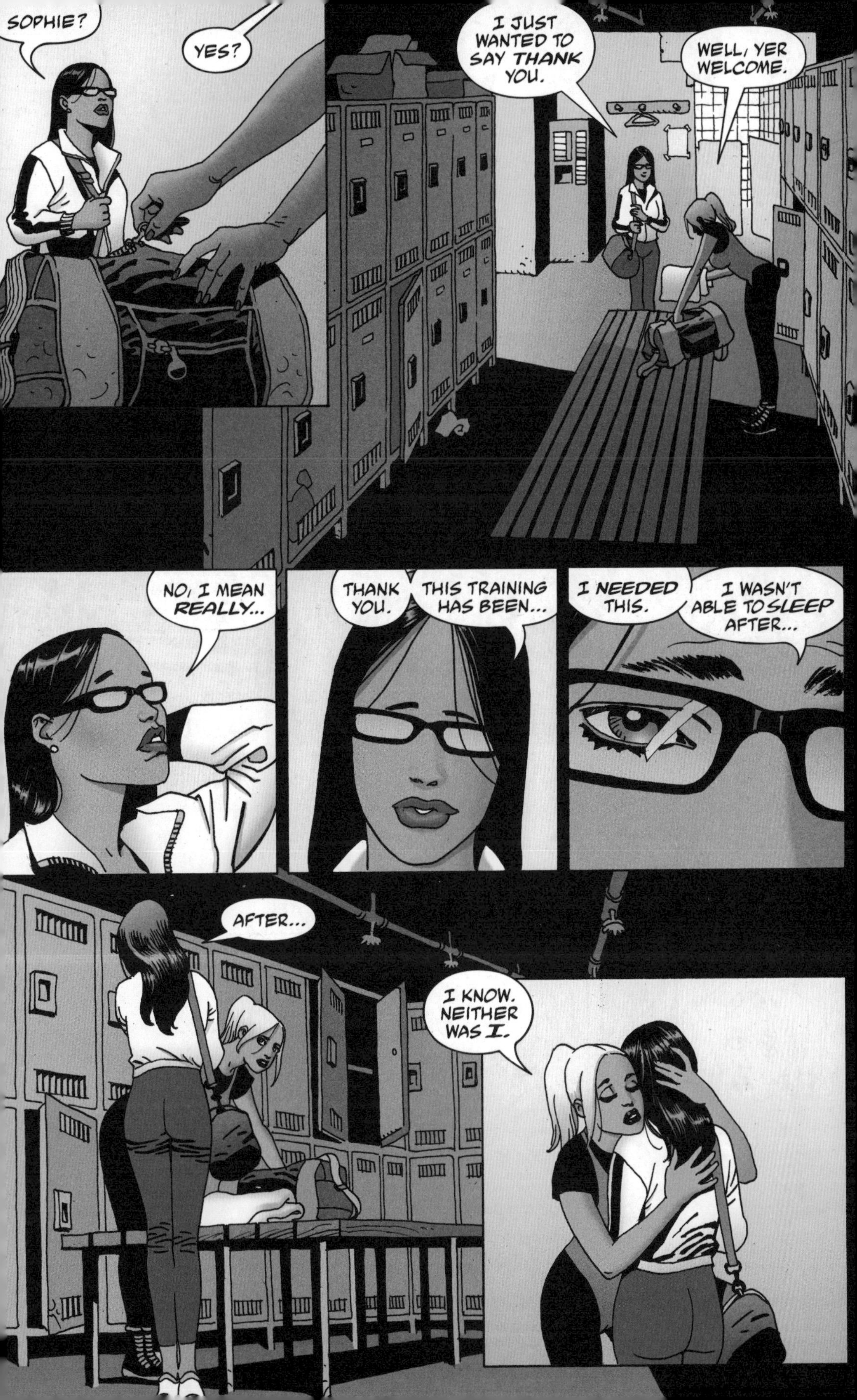

SOPHIE?
YES?
I JUST WANTED TO SAY THANK YOU.
WELL, YER WELCOME.
NO, I MEAN REALLY...
THANK YOU.
THIS TRAINING HAS BEEN...
I NEEDED THIS.
I WASN'T ABLE TO SLEEP AFTER...
AFTER...
I KNOW. NEITHER WAS I.

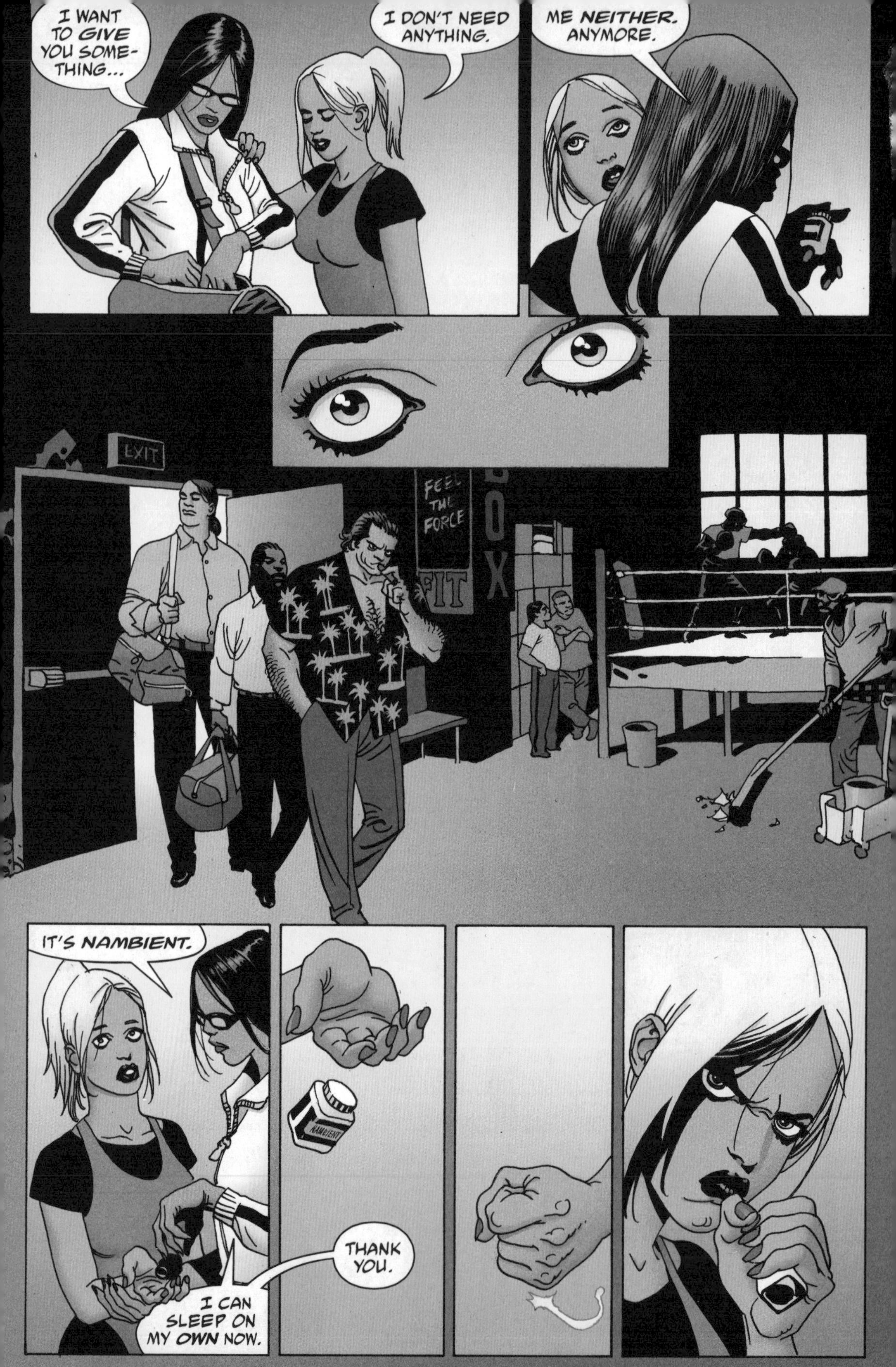

I WANT TO GIVE YOU SOME-THING...
I DON'T NEED ANYTHING.
ME NEITHER. ANYMORE.
EXIT
FEEL THE FORCE
FIT
BOX
IT'S NAMBIENT.
NAMBIENT
THANK YOU.
I CAN SLEEP ON MY OWN NOW.

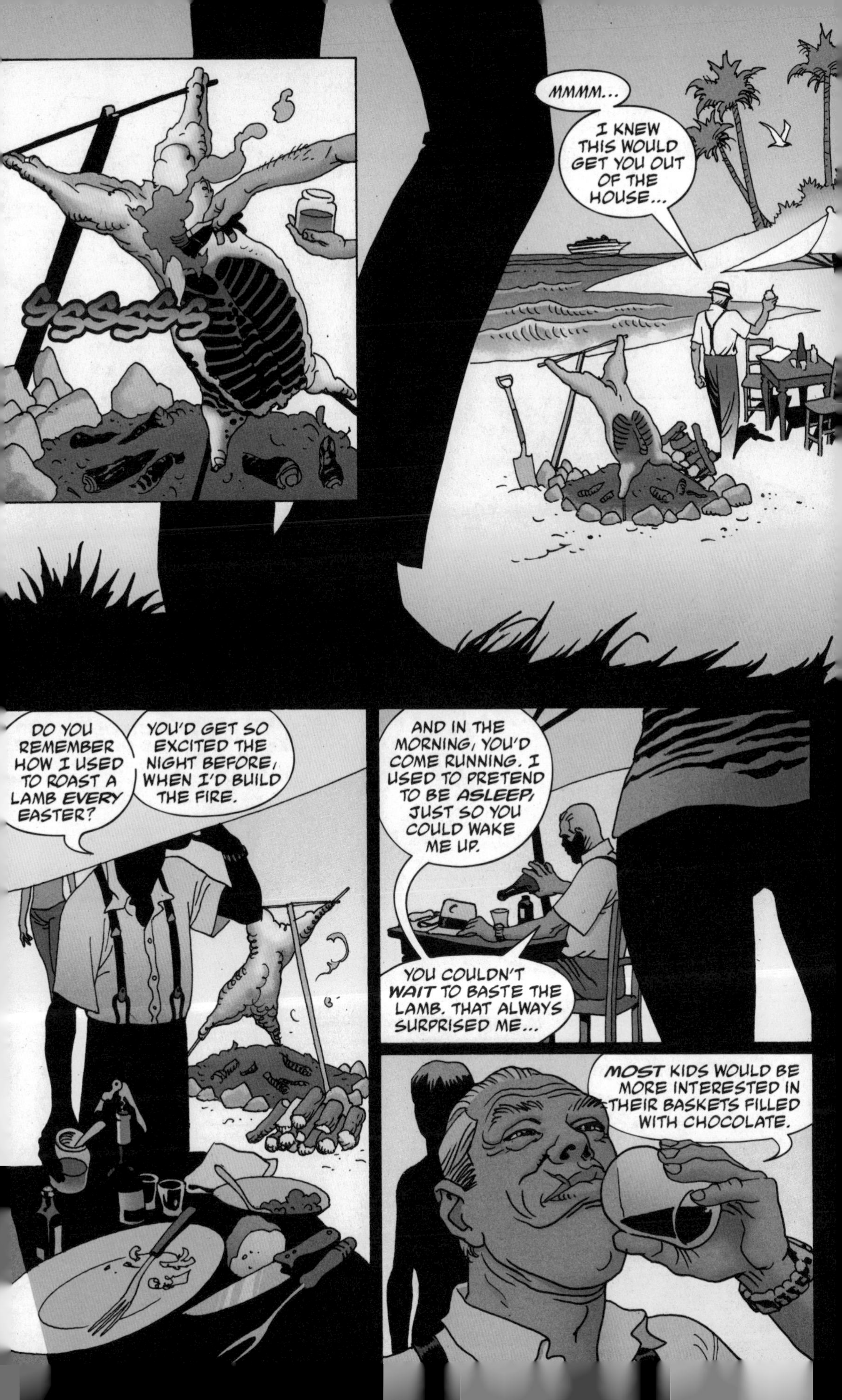
SSSSSS
MMMM...
I KNEW THIS WOULD GET YOU OUT OF THE HOUSE...
DO YOU REMEMBER HOW I USED TO ROAST A LAMB EVERY EASTER?
YOU'D GET SO EXCITED THE NIGHT BEFORE, WHEN I'D BUILD THE FIRE.
AND IN THE MORNING, YOU'D COME RUNNING. I USED TO PRETEND TO BE ASLEEP, JUST SO YOU COULD WAKE ME UP.
YOU COULDN'T WAIT TO BASTE THE LAMB. THAT ALWAYS SURPRISED ME...
MOST KIDS WOULD BE MORE INTERESTED IN THEIR BASKETS FILLED WITH CHOCOLATE.

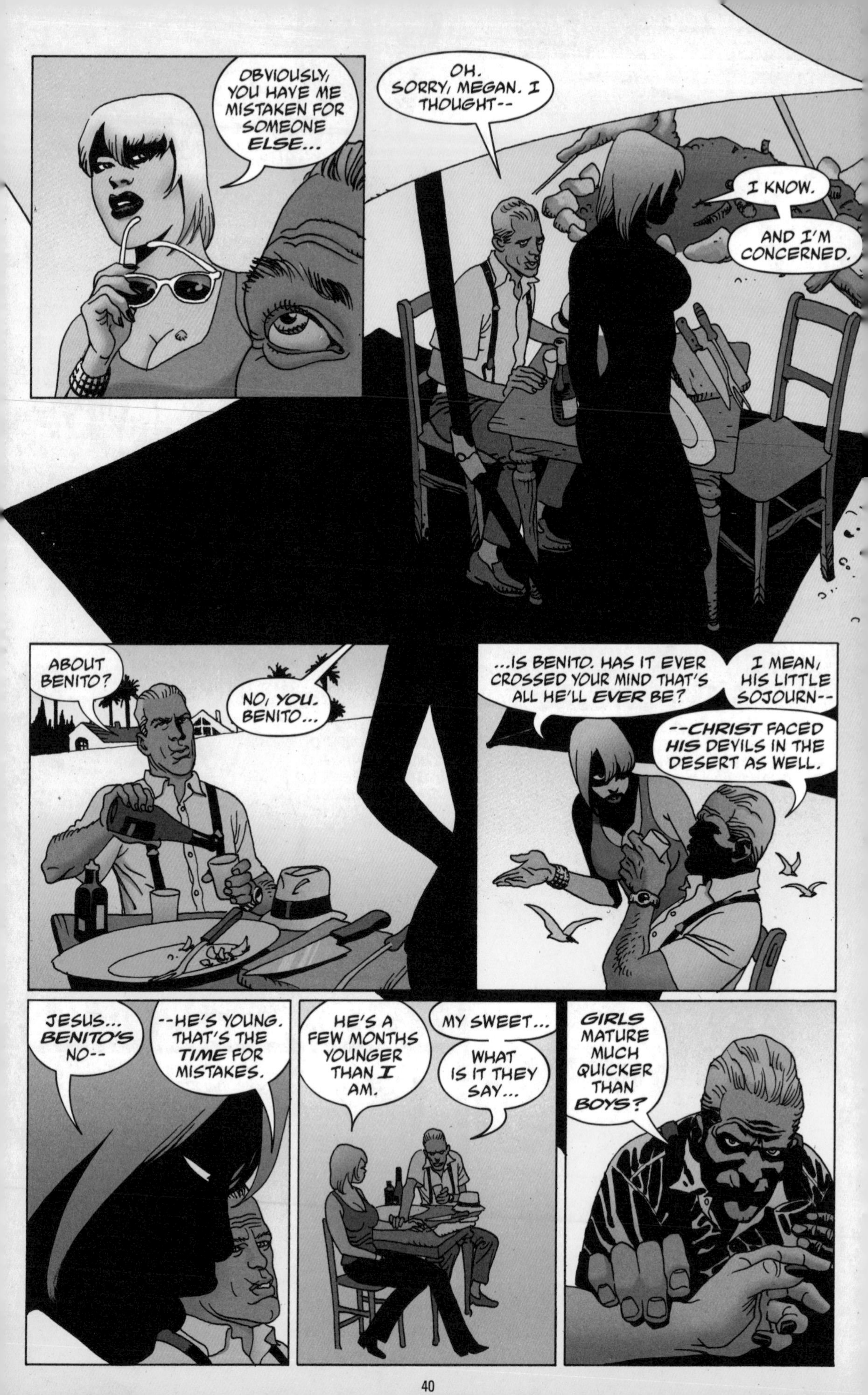
OBVIOUSLY, YOU HAVE ME MISTAKEN FOR SOMEONE ELSE...
OH. SORRY, MEGAN. I THOUGHT--
I KNOW.
AND I'M CONCERNED.
ABOUT BENITO?
NO, YOU. BENITO...
...IS BENITO. HAS IT EVER CROSSED YOUR MIND THAT'S ALL HE'LL EVER BE?
I MEAN, HIS LITTLE SOJOURN--
--CHRIST FACED HIS DEVILS IN THE DESERT AS WELL.
JESUS... BENITO'S NO--
--HE'S YOUNG. THAT'S THE TIME FOR MISTAKES.
HE'S A FEW MONTHS YOUNGER THAN I AM.
MY SWEET...
WHAT IS IT THEY SAY...
GIRLS MATURE MUCH QUICKER THAN BOYS?

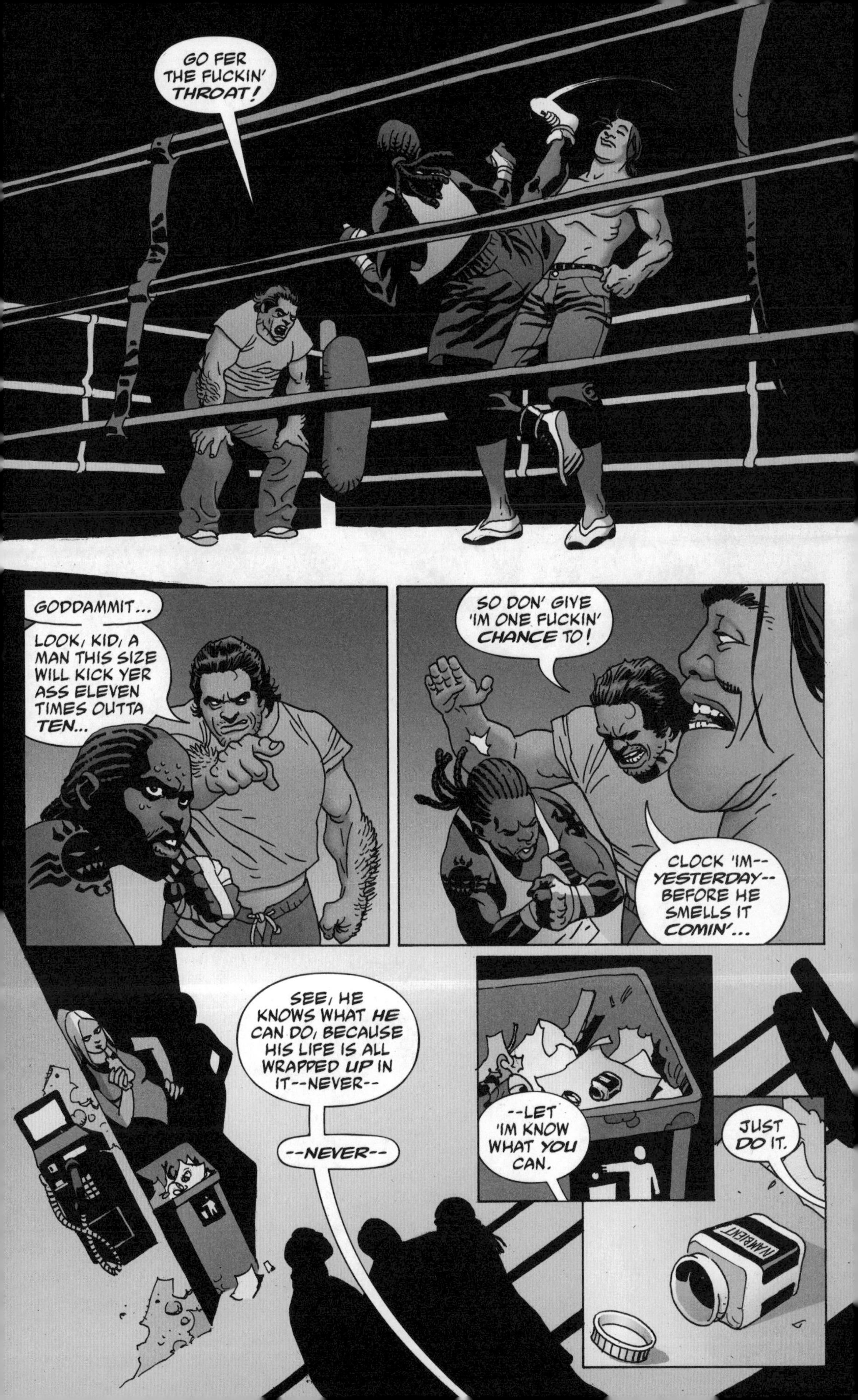
GO FER THE FUCKIN' THROAT!
GODDAMMIT...
LOOK, KID, A MAN THIS SIZE WILL KICK YER ASS ELEVEN TIMES OUTTA TEN...
SO DON' GIVE 'IM ONE FUCKIN' CHANCE TO!
CLOCK 'IM--YESTERDAY--BEFORE HE SMELLS IT COMIN'...
SEE, HE KNOWS WHAT HE CAN DO, BECAUSE HIS LIFE IS ALL WRAPPED UP IN IT--NEVER--
--NEVER--
--LET 'IM KNOW WHAT YOU CAN.
JUST DO IT.

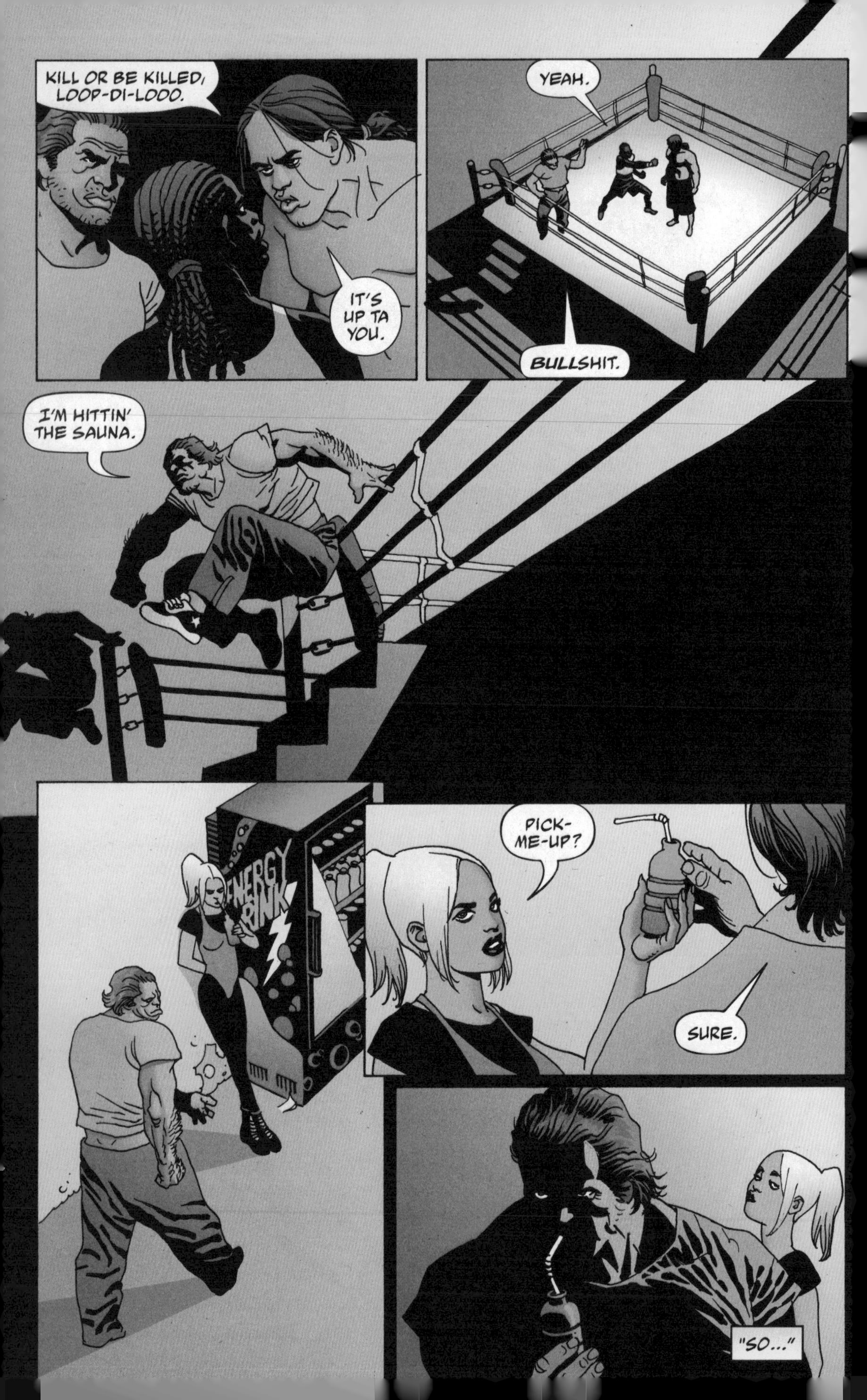
KILL OR BE KILLED, LOOP-DI-LOOO.
IT'S UP TA YOU.
YEAH.
BULLSHIT.
I'M HITTIN' THE SAUNA.
ENERGY DRINK
PICK-ME-UP?
SURE.
"SO..."

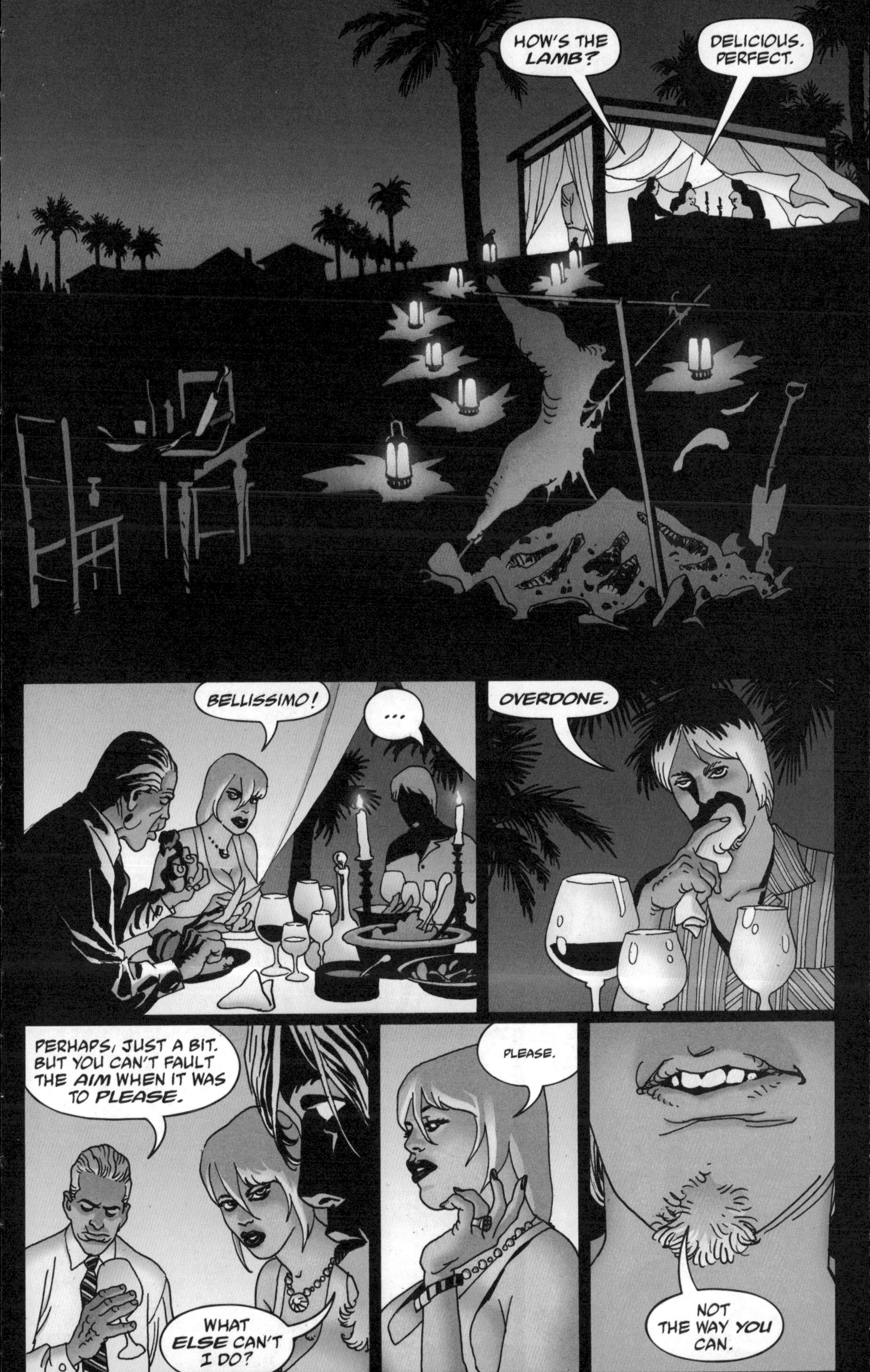
HOW'S THE LAMB?
DELICIOUS. PERFECT.
BELLISSIMO!
...
OVERDONE.
PERHAPS, JUST A BIT. BUT YOU CAN'T FAULT THE AIM WHEN IT WAS TO PLEASE.
WHAT ELSE CAN'T I DO?
PLEASE.
NOT THE WAY YOU CAN.

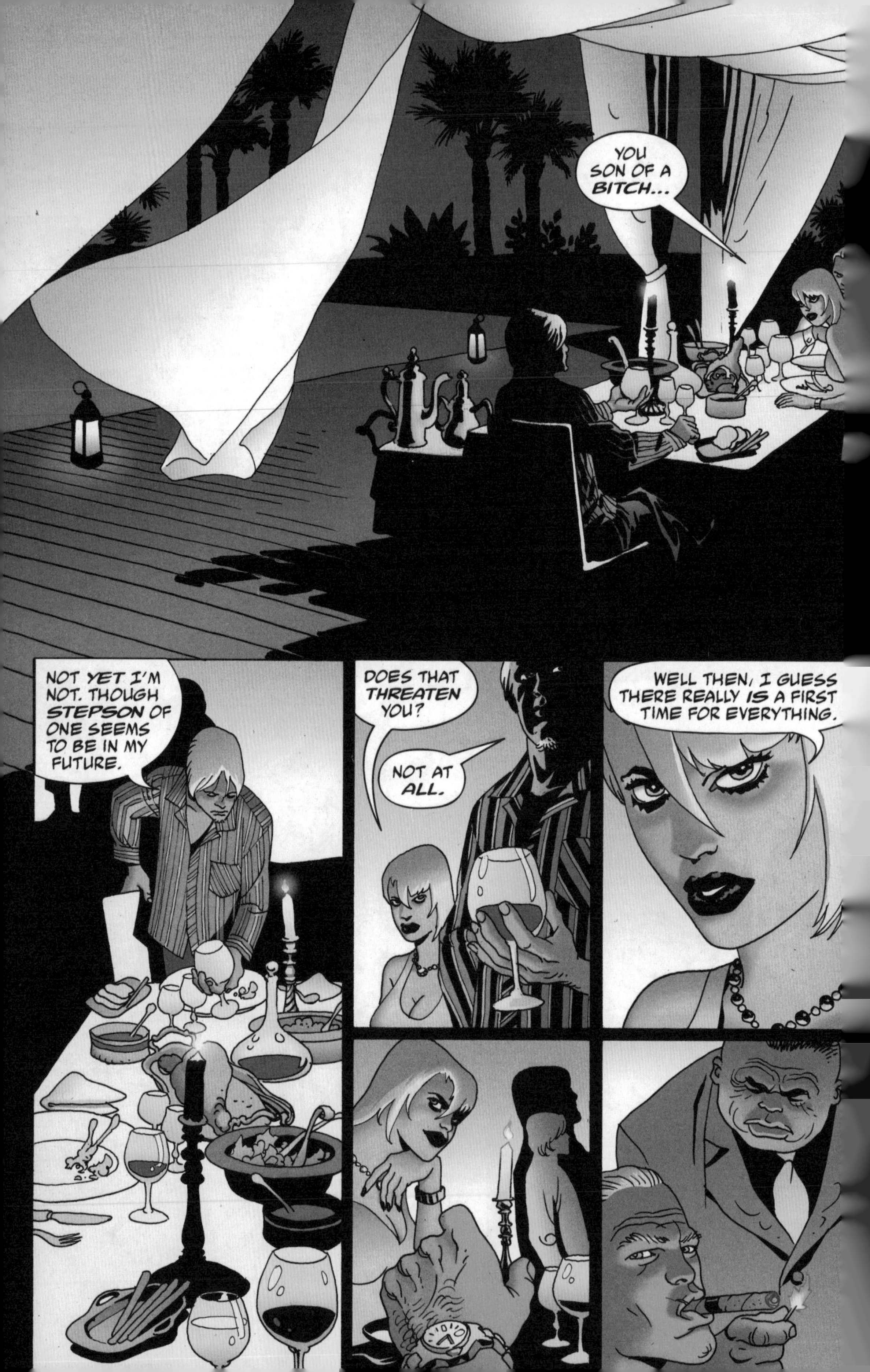
YOU SON OF A BITCH...
NOT YET I'M NOT. THOUGH STEPSON OF ONE SEEMS TO BE IN MY FUTURE.
DOES THAT THREATEN YOU?
NOT AT ALL.
WELL THEN, I GUESS THERE REALLY IS A FIRST TIME FOR EVERYTHING.

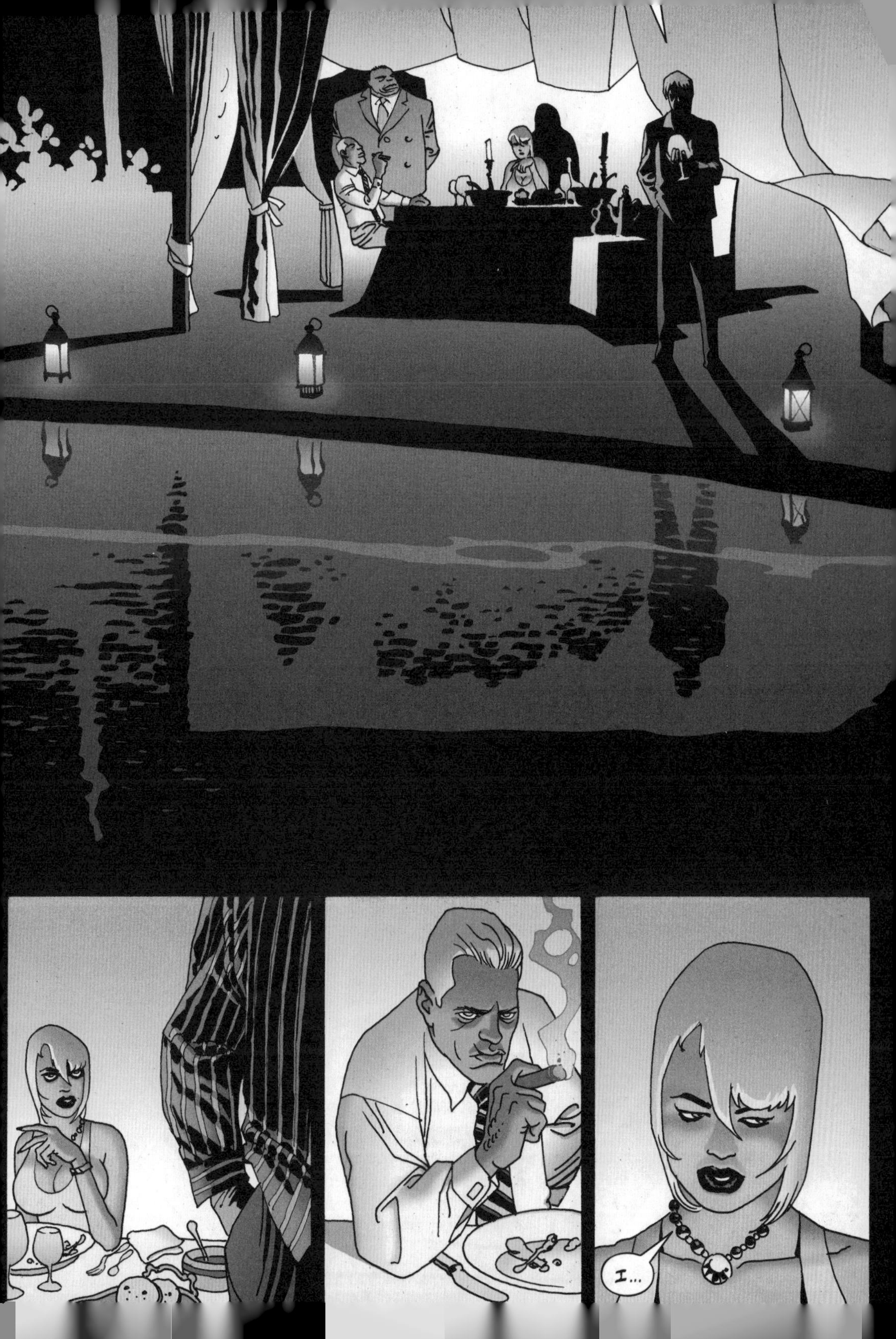
I...

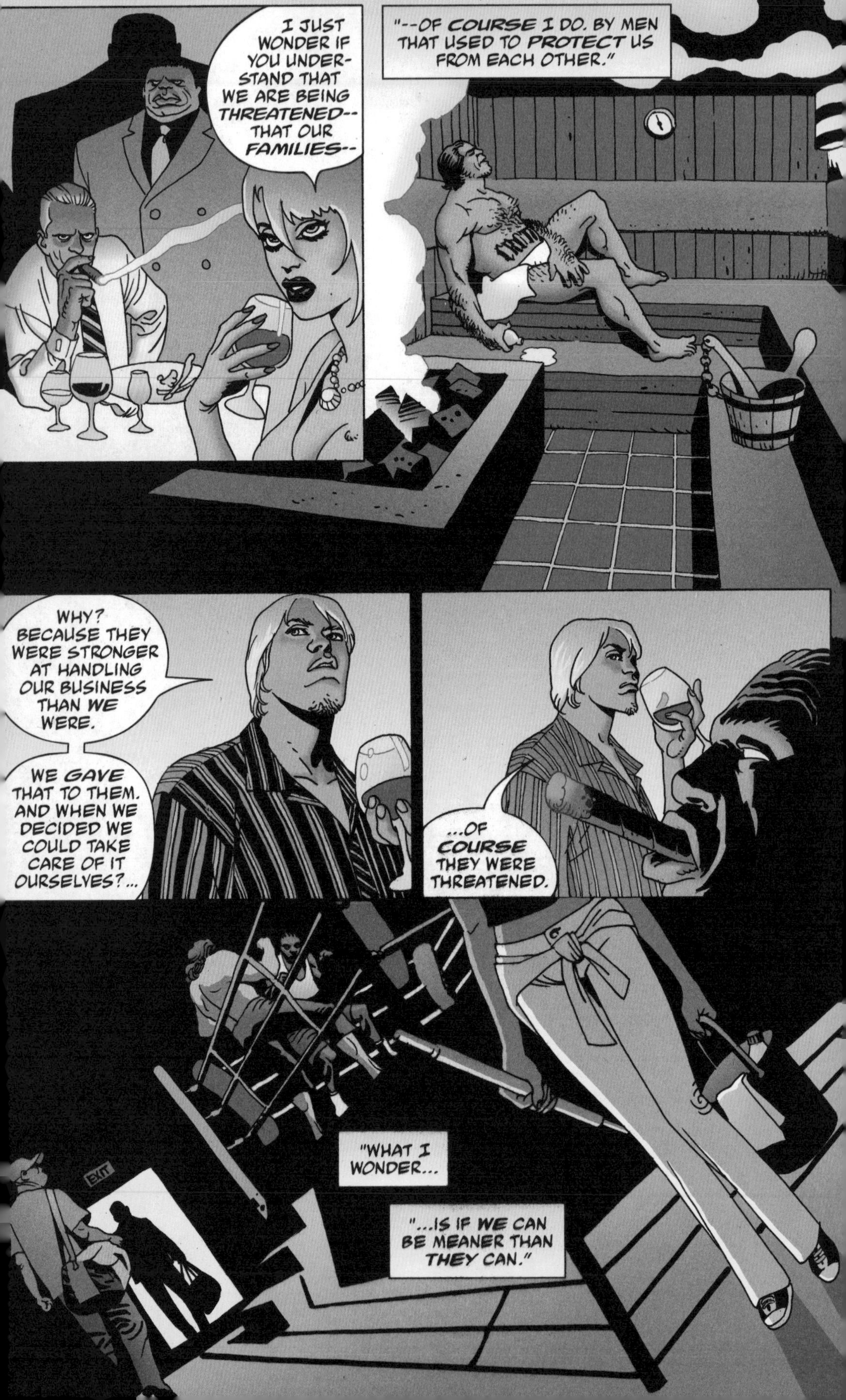
I JUST WONDER IF YOU UNDERSTAND THAT WE ARE BEING THREATENED-- THAT OUR FAMILIES--
"--OF COURSE I DO. BY MEN THAT USED TO PROTECT US FROM EACH OTHER."
WHY? BECAUSE THEY WERE STRONGER AT HANDLING OUR BUSINESS THAN WE WERE.
WE GAVE THAT TO THEM. AND WHEN WE DECIDED WE COULD TAKE CARE OF IT OURSELVES?...
...OF COURSE THEY WERE THREATENED.
"WHAT I WONDER...
"...IS IF WE CAN BE MEANER THAN THEY CAN."
EXIT

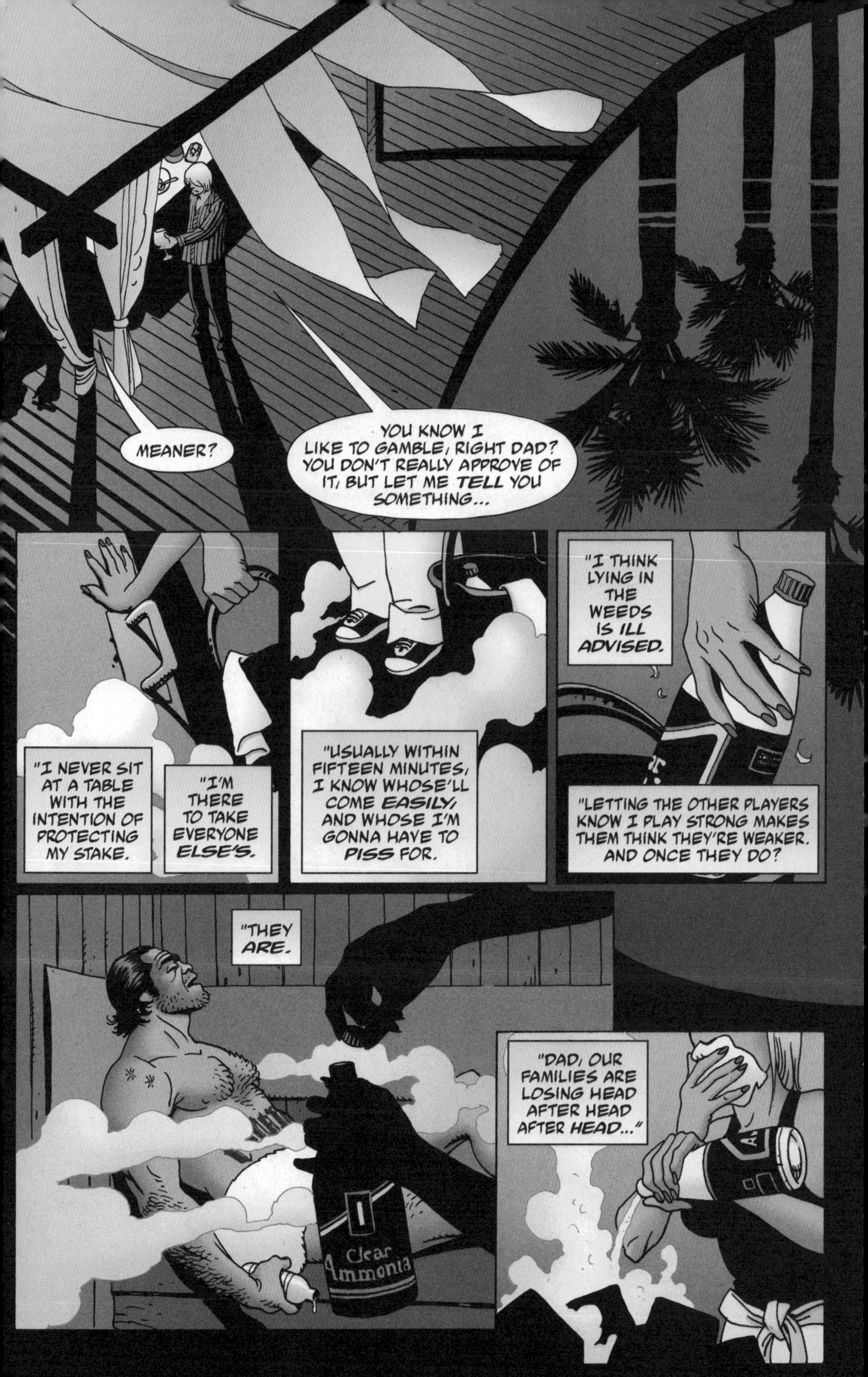
MEANER?
YOU KNOW I LIKE TO GAMBLE, RIGHT DAD? YOU DON'T REALLY APPROVE OF IT, BUT LET ME TELL YOU SOMETHING...
"I NEVER SIT AT A TABLE WITH THE INTENTION OF PROTECTING MY STAKE.
"I'M THERE TO TAKE EVERYONE ELSE'S.
"USUALLY WITHIN FIFTEEN MINUTES, I KNOW WHOSE'LL COME EASILY, AND WHOSE I'M GONNA HAVE TO PISS FOR.
"I THINK LYING IN THE WEEDS IS ILL ADVISED.
"LETTING THE OTHER PLAYERS KNOW I PLAY STRONG MAKES THEM THINK THEY'RE WEAKER. AND ONCE THEY DO?
"THEY ARE.
Clear Ammonia
"DAD, OUR FAMILIES ARE LOSING HEAD AFTER HEAD AFTER HEAD..."

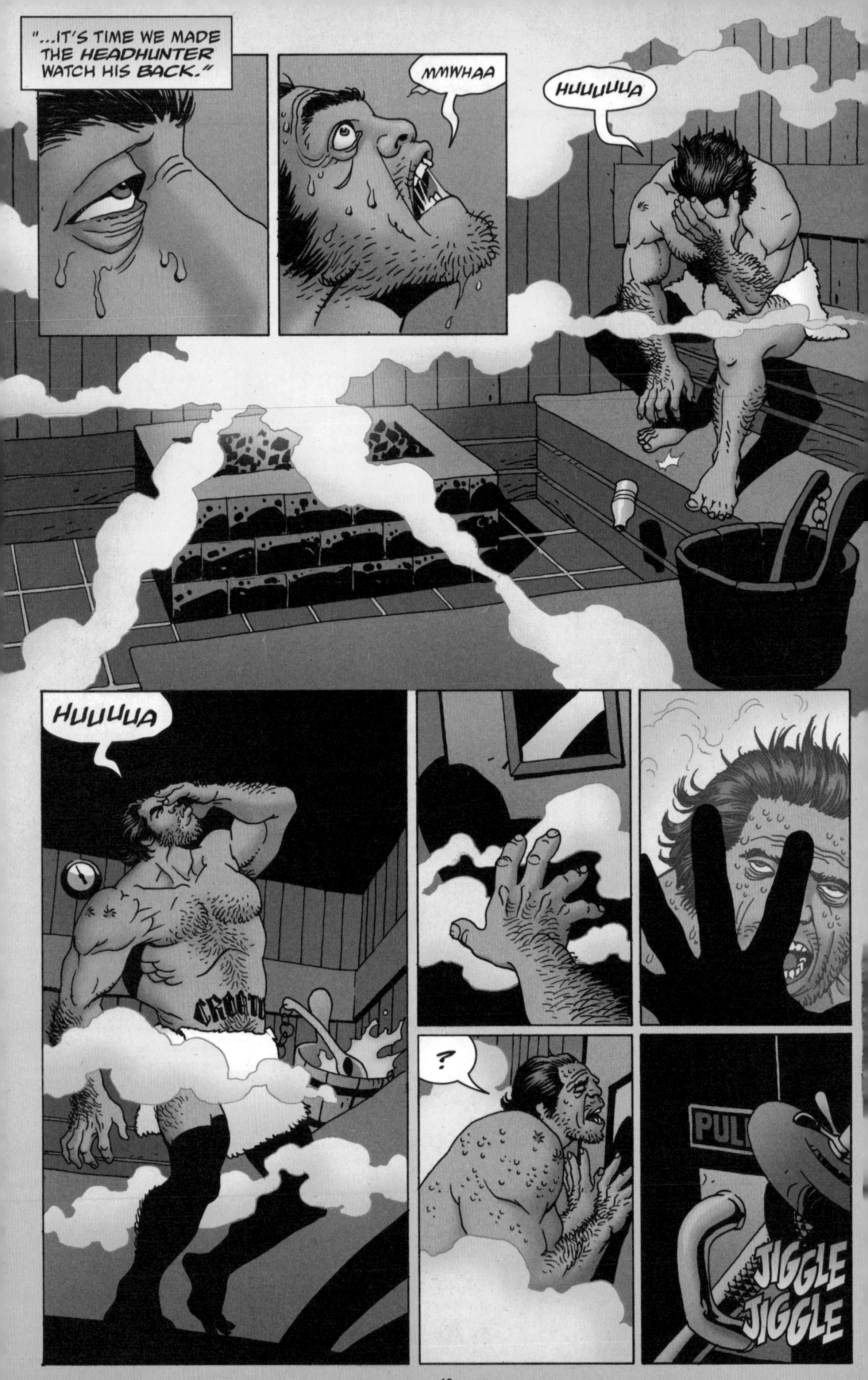
"...IT'S TIME WE MADE THE HEADHUNTER WATCH HIS BACK."
MMWHAA
HUUUUUA
HUUUUA
CROATIA
?
PUL
JIGGLE JIGGLE

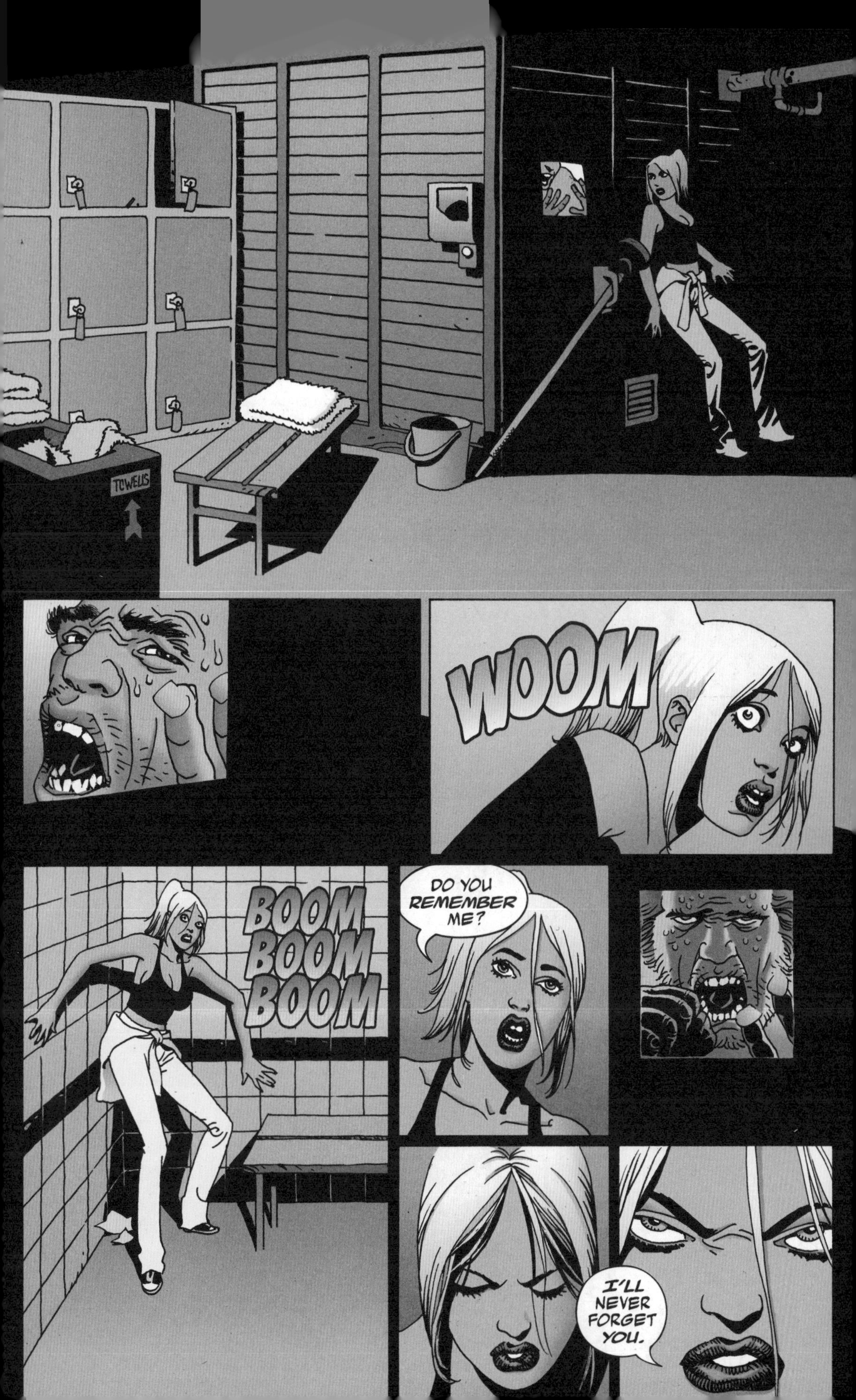
WOOM
BOOM
BOOM
BOOM
DO YOU REMEMBER ME?
I'LL NEVER FORGET YOU.

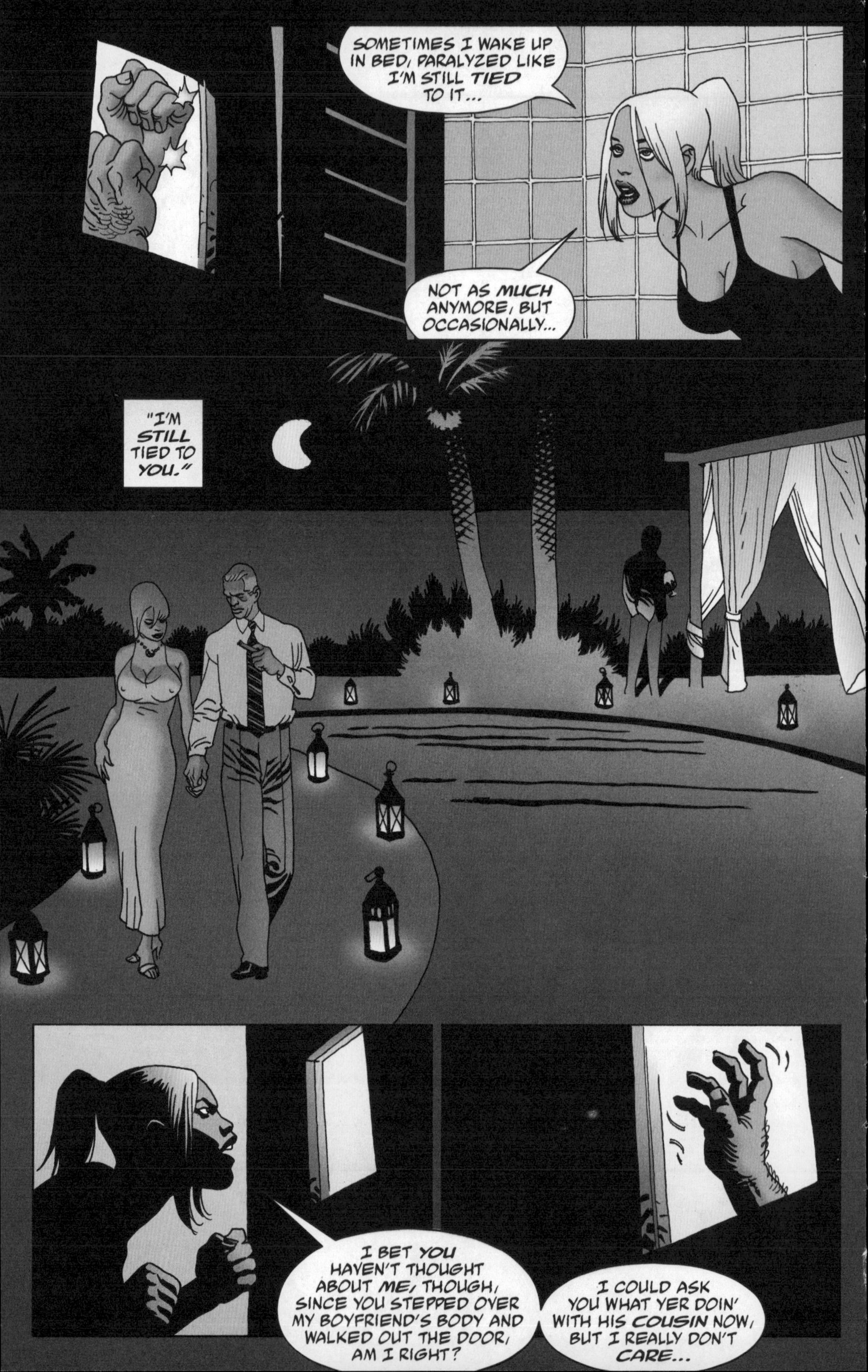
SOMETIMES I WAKE UP IN BED, PARALYZED LIKE I'M STILL TIED TO IT...
NOT AS MUCH ANYMORE, BUT OCCASIONALLY...
"I'M STILL TIED TO YOU."
I BET YOU HAVEN'T THOUGHT ABOUT ME, THOUGH, SINCE YOU STEPPED OVER MY BOYFRIEND'S BODY AND WALKED OUT THE DOOR, AM I RIGHT?
I COULD ASK YOU WHAT YER DOIN' WITH HIS COUSIN NOW, BUT I REALLY DON'T CARE...

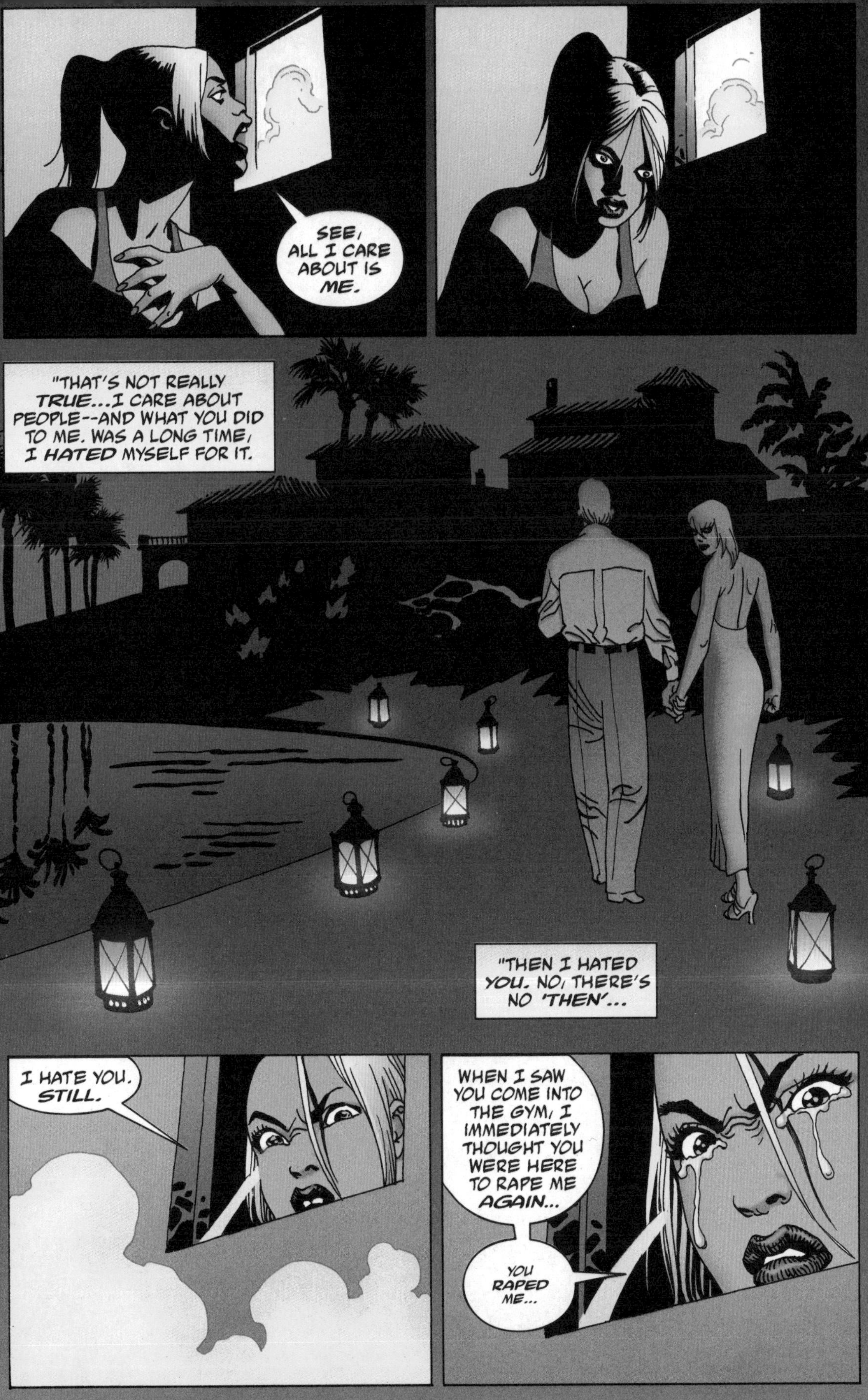
SEE, ALL I CARE ABOUT IS ME.
"THAT'S NOT REALLY TRUE...I CARE ABOUT PEOPLE--AND WHAT YOU DID TO ME. WAS A LONG TIME, I HATED MYSELF FOR IT.
"THEN I HATED YOU. NO, THERE'S NO 'THEN'...
I HATE YOU. STILL.
WHEN I SAW YOU COME INTO THE GYM, I IMMEDIATELY THOUGHT YOU WERE HERE TO RAPE ME AGAIN...
YOU RAPED ME...

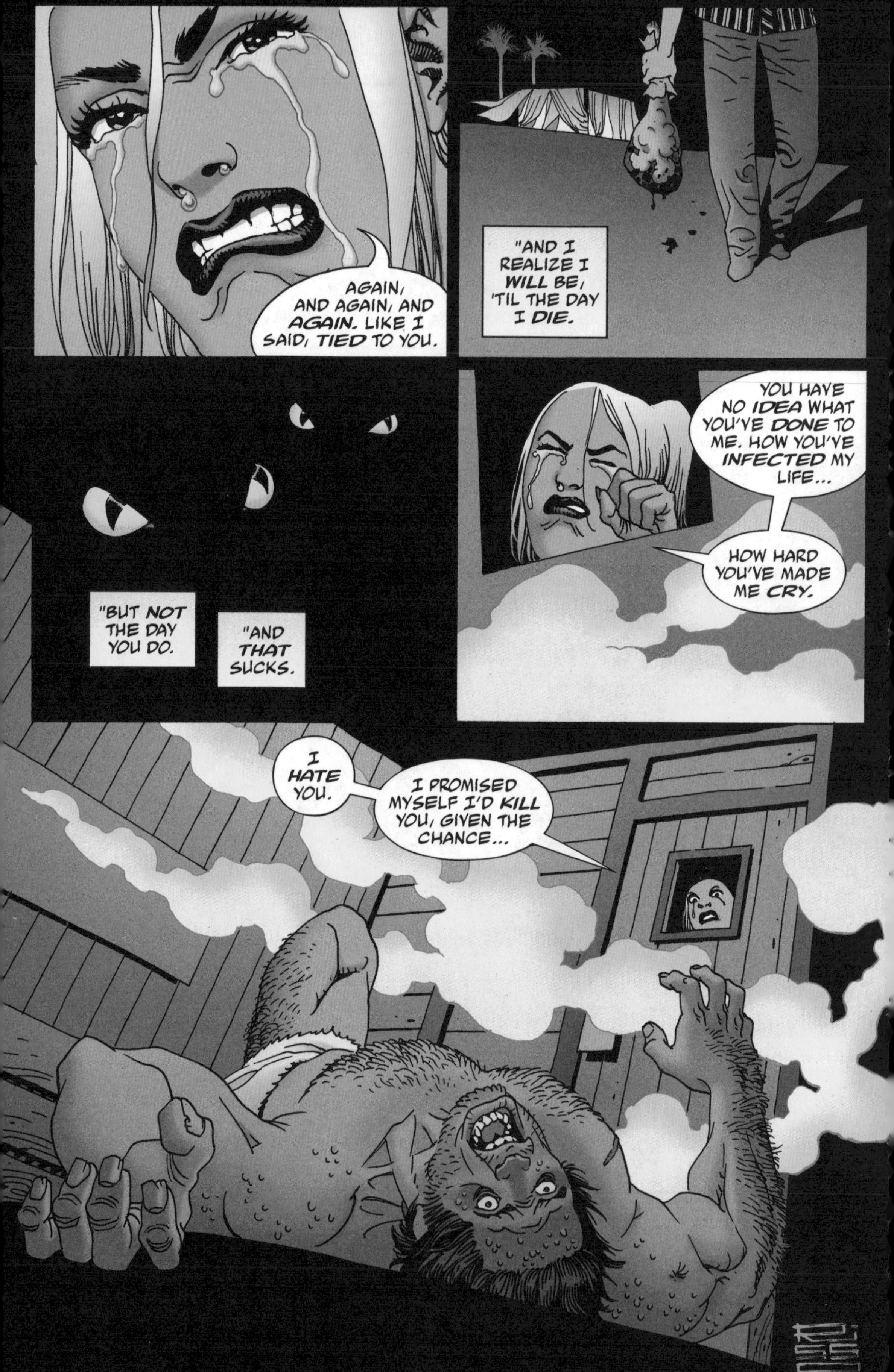
AGAIN, AND AGAIN, AND AGAIN. LIKE I SAID, TIED TO YOU.
"AND I REALIZE I WILL BE, 'TIL THE DAY I DIE.
"BUT NOT THE DAY YOU DO.
"AND THAT SUCKS.
YOU HAVE NO IDEA WHAT YOU'VE DONE TO ME. HOW YOU'VE INFECTED MY LIFE...
HOW HARD YOU'VE MADE ME CRY.
I HATE YOU.
I PROMISED MYSELF I'D KILL YOU, GIVEN THE CHANCE...

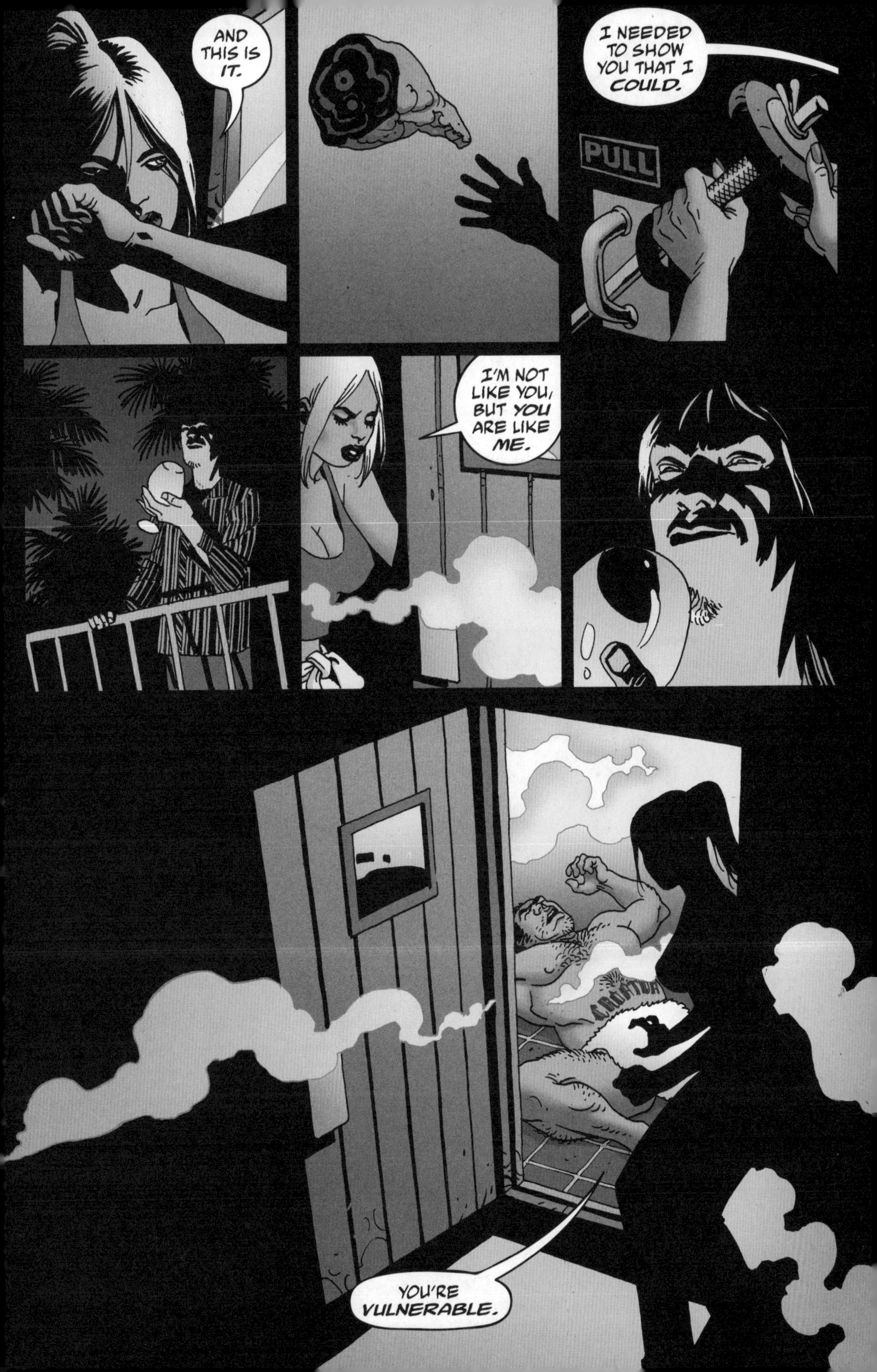
AND THIS IS IT.
I NEEDED TO SHOW YOU THAT I COULD.
PULL
I'M NOT LIKE YOU, BUT YOU ARE LIKE ME.
YOU'RE VULNERABLE.

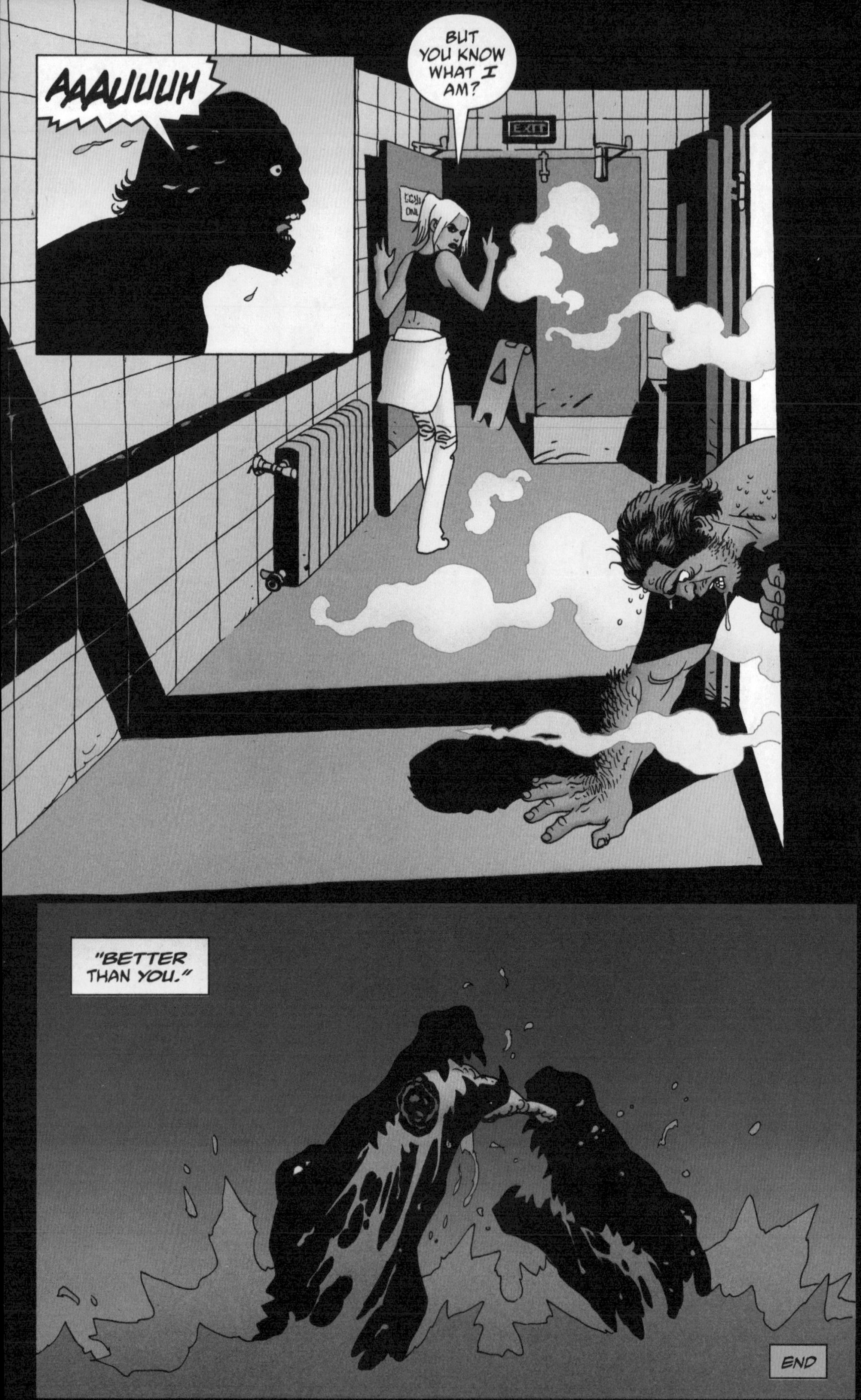
AAAUUUUH
BUT YOU KNOW WHAT I AM?
EXIT
"BETTER THAN YOU."
END

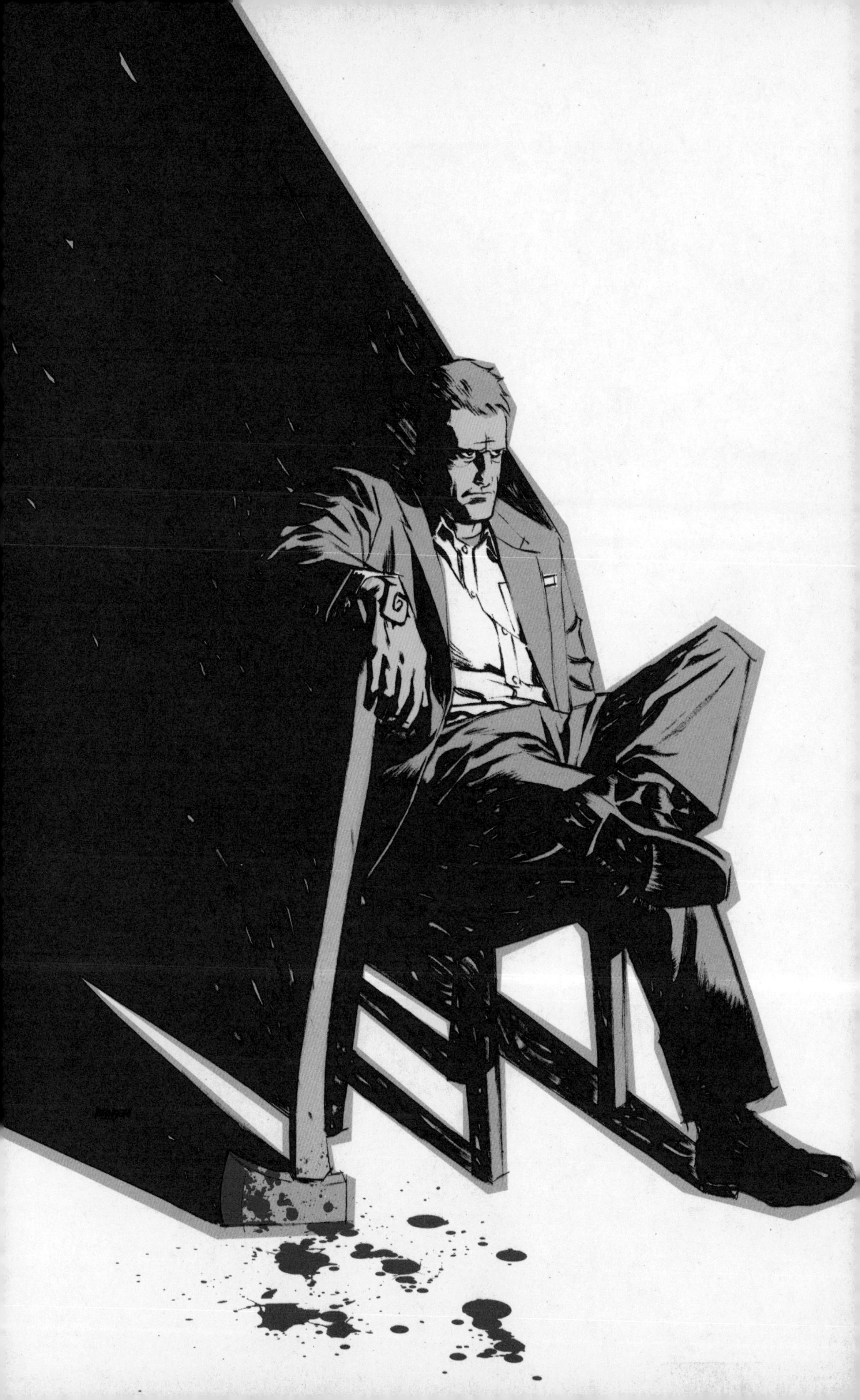

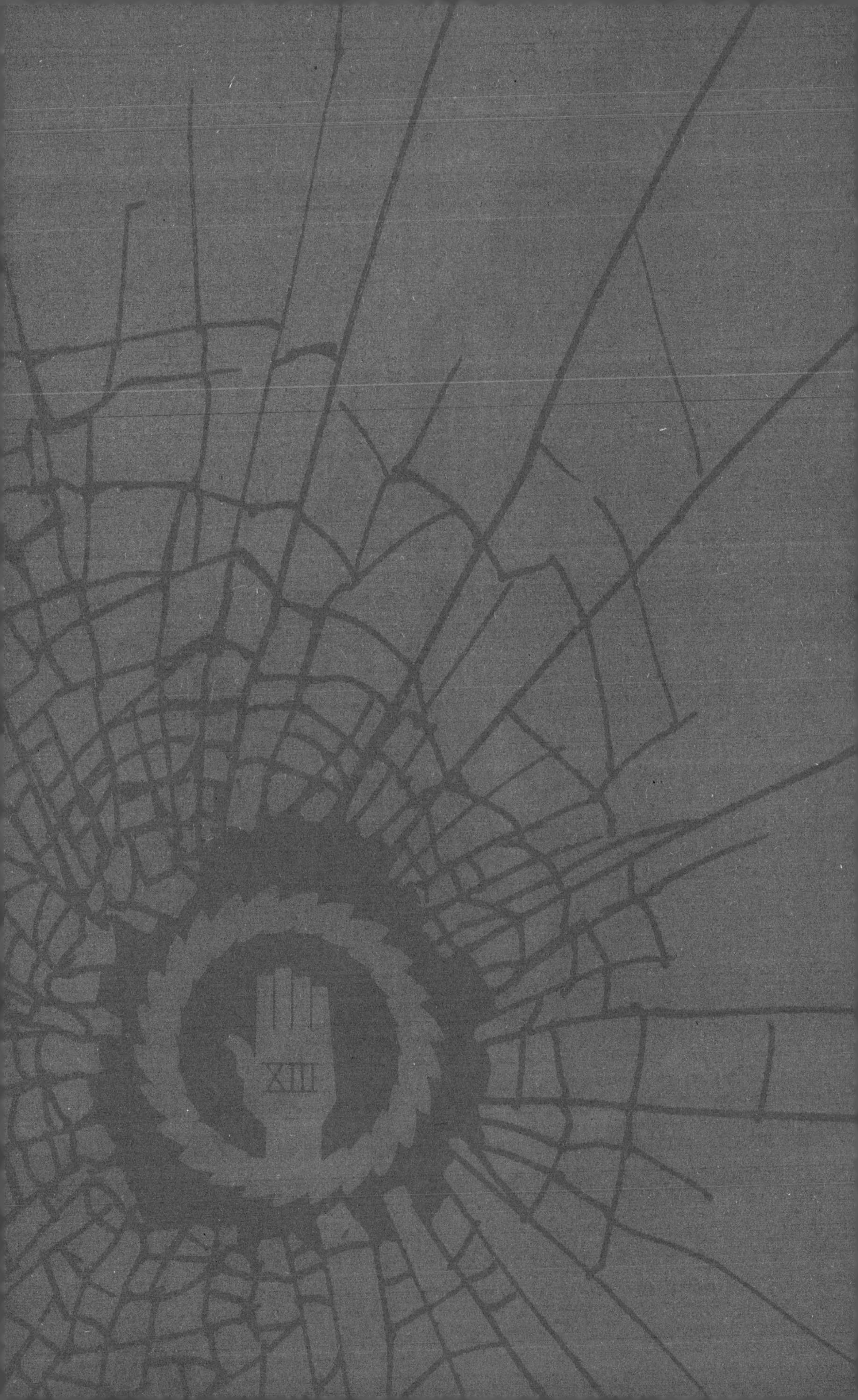
XIII

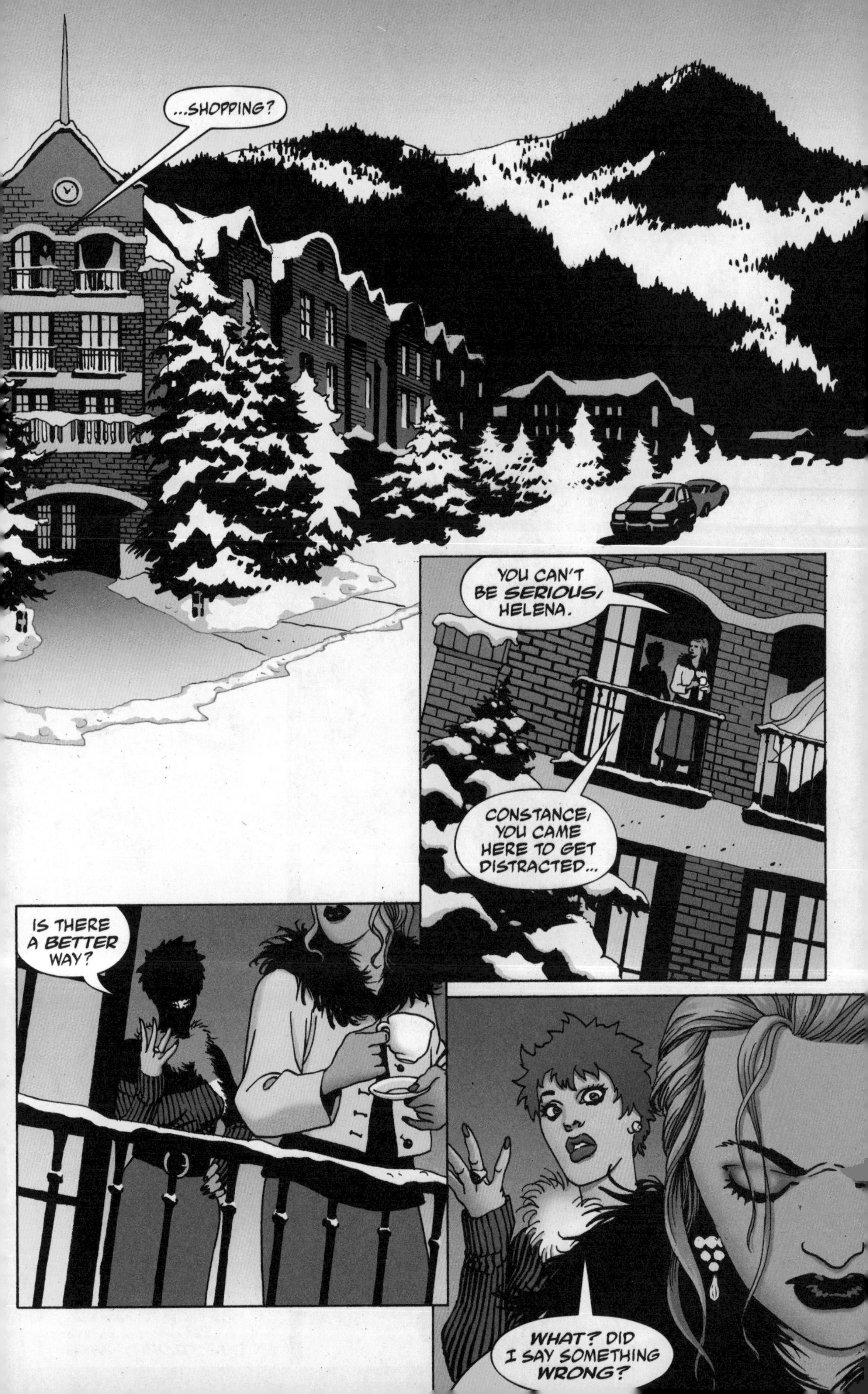
...SHOPPING?
YOU CAN'T BE SERIOUS, HELENA.
CONSTANCE, YOU CAME HERE TO GET DISTRACTED...
IS THERE A BETTER WAY?
WHAT? DID I SAY SOMETHING WRONG?

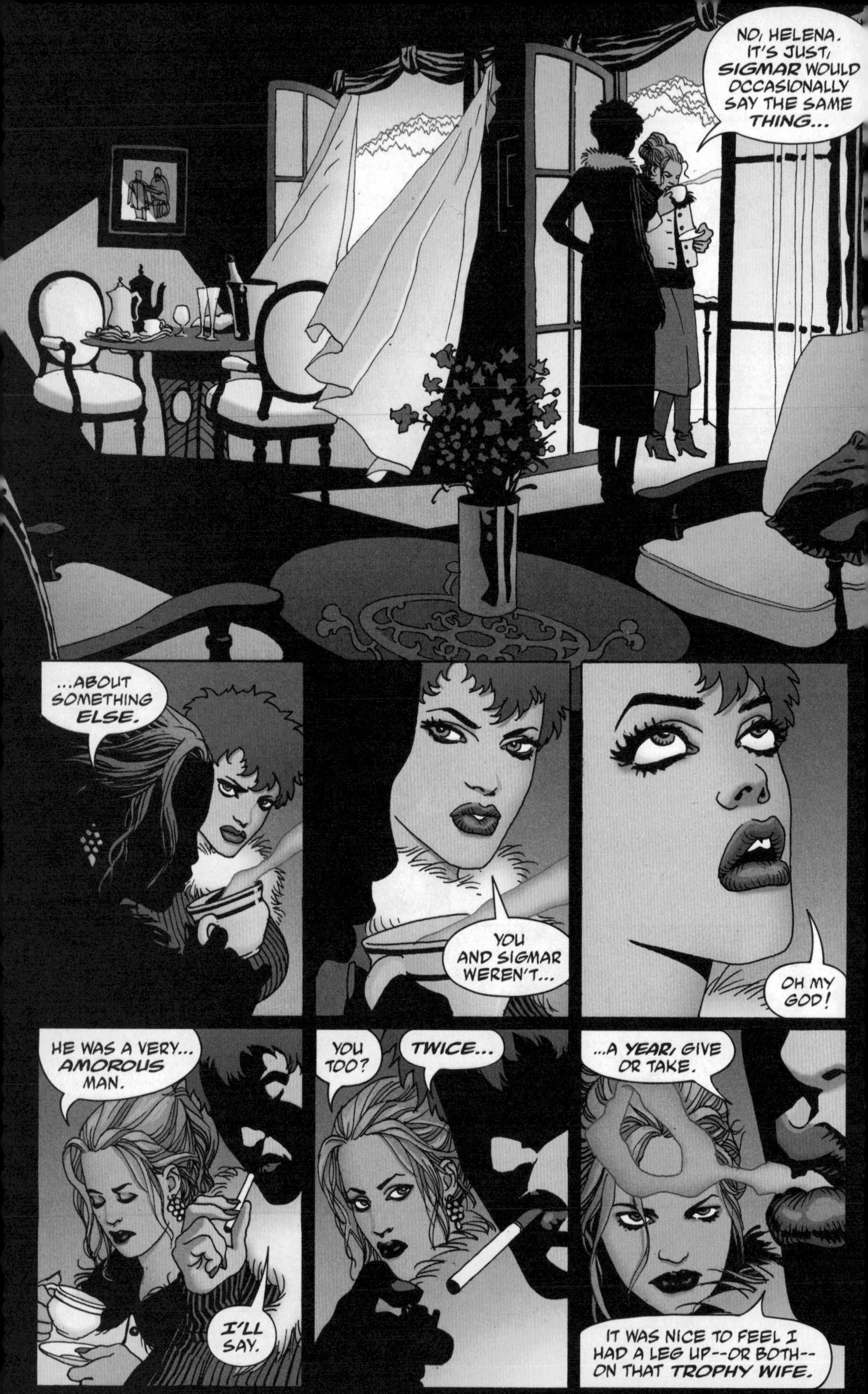
NO, HELENA. IT'S JUST, SIGMAR WOULD OCCASIONALLY SAY THE SAME THING...
...ABOUT SOMETHING ELSE.
YOU AND SIGMAR WEREN'T...
OH MY GOD!
HE WAS A VERY... AMOROUS MAN.
I'LL SAY.
YOU TOO?
TWICE...
...A YEAR, GIVE OR TAKE.
IT WAS NICE TO FEEL I HAD A LEG UP--OR BOTH--ON THAT TROPHY WIFE.

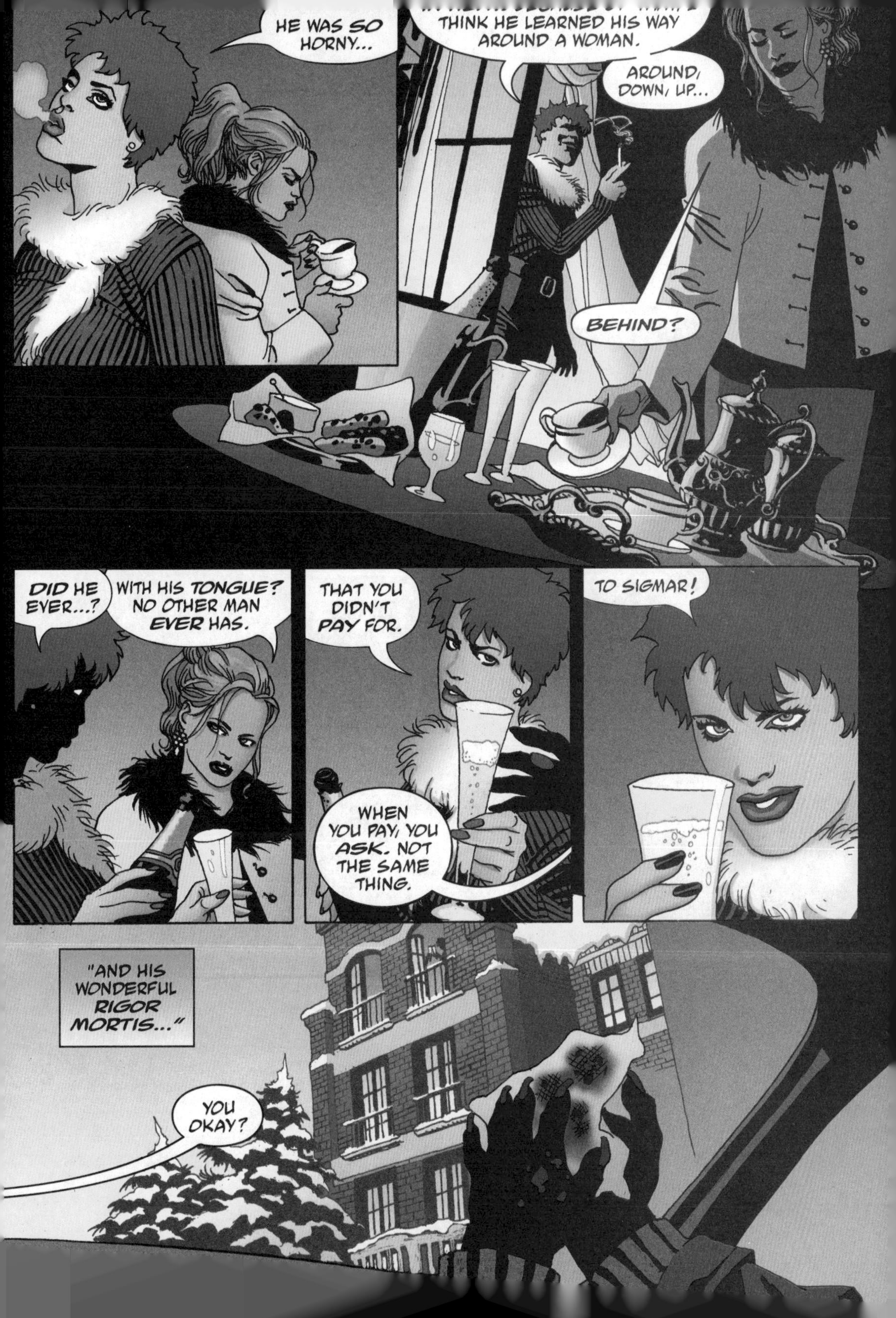
HE WAS SO HORNY...
THINK HE LEARNED HIS WAY AROUND A WOMAN.
AROUND, DOWN, UP...
BEHIND?
DID HE EVER...?
WITH HIS TONGUE? NO OTHER MAN EVER HAS.
THAT YOU DIDN'T PAY FOR.
WHEN YOU PAY, YOU ASK. NOT THE SAME THING.
TO SIGMAR!
"AND HIS WONDERFUL RIGOR MORTIS..."
YOU OKAY?

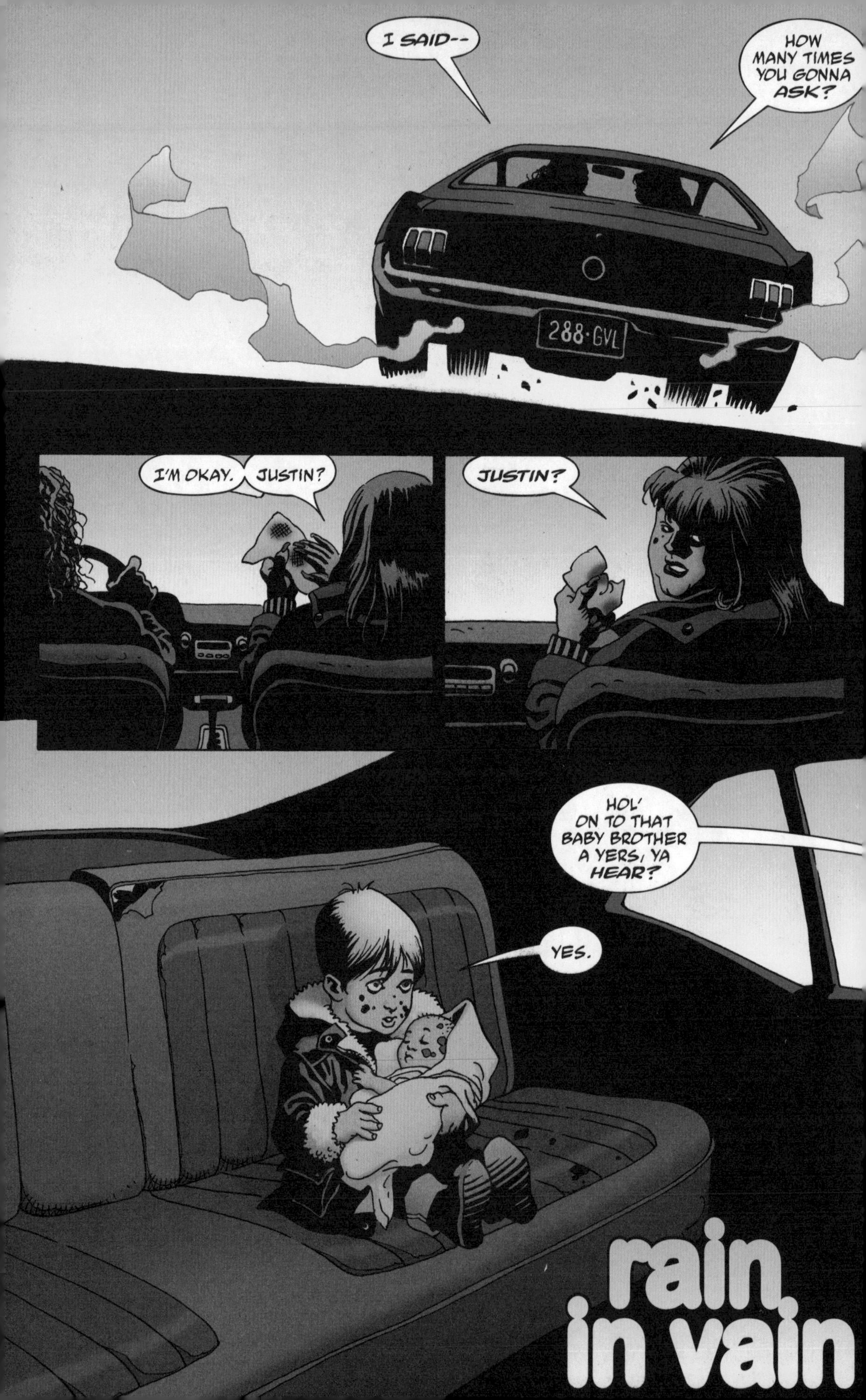
I SAID--
HOW MANY TIMES YOU GONNA ASK?
I'M OKAY.
JUSTIN?
JUSTIN?
HOL' ON TO THAT BABY BROTHER A YERS, YA HEAR?
YES.
rain in vain

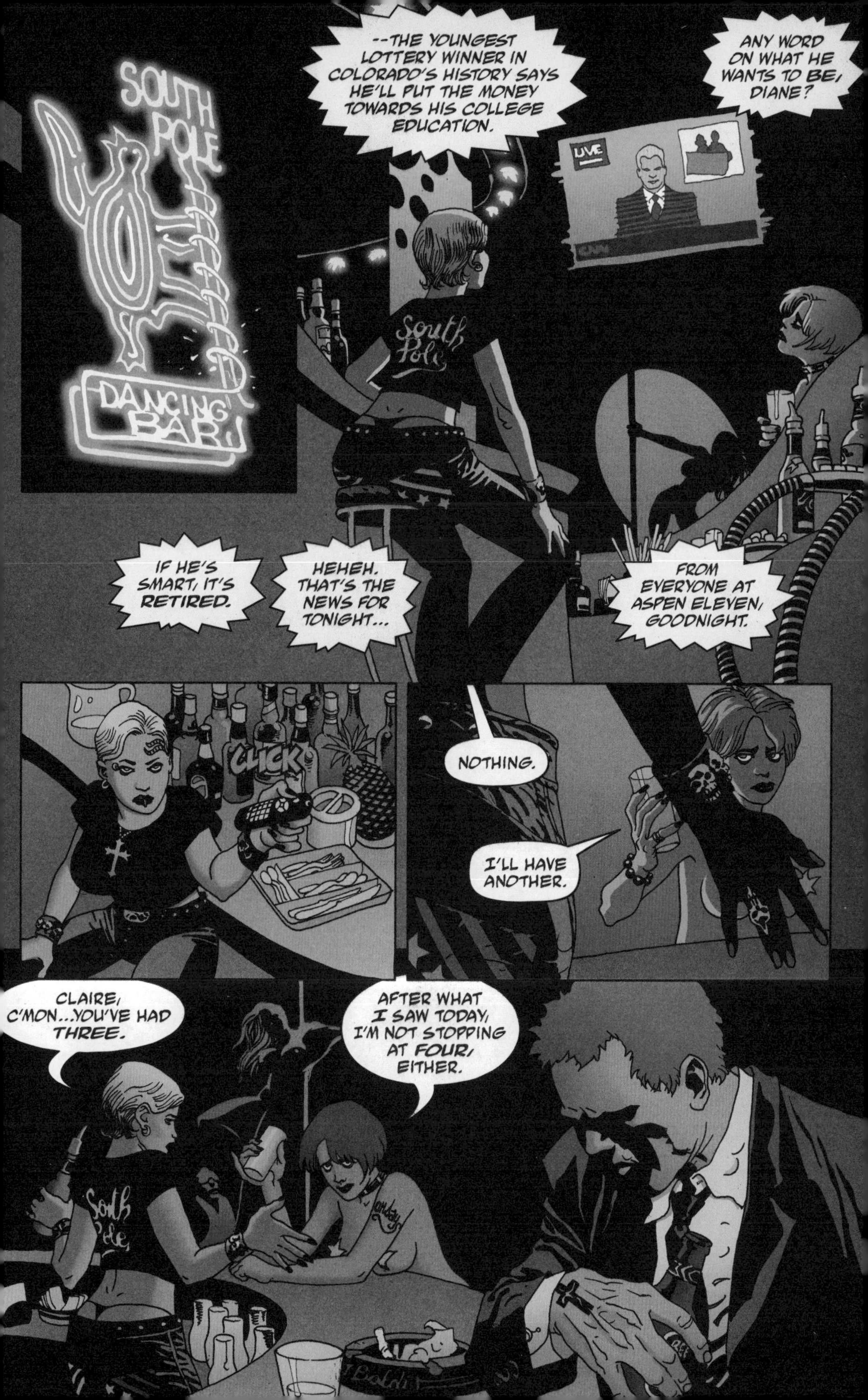
SOUTH POLE
DANCING BAR
--THE YOUNGEST LOTTERY WINNER IN COLORADO'S HISTORY SAYS HE'LL PUT THE MONEY TOWARDS HIS COLLEGE EDUCATION.
ANY WORD ON WHAT HE WANTS TO BE, DIANE?
LIVE
South Pole
IF HE'S SMART, IT'S RETIRED.
HEHEH. THAT'S THE NEWS FOR TONIGHT...
FROM EVERYONE AT ASPEN ELEVEN, GOODNIGHT.
CLICK
NOTHING.
I'LL HAVE ANOTHER.
CLAIRE, C'MON...YOU'VE HAD THREE.
AFTER WHAT I SAW TODAY, I'M NOT STOPPING AT FOUR, EITHER.
South Pole

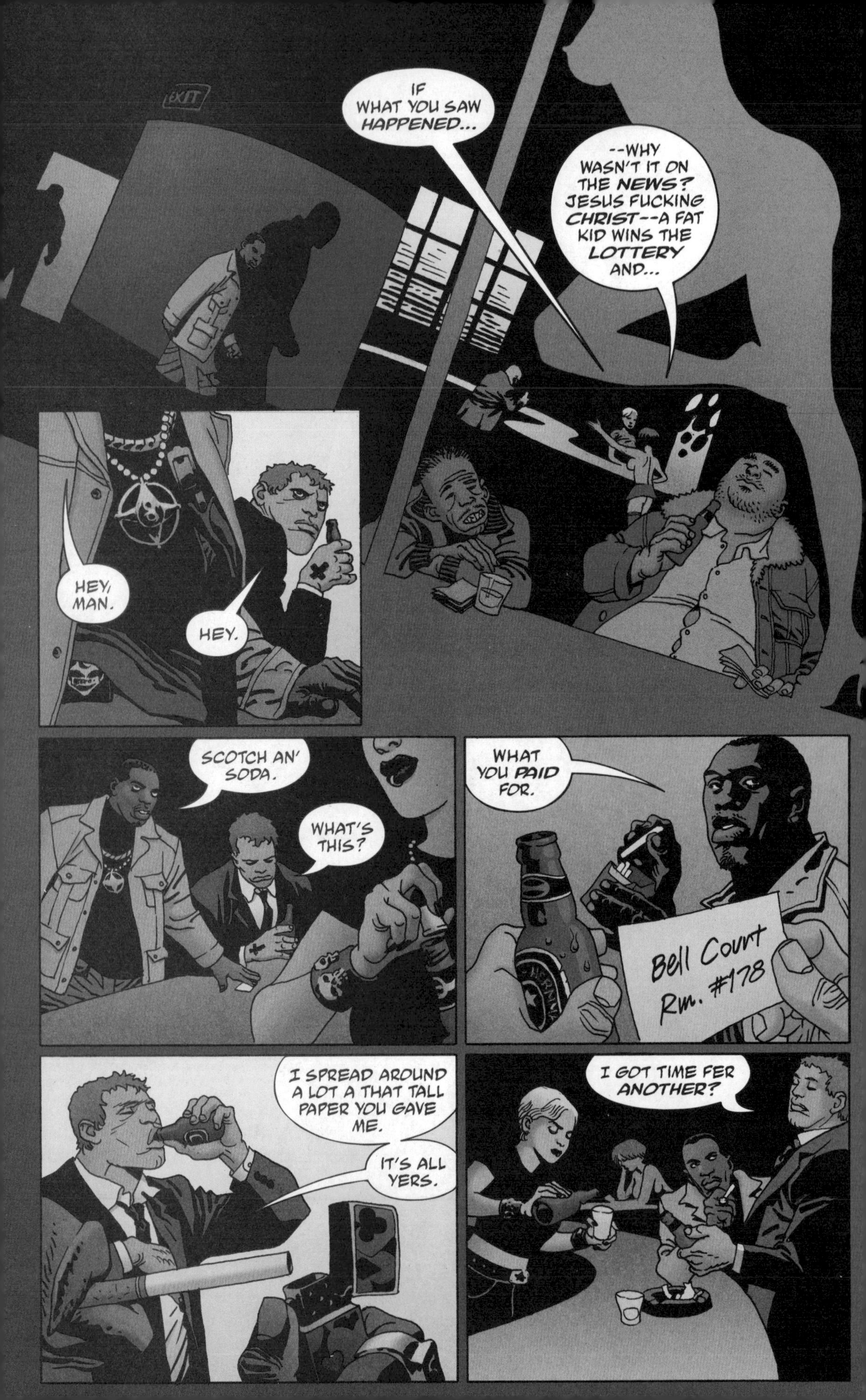
EXIT
IF WHAT YOU SAW HAPPENED...
--WHY WASN'T IT ON THE NEWS? JESUS FUCKING CHRIST--A FAT KID WINS THE LOTTERY AND...
HEY, MAN.
HEY.
SCOTCH AN' SODA.
WHAT'S THIS?
WHAT YOU PAID FOR.
Bell Court Rm. #178
I SPREAD AROUND A LOT A THAT TALL PAPER YOU GAVE ME.
IT'S ALL YERS.
I GOT TIME FER ANOTHER?

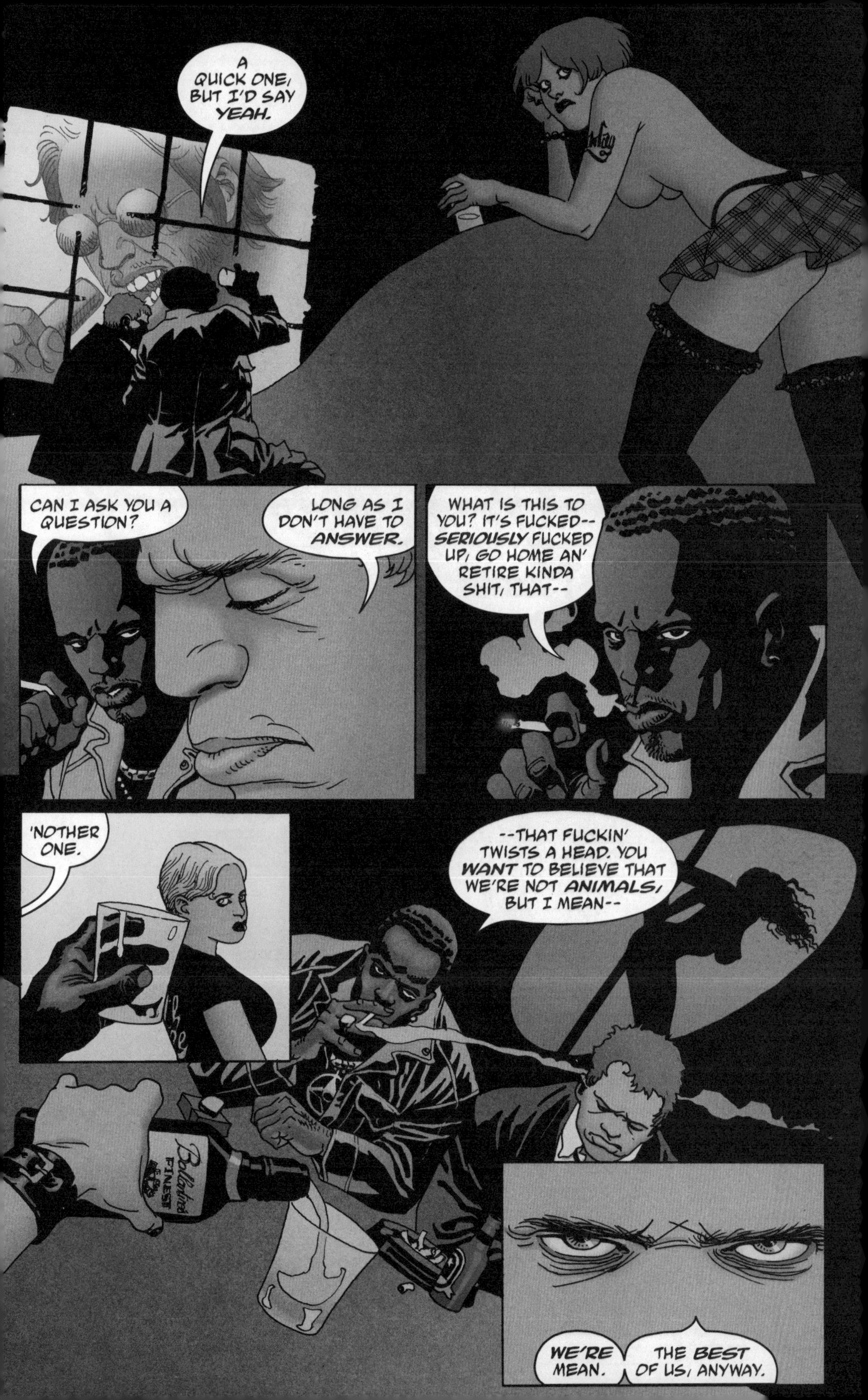
A QUICK ONE, BUT I'D SAY YEAH.
CAN I ASK YOU A QUESTION?
LONG AS I DON'T HAVE TO ANSWER.
WHAT IS THIS TO YOU? IT'S FUCKED-- SERIOUSLY FUCKED UP, GO HOME AN' RETIRE KINDA SHIT, THAT--
'NOTHER ONE.
--THAT FUCKIN' TWISTS A HEAD. YOU WANT TO BELIEVE THAT WE'RE NOT ANIMALS, BUT I MEAN--
WE'RE MEAN.
THE BEST OF US, ANYWAY.

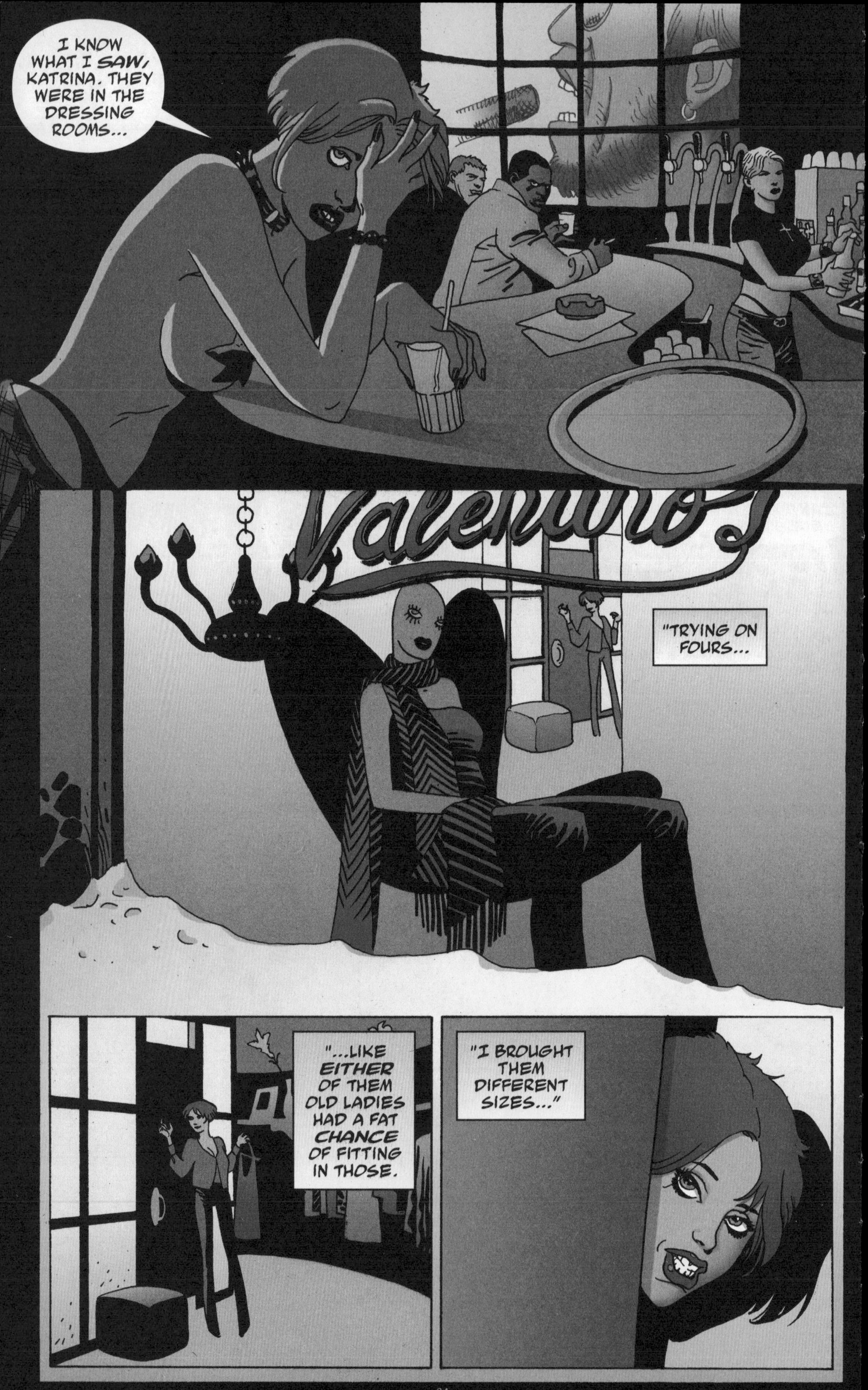
I KNOW WHAT I SAW, KATRINA. THEY WERE IN THE DRESSING ROOMS...
"TRYING ON FOURS...
"...LIKE EITHER OF THEM OLD LADIES HAD A FAT CHANCE OF FITTING IN THOSE.
"I BROUGHT THEM DIFFERENT SIZES..."

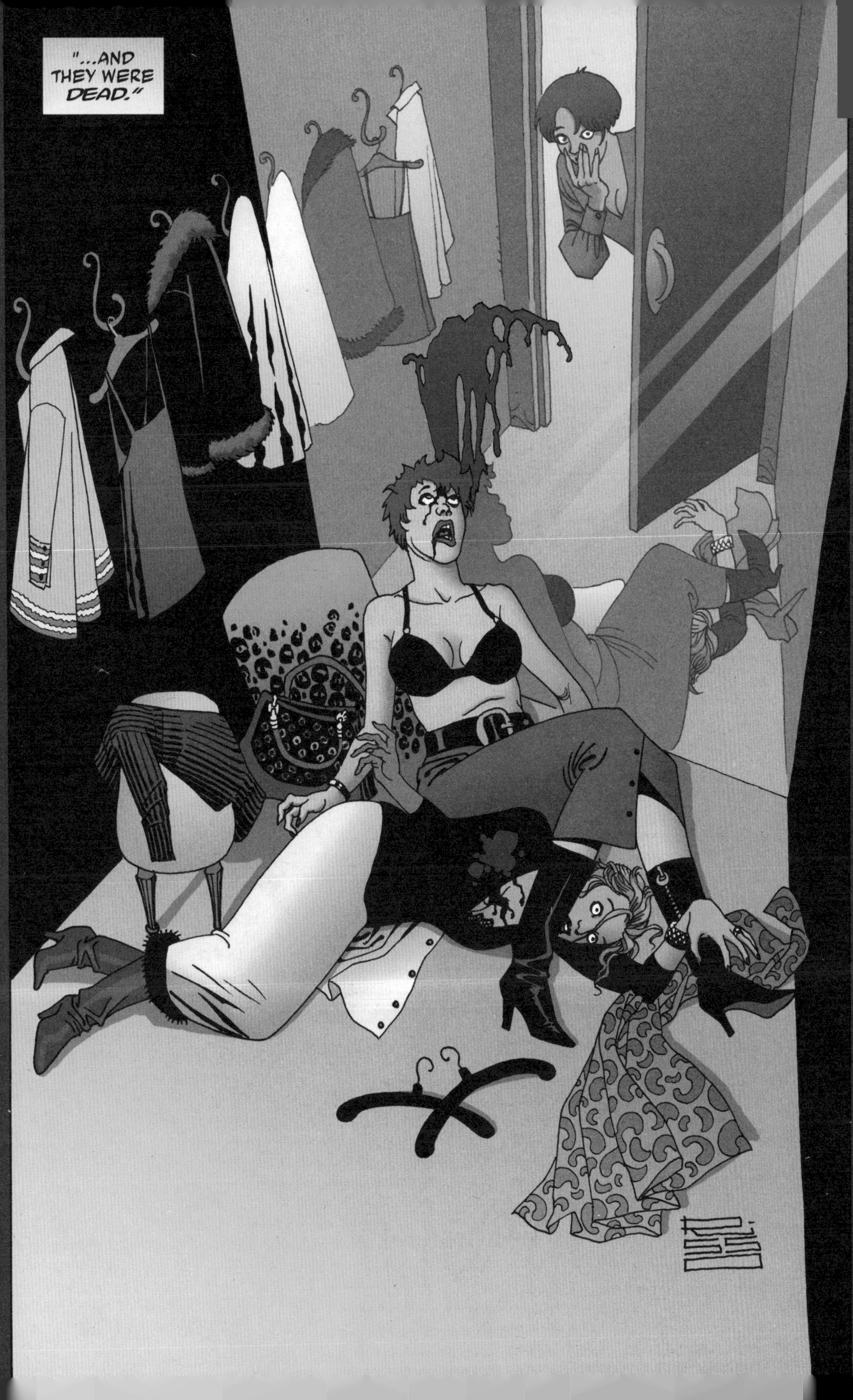
"...AND THEY WERE DEAD."

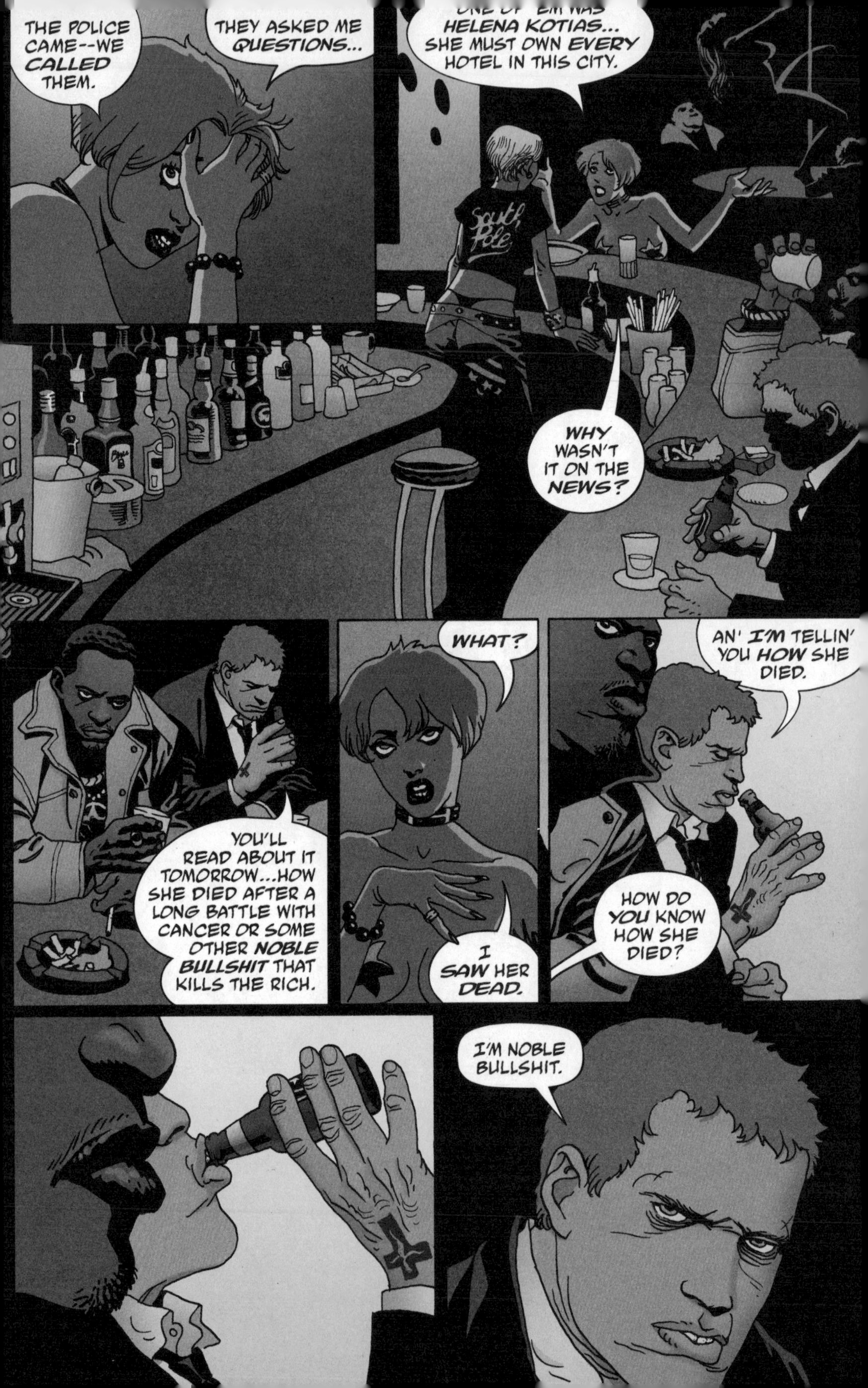
THE POLICE CAME--WE CALLED THEM.
THEY ASKED ME QUESTIONS...
HELENA KOTIAS... SHE MUST OWN EVERY HOTEL IN THIS CITY.
South Pole
WHY WASN'T IT ON THE NEWS?
YOU'LL READ ABOUT IT TOMORROW...HOW SHE DIED AFTER A LONG BATTLE WITH CANCER OR SOME OTHER NOBLE BULLSHIT THAT KILLS THE RICH.
WHAT?
I SAW HER DEAD.
AN' I'M TELLIN' YOU HOW SHE DIED.
HOW DO YOU KNOW HOW SHE DIED?
I'M NOBLE BULLSHIT.

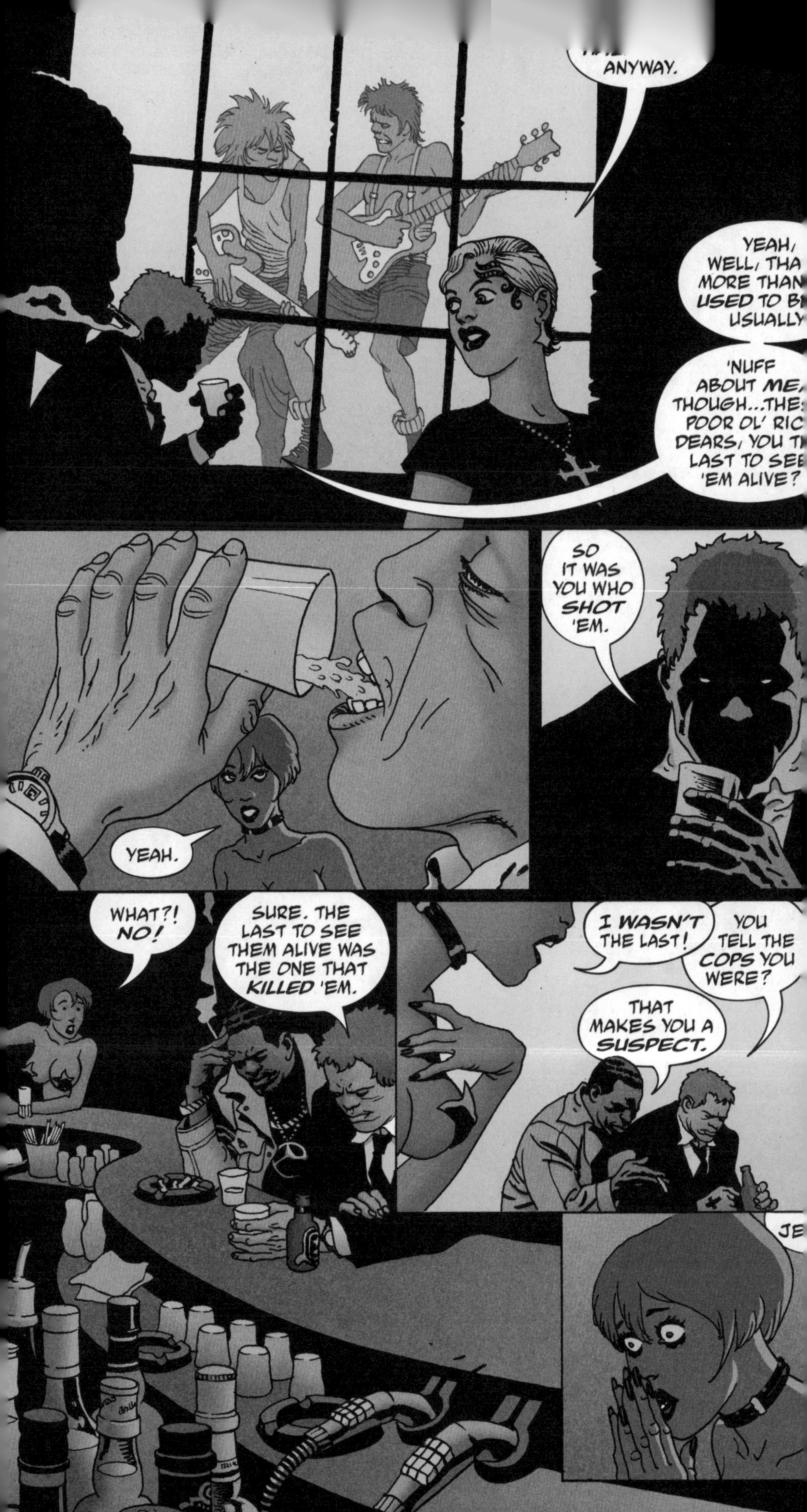

ANYWAY.
YEAH, WELL, THA MORE THAN USED TO B USUALLY
'NUFF ABOUT ME, THOUGH...THE POOR OL' RIC DEARS, YOU T LAST TO SEE 'EM ALIVE?
SO IT WAS YOU WHO SHOT 'EM.
YEAH.
WHAT?! NO!
SURE. THE LAST TO SEE THEM ALIVE WAS THE ONE THAT KILLED 'EM.
I WASN'T THE LAST!
YOU TELL THE COPS YOU WERE?
THAT MAKES YOU A SUSPECT.
JE

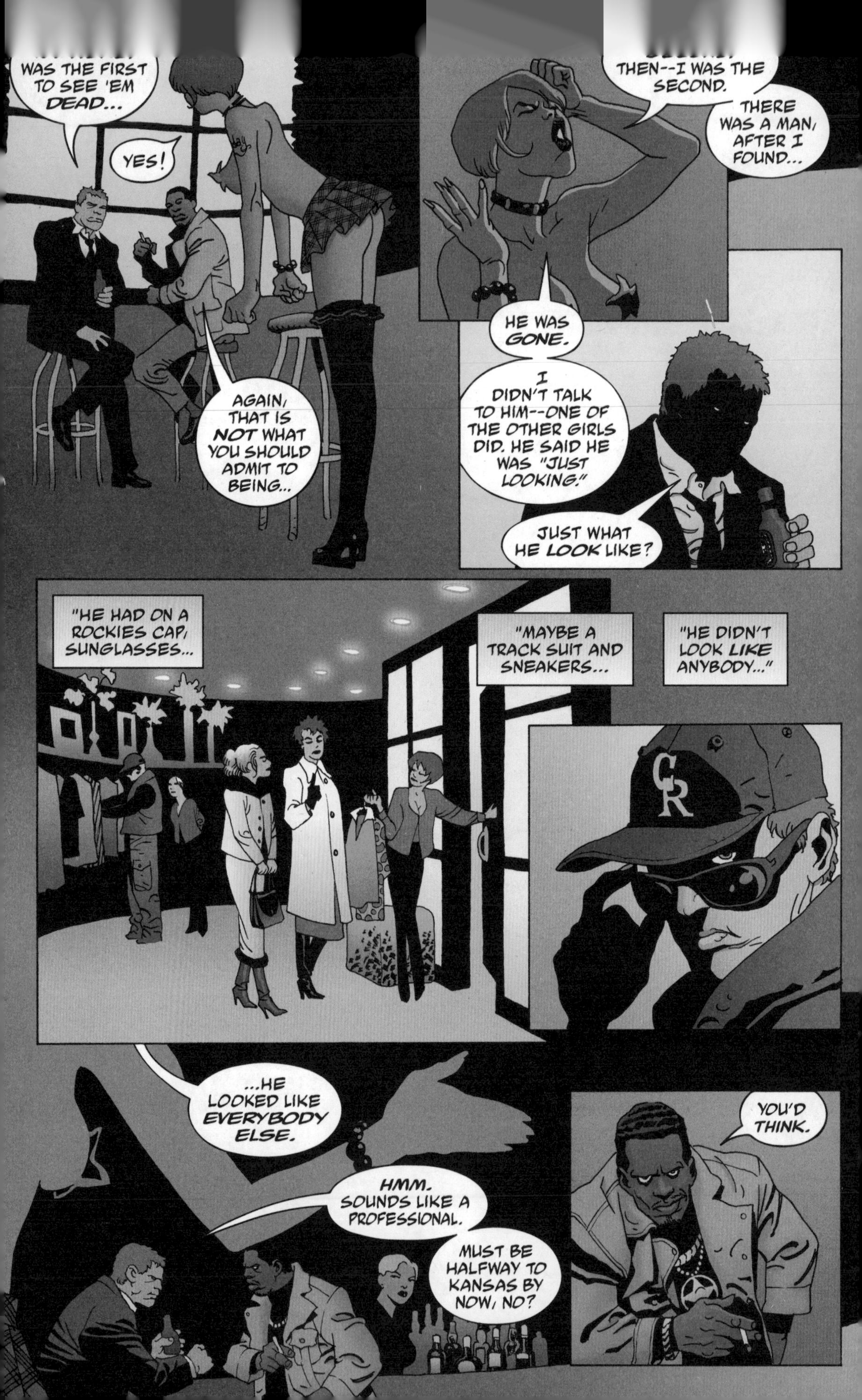
WAS THE FIRST TO SEE 'EM DEAD...
YES!
AGAIN, THAT IS NOT WHAT YOU SHOULD ADMIT TO BEING...
THEN--I WAS THE SECOND.
THERE WAS A MAN, AFTER I FOUND...
HE WAS GONE.
I DIDN'T TALK TO HIM--ONE OF THE OTHER GIRLS DID. HE SAID HE WAS "JUST LOOKING."
JUST WHAT HE LOOK LIKE?
"HE HAD ON A ROCKIES CAP, SUNGLASSES...
"MAYBE A TRACK SUIT AND SNEAKERS...
"HE DIDN'T LOOK LIKE ANYBODY..."
CR
...HE LOOKED LIKE EVERYBODY ELSE.
HMM. SOUNDS LIKE A PROFESSIONAL.
MUST BE HALFWAY TO KANSAS BY NOW, NO?
YOU'D THINK.

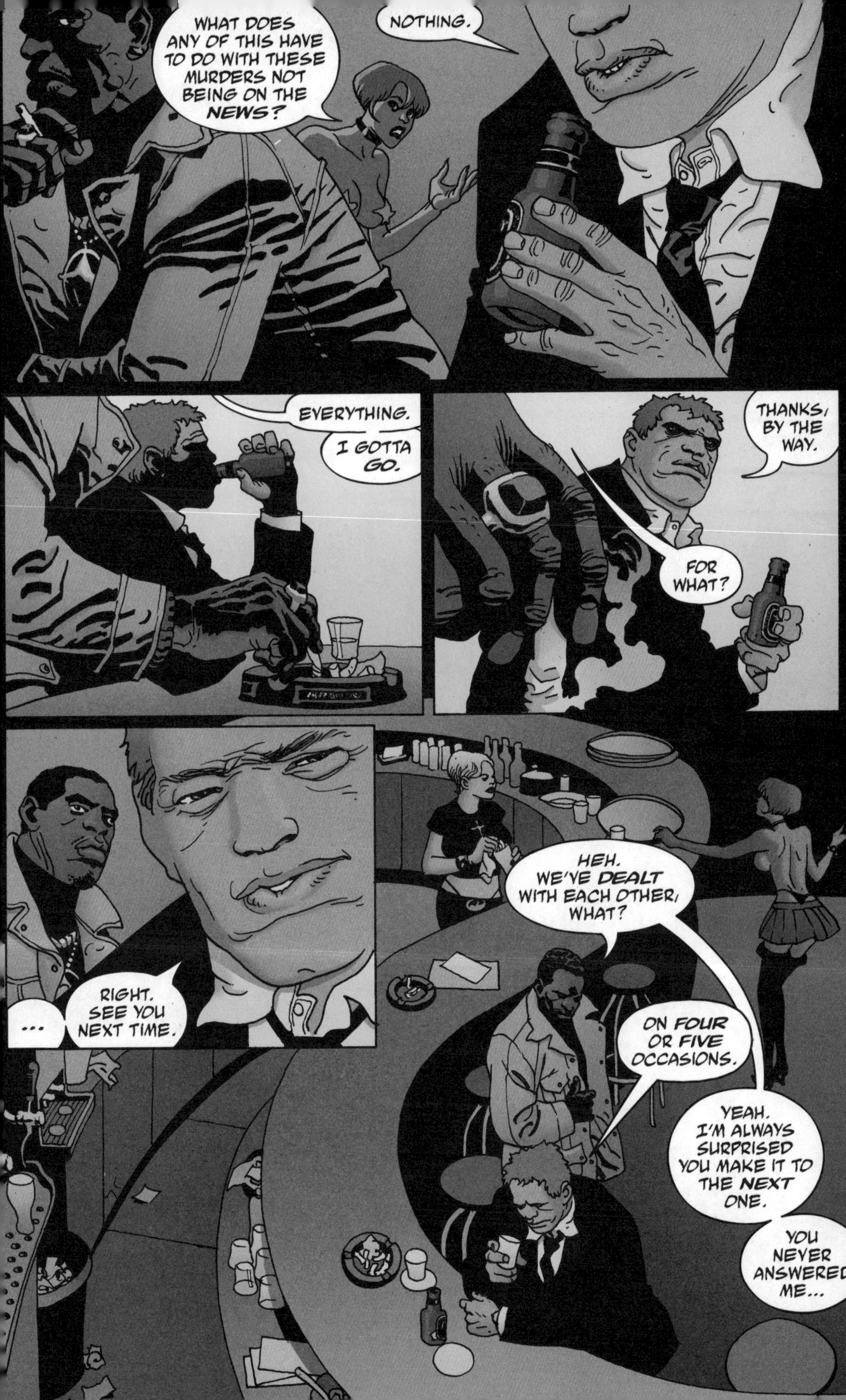
WHAT DOES ANY OF THIS HAVE TO DO WITH THESE MURDERS NOT BEING ON THE NEWS?
NOTHING.
EVERYTHING.
I GOTTA GO.
THANKS, BY THE WAY.
FOR WHAT?
...
RIGHT. SEE YOU NEXT TIME.
HEH. WE'VE DEALT WITH EACH OTHER, WHAT?
ON FOUR OR FIVE OCCASIONS.
YEAH. I'M ALWAYS SURPRISED YOU MAKE IT TO THE NEXT ONE.
YOU NEVER ANSWERED ME...

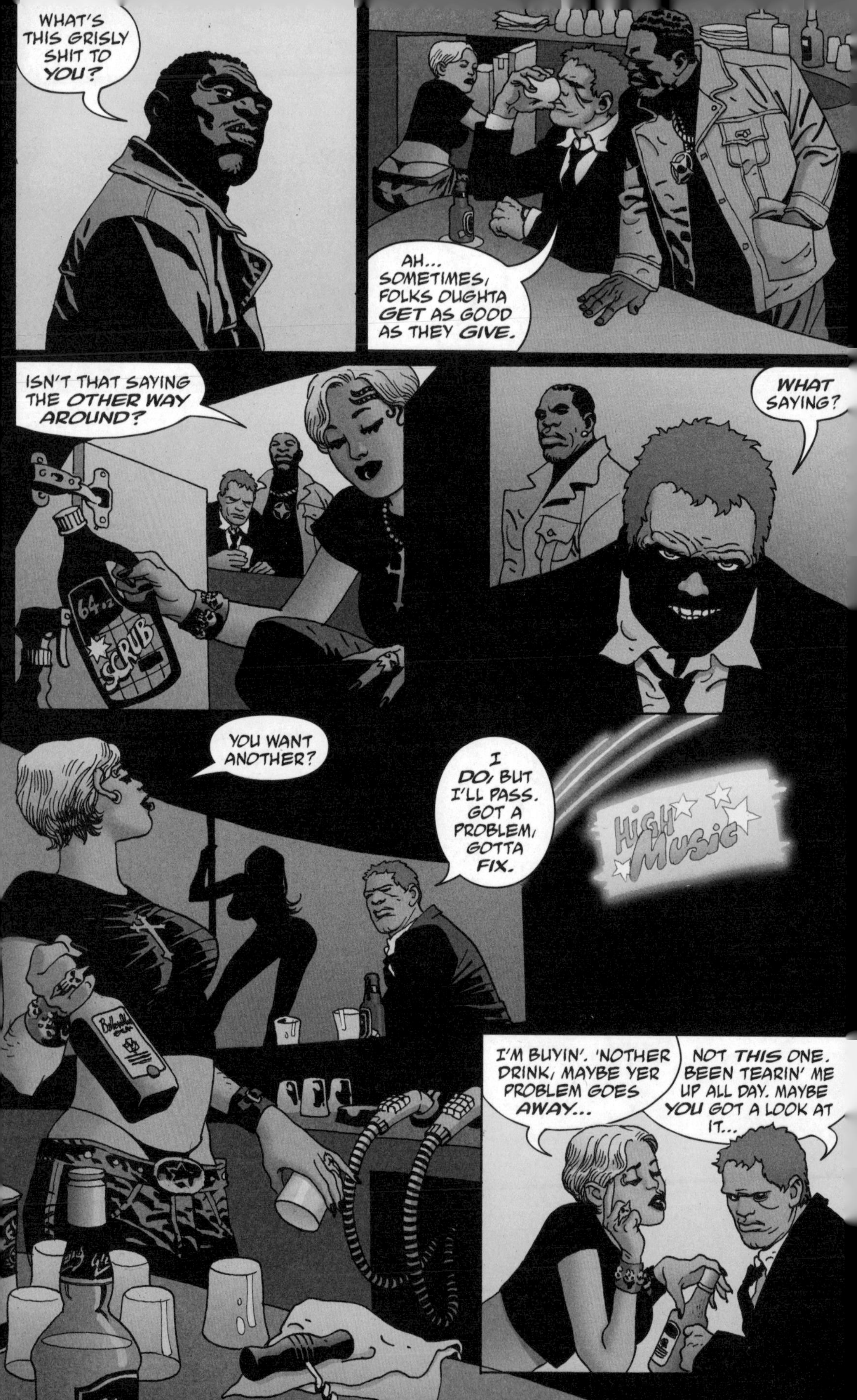
WHAT'S THIS GRISLY SHIT TO YOU?
AH... SOMETIMES, FOLKS OUGHTA GET AS GOOD AS THEY GIVE.
ISN'T THAT SAYING THE OTHER WAY AROUND?
64oz
SCRUB
WHAT SAYING?
YOU WANT ANOTHER?
I DO, BUT I'LL PASS. GOT A PROBLEM, GOTTA FIX.
High Music
I'M BUYIN'. 'NOTHER DRINK, MAYBE YER PROBLEM GOES AWAY...
NOT THIS ONE. BEEN TEARIN' ME UP ALL DAY. MAYBE YOU GOT A LOOK AT IT...

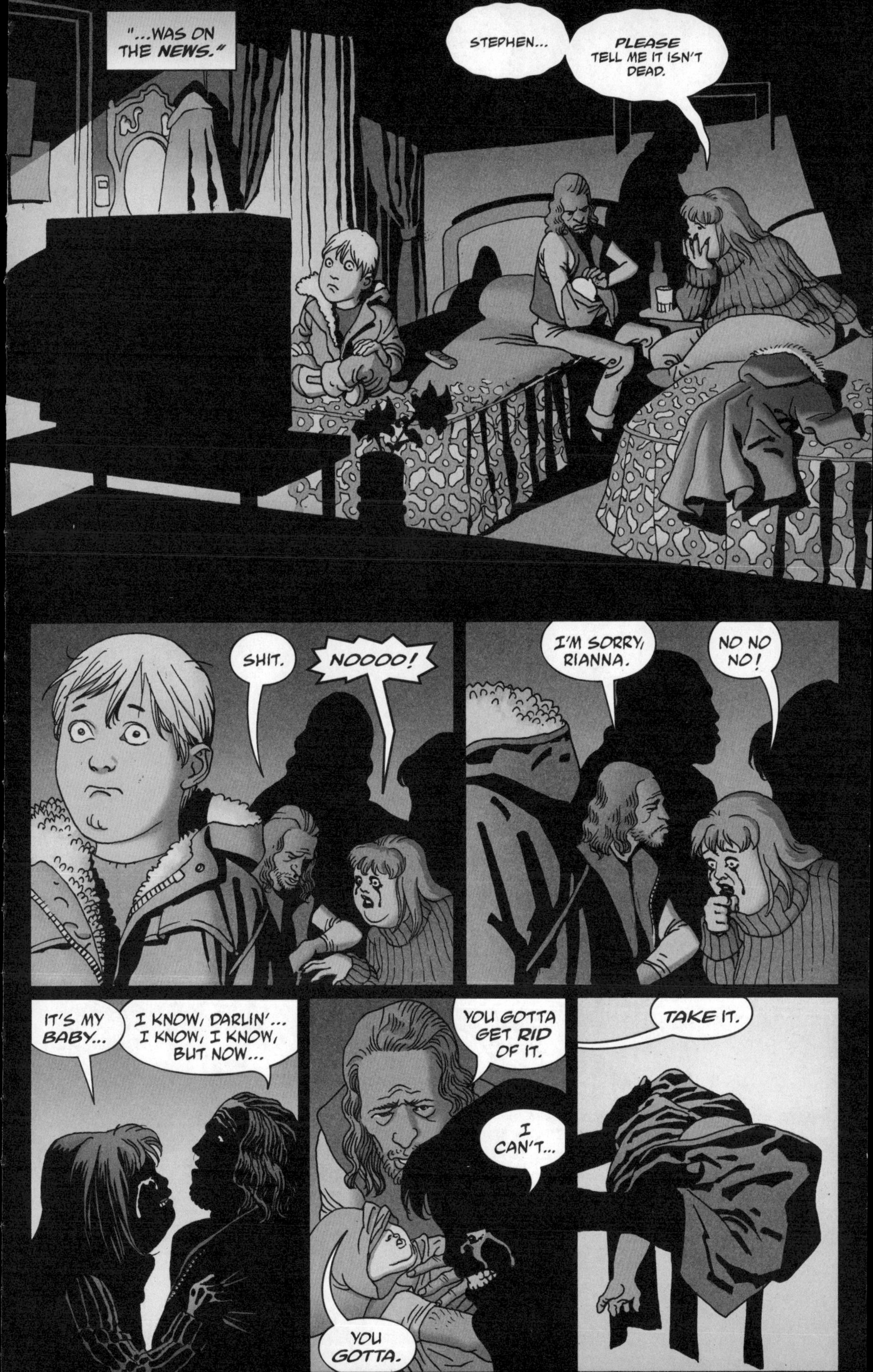
"...WAS ON THE NEWS."
STEPHEN...
PLEASE TELL ME IT ISN'T DEAD.
SHIT.
NOOOO!
I'M SORRY, RIANNA.
NO NO NO!
IT'S MY BABY...
I KNOW, DARLIN'... I KNOW, I KNOW, BUT NOW...
YOU GOTTA GET RID OF IT.
I CAN'T...
YOU GOTTA.
TAKE IT.

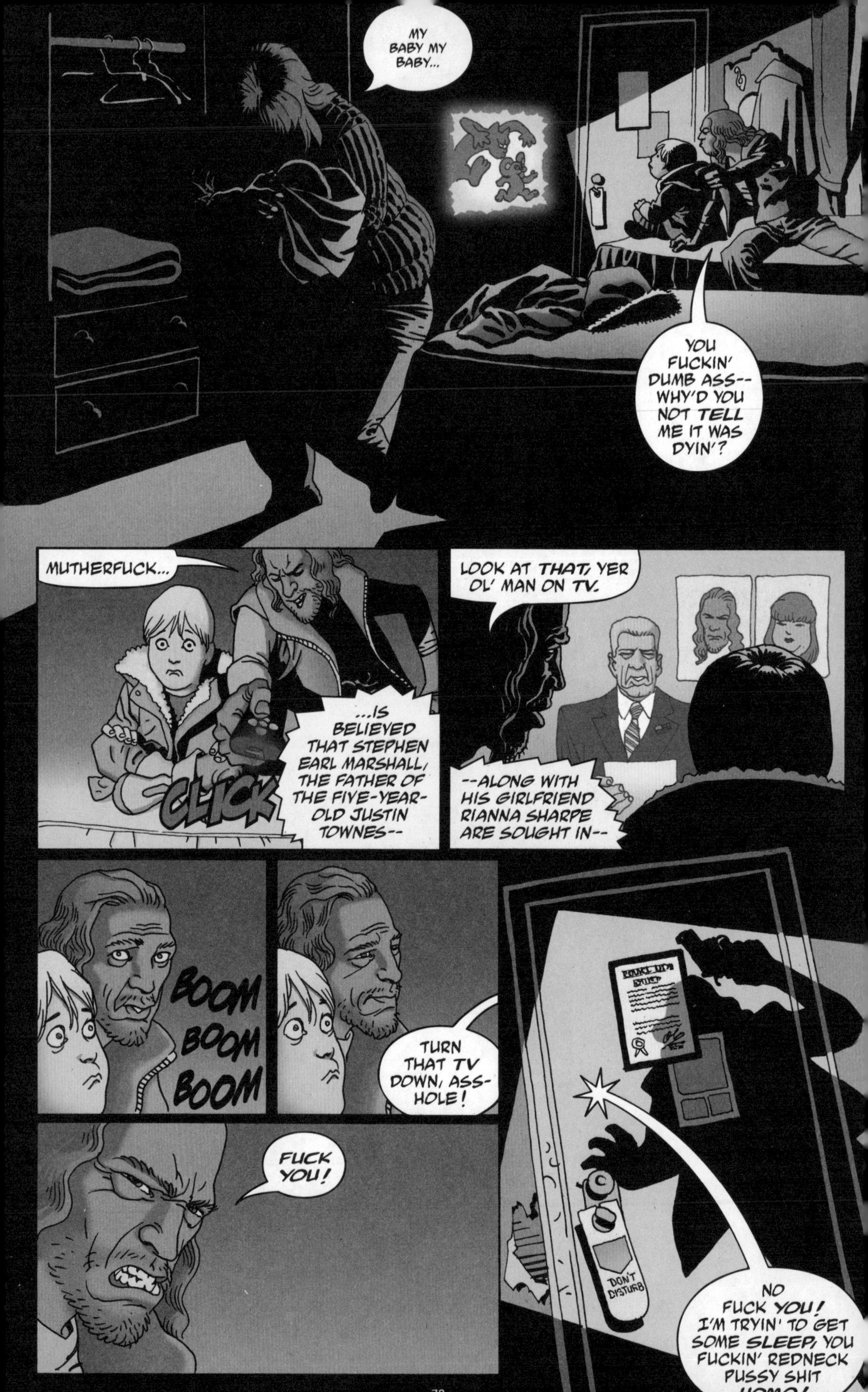
MY BABY MY BABY...
YOU FUCKIN' DUMB ASS--WHY'D YOU NOT TELL ME IT WAS DYIN'?
MUTHERFUCK...
...IS BELIEVED THAT STEPHEN EARL MARSHALL, THE FATHER OF THE FIVE-YEAR-OLD JUSTIN TOWNES--
CLICK
LOOK AT THAT, YER OL' MAN ON TV.
--ALONG WITH HIS GIRLFRIEND RIANNA SHARPE ARE SOUGHT IN--
BOOM BOOM BOOM
TURN THAT TV DOWN, ASS-HOLE!
FUCK YOU!
DON'T DISTURB
NO FUCK YOU! I'M TRYIN' TO GET SOME SLEEP, YOU FUCKIN' REDNECK PUSSY SHIT HOMO!

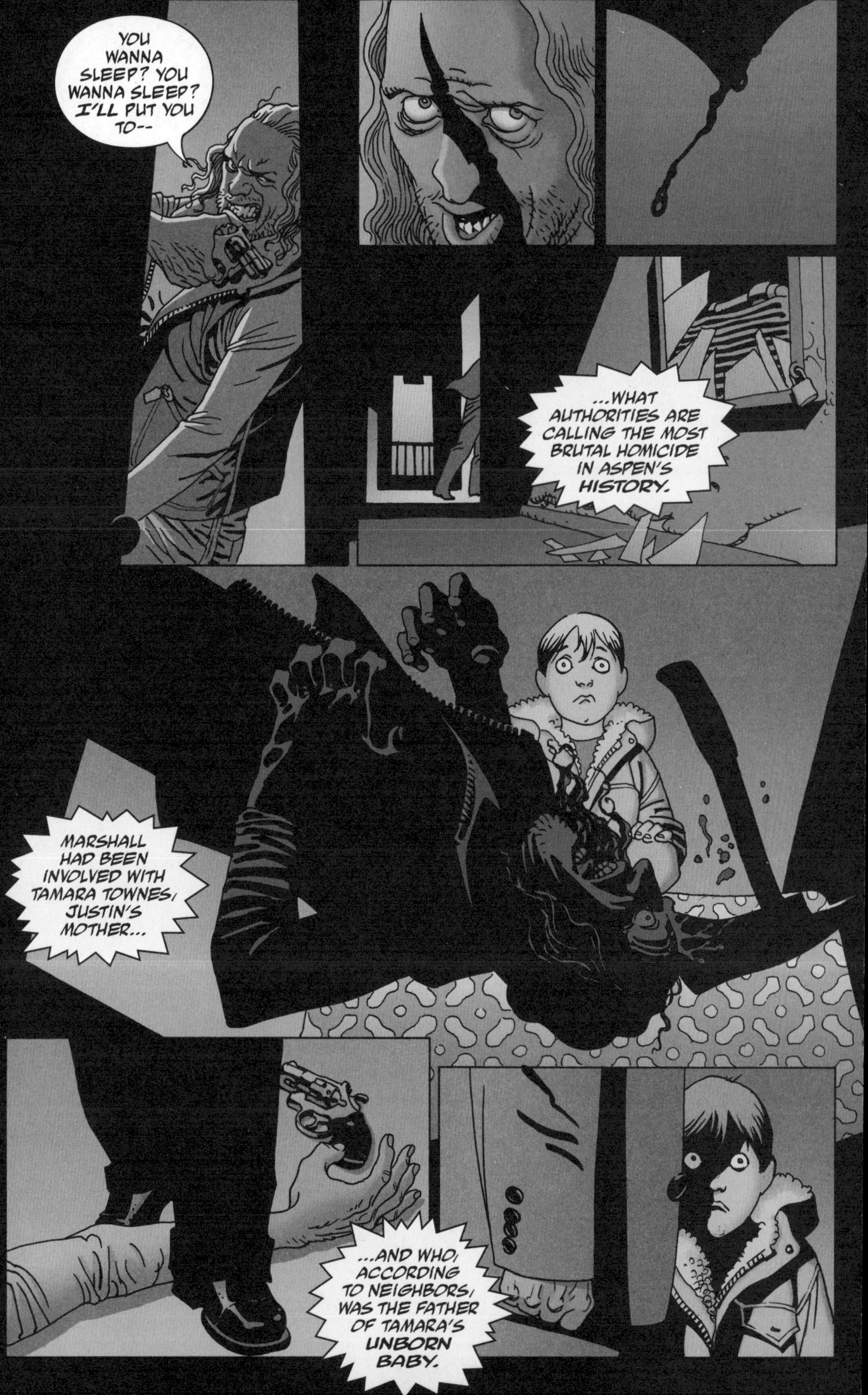
YOU WANNA SLEEP? YOU WANNA SLEEP? I'LL PUT YOU TO--
...WHAT AUTHORITIES ARE CALLING THE MOST BRUTAL HOMICIDE IN ASPEN'S HISTORY.
MARSHALL HAD BEEN INVOLVED WITH TAMARA TOWNES, JUSTIN'S MOTHER...
...AND WHO, ACCORDING TO NEIGHBORS, WAS THE FATHER OF TAMARA'S UNBORN BABY.

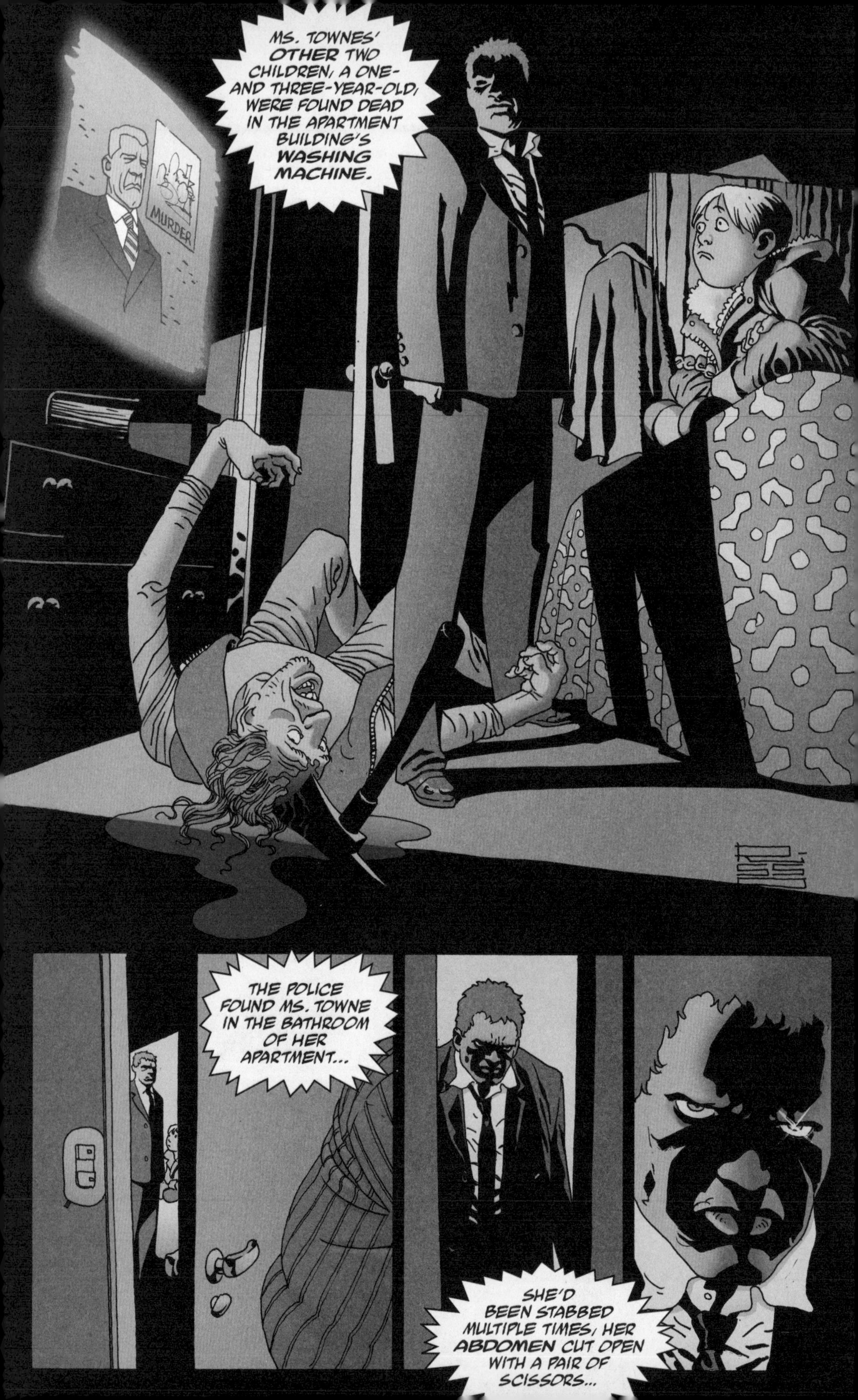
MS. TOWNES' OTHER TWO CHILDREN, A ONE- AND THREE-YEAR-OLD, WERE FOUND DEAD IN THE APARTMENT BUILDING'S WASHING MACHINE.
MURDER
THE POLICE FOUND MS. TOWNE IN THE BATHROOM OF HER APARTMENT...
SHE'D BEEN STABBED MULTIPLE TIMES, HER ABDOMEN CUT OPEN WITH A PAIR OF SCISSORS...

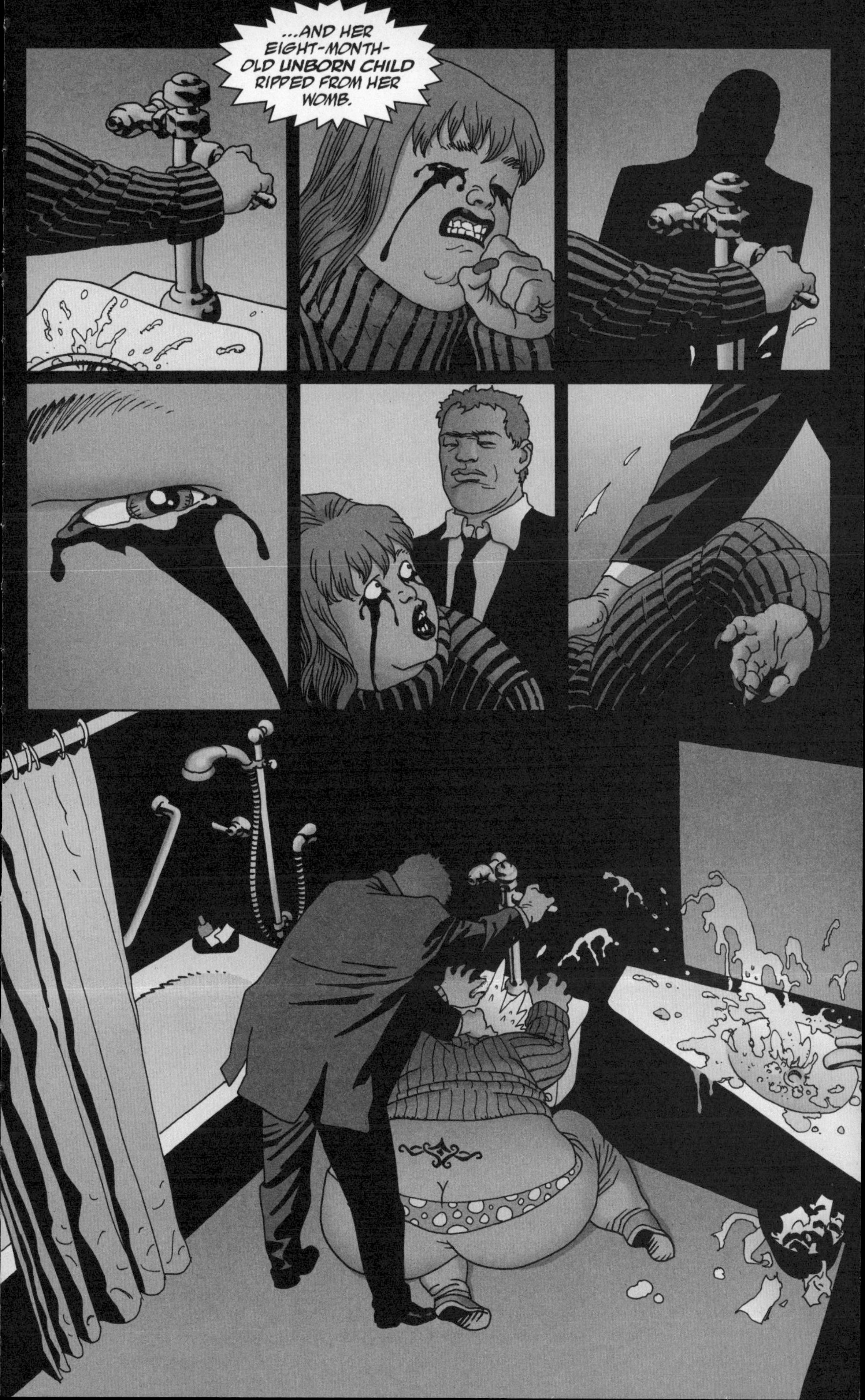
...AND HER EIGHT-MONTH-OLD UNBORN CHILD RIPPED FROM HER WOMB.

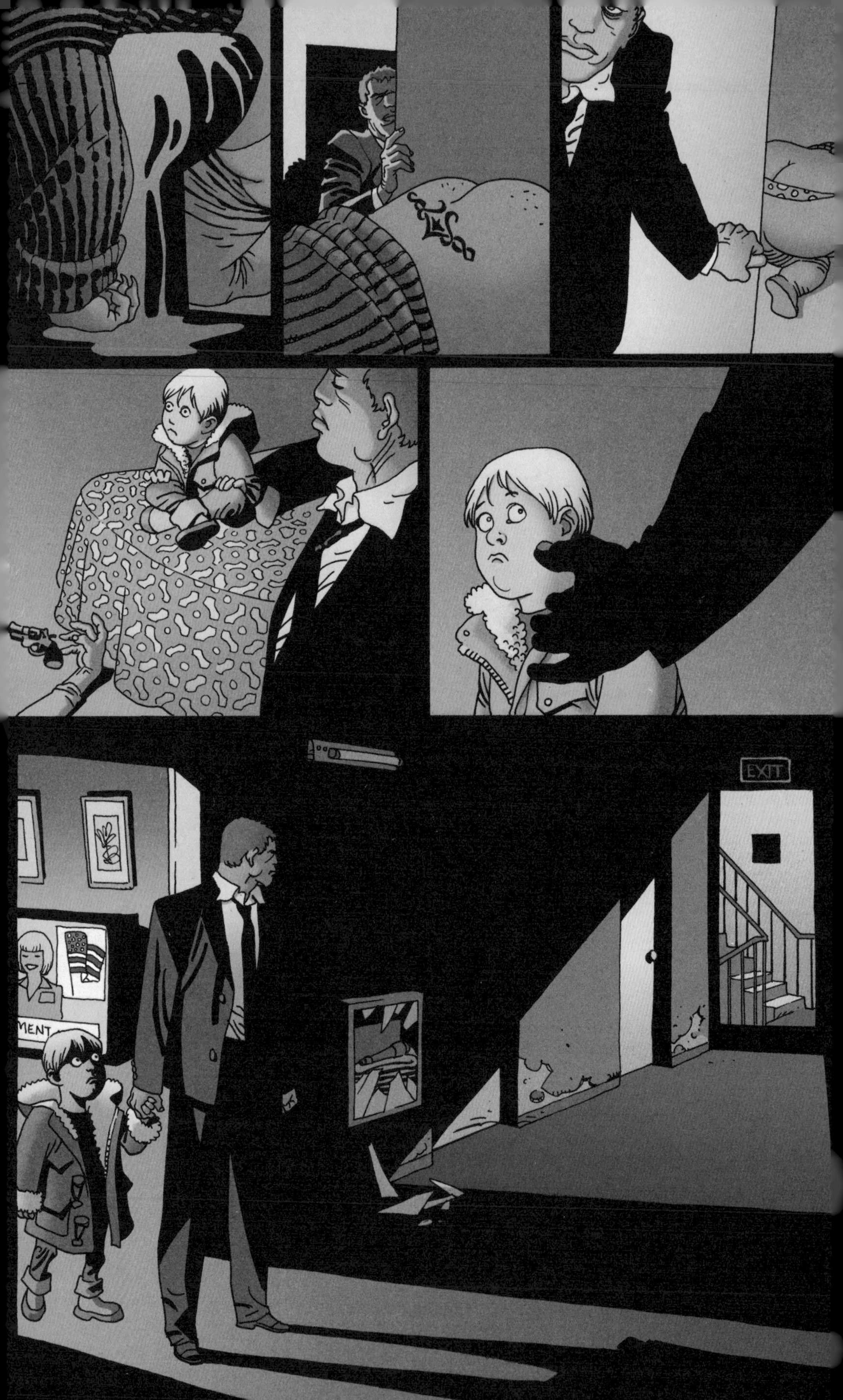
EXIT
MENT

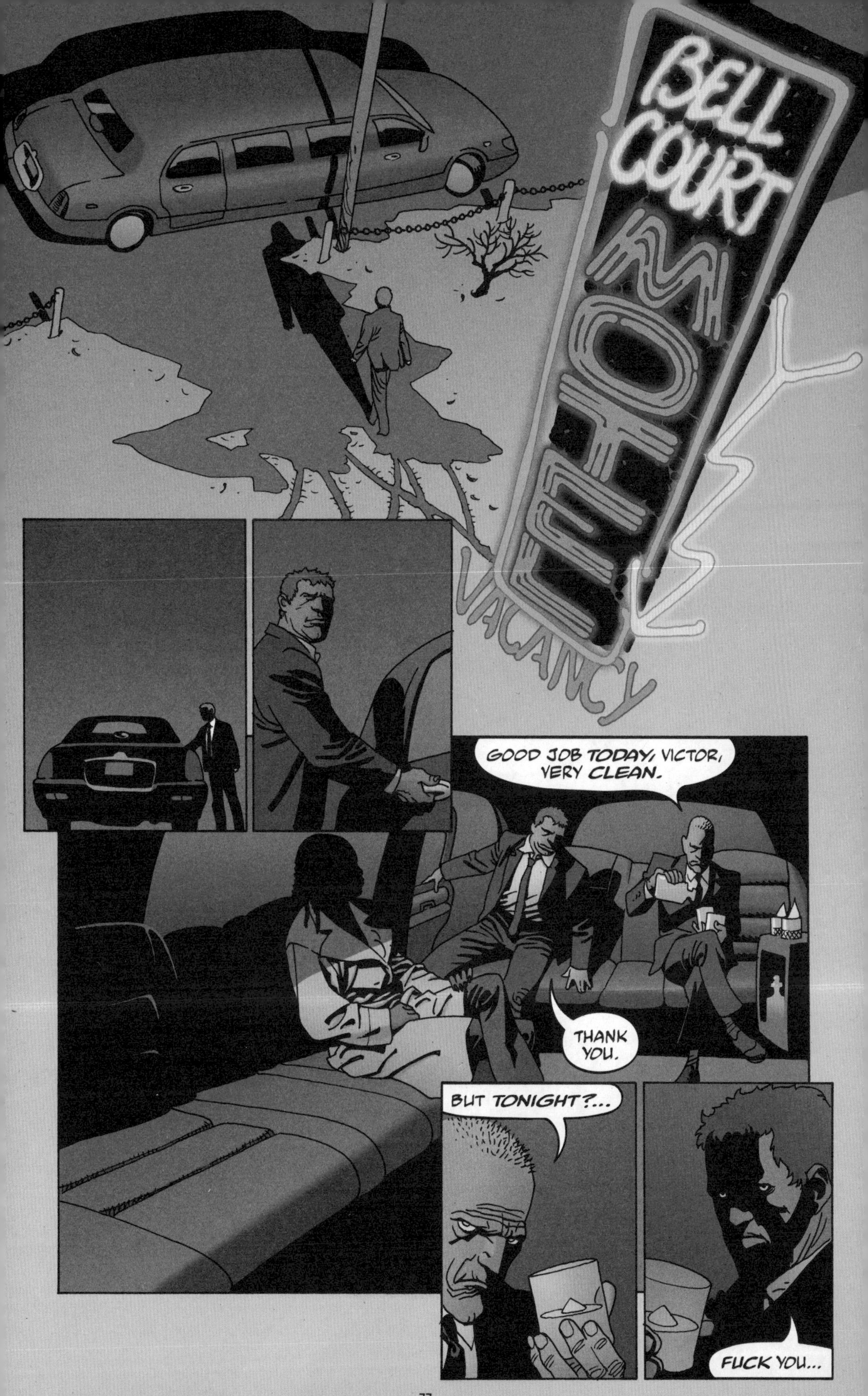
BELL COURT
MOTEL
VACANCY
GOOD JOB TODAY, VICTOR, VERY CLEAN.
THANK YOU.
BUT TONIGHT?...
FUCK YOU...

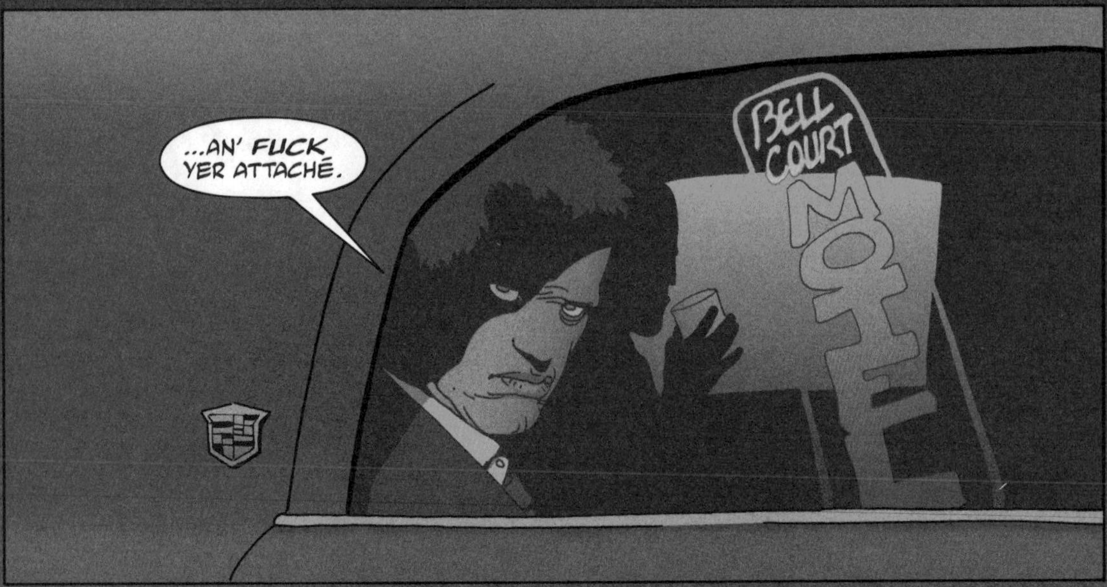
...AN' FUCK YER ATTACHÉ.
BELL COURT MOTEL

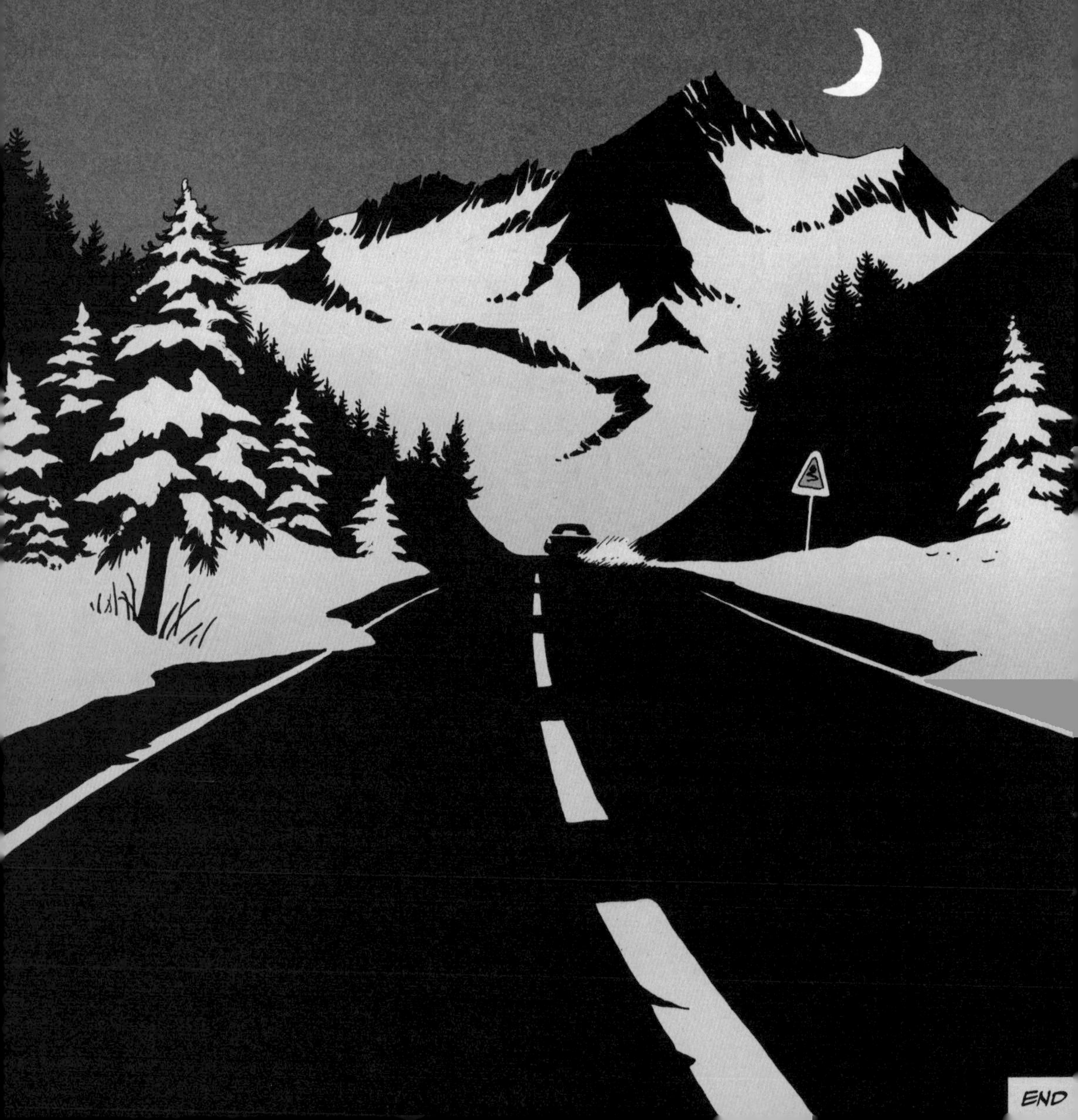
END

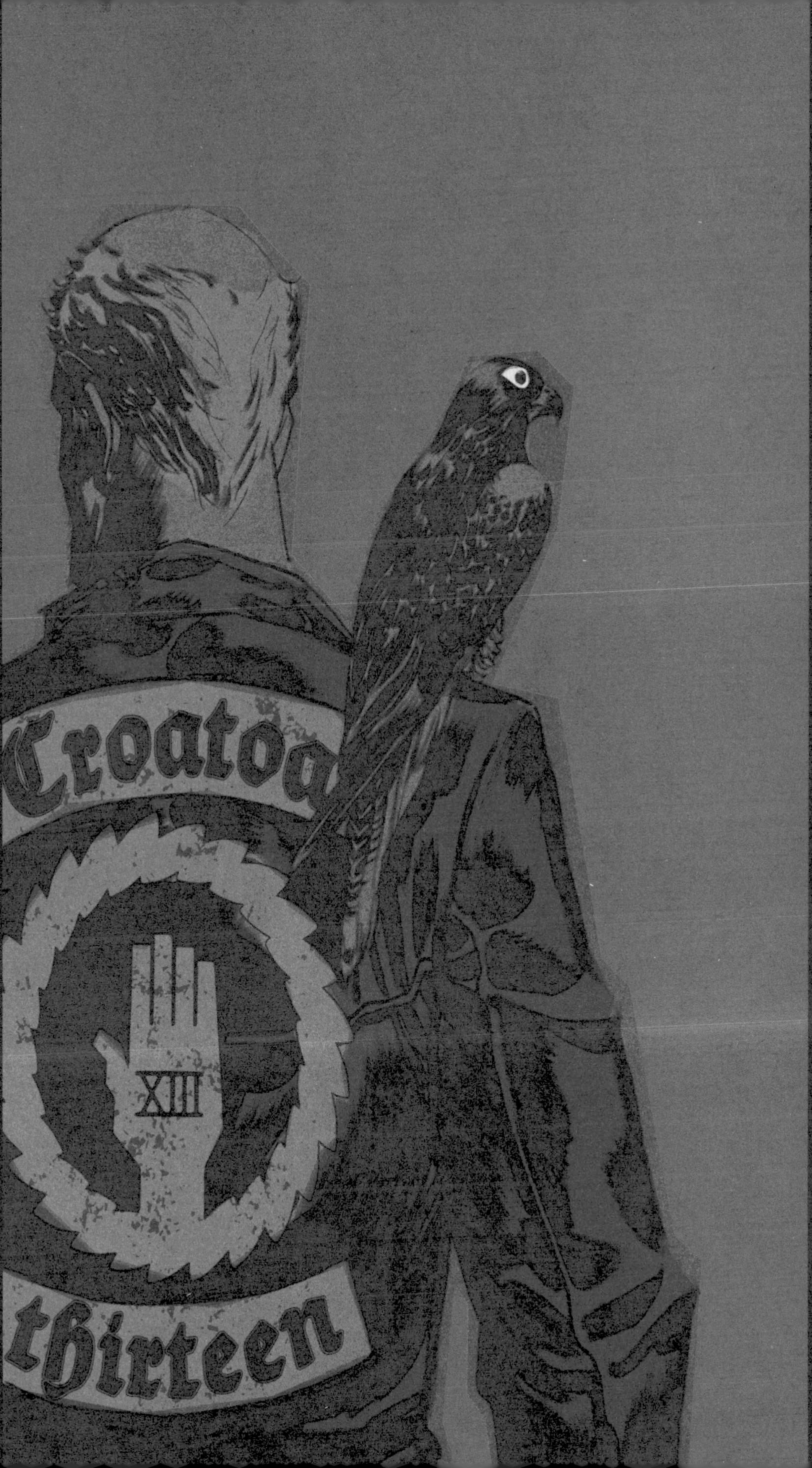
Croatoa
XIII
thirteen

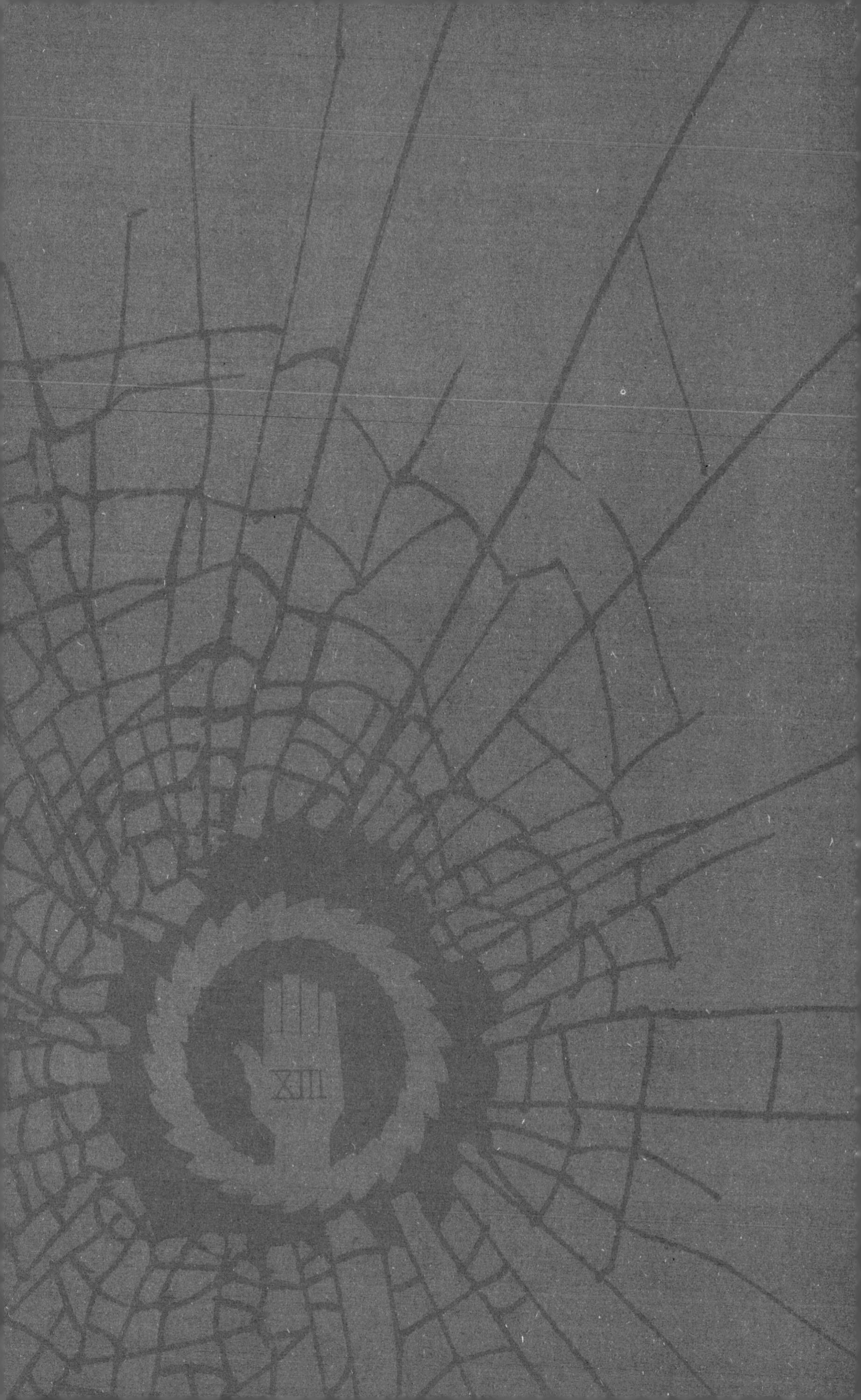
XIII

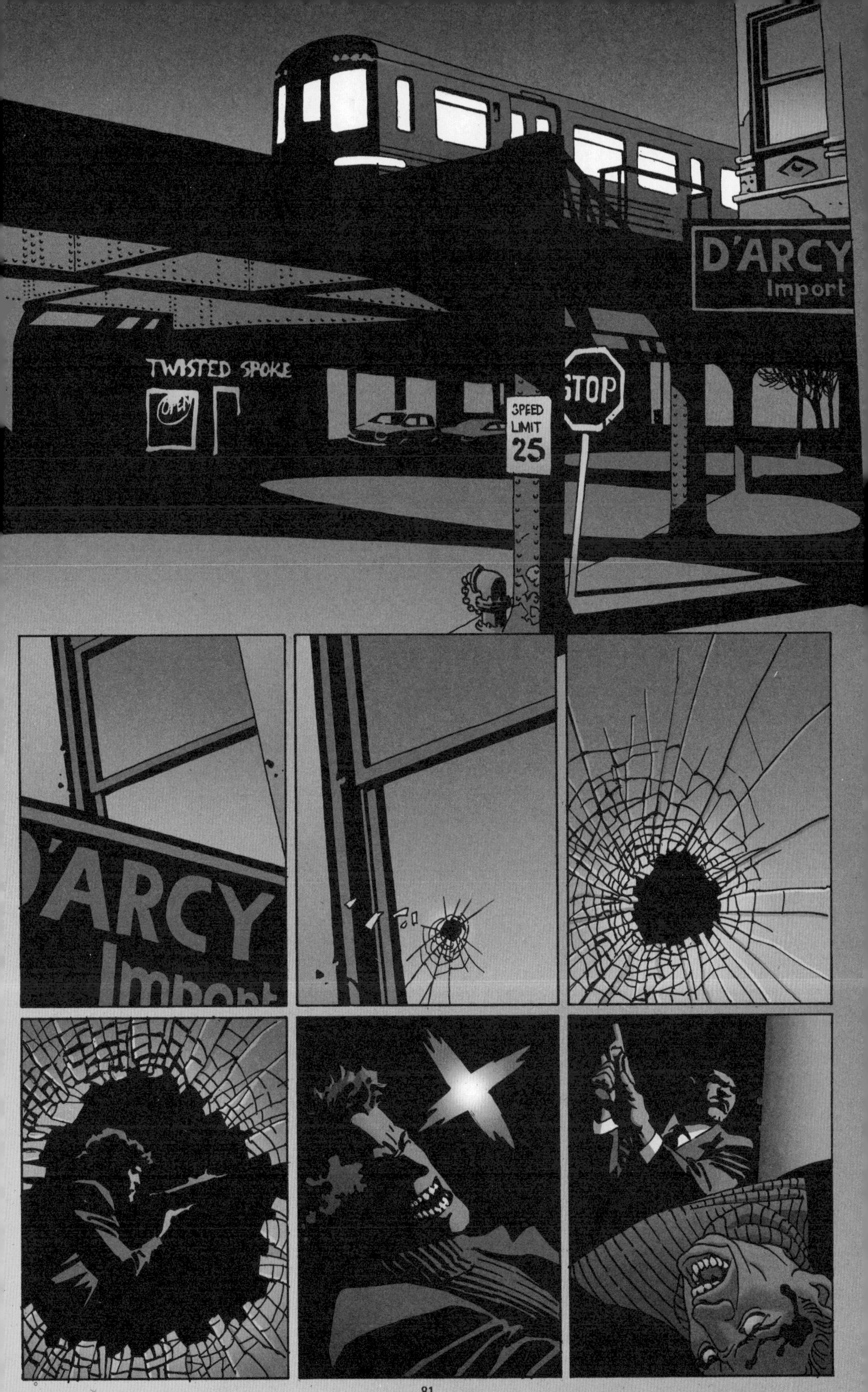
D'ARCY
Import
TWISTED SPOKE
OPEN
STOP
SPEED
LIMIT
25
D'ARCY

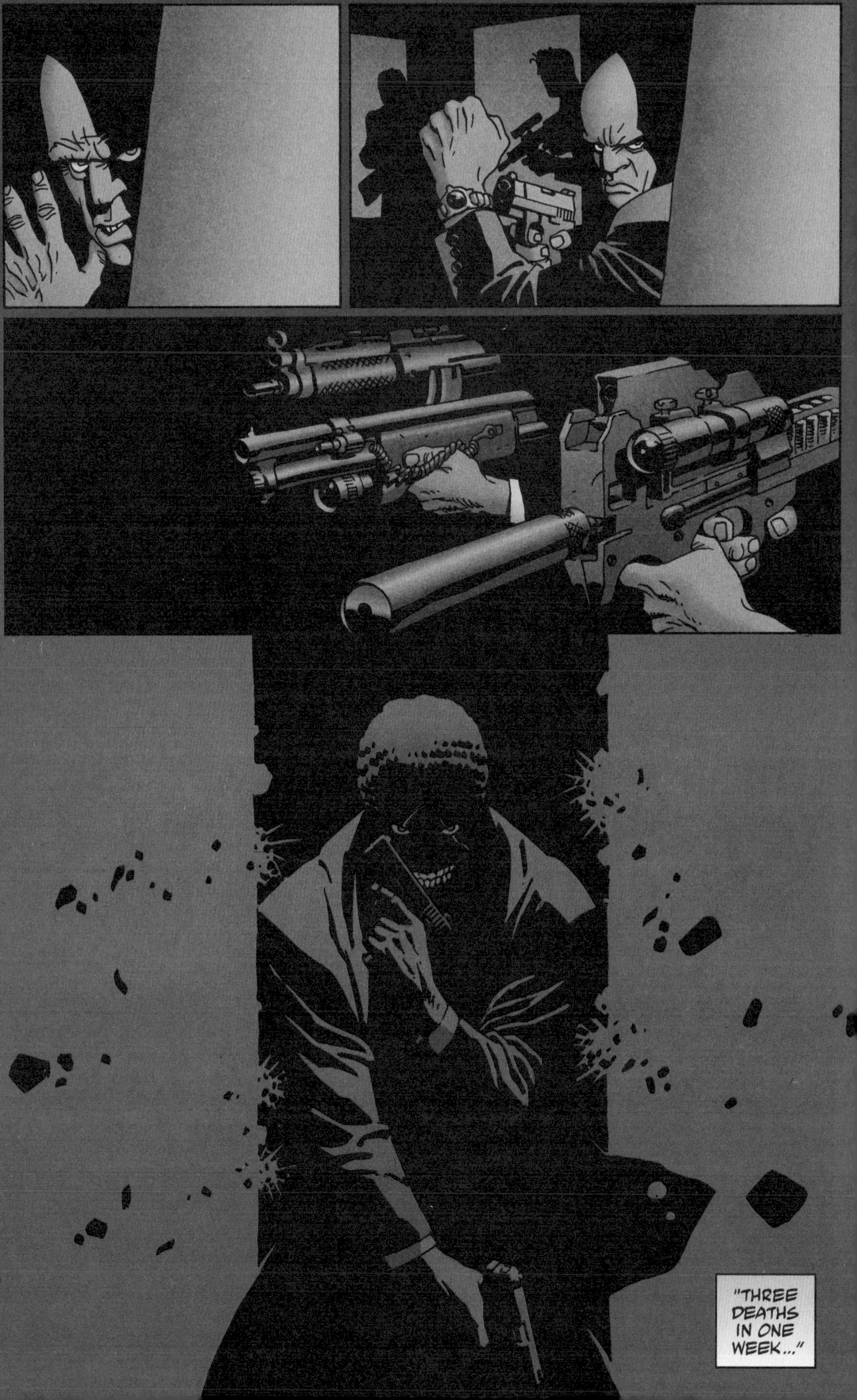
"THREE DEATHS IN ONE WEEK..."

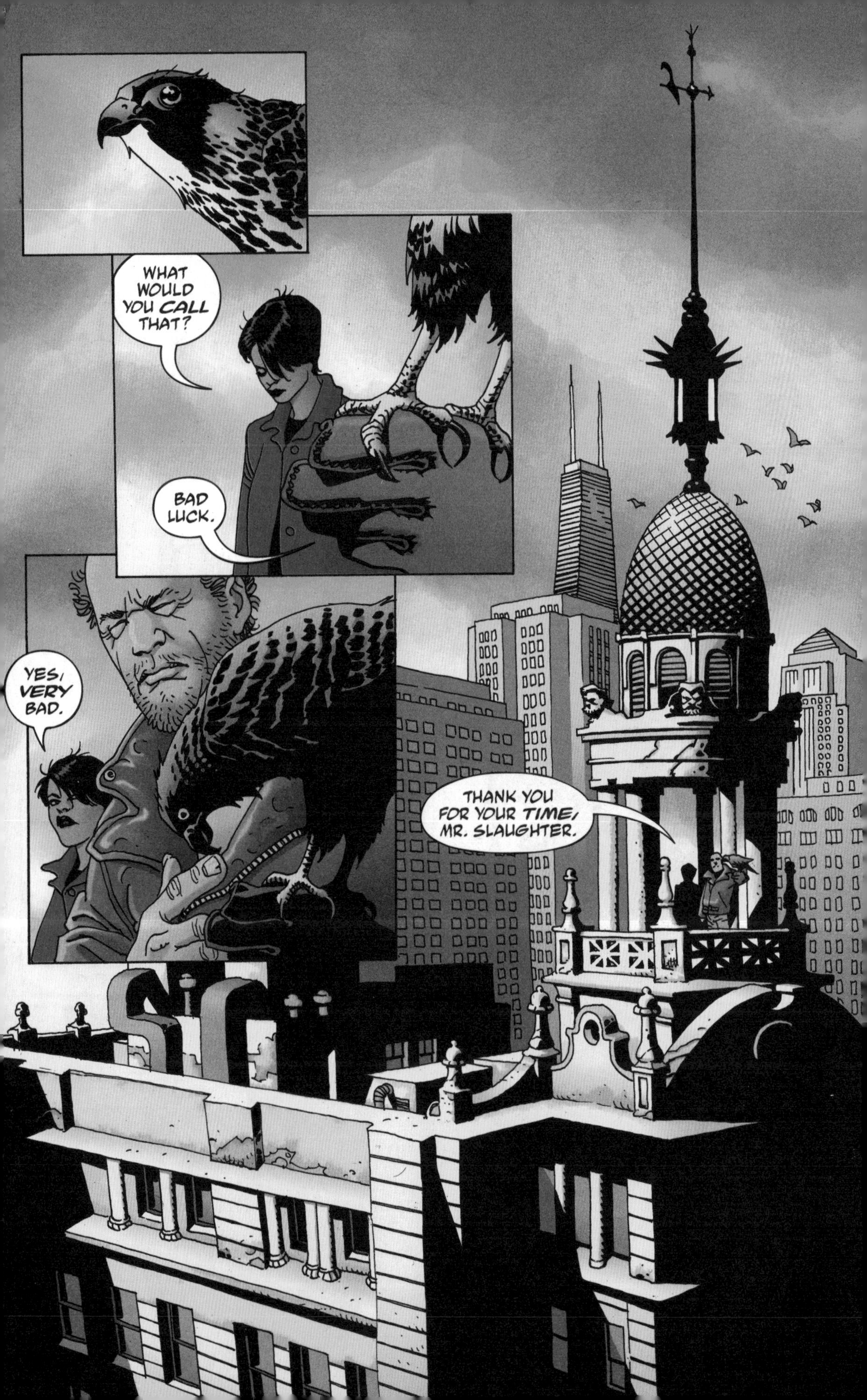
WHAT WOULD YOU CALL THAT?
BAD LUCK.
YES, VERY BAD.
THANK YOU FOR YOUR TIME, MR. SLAUGHTER.

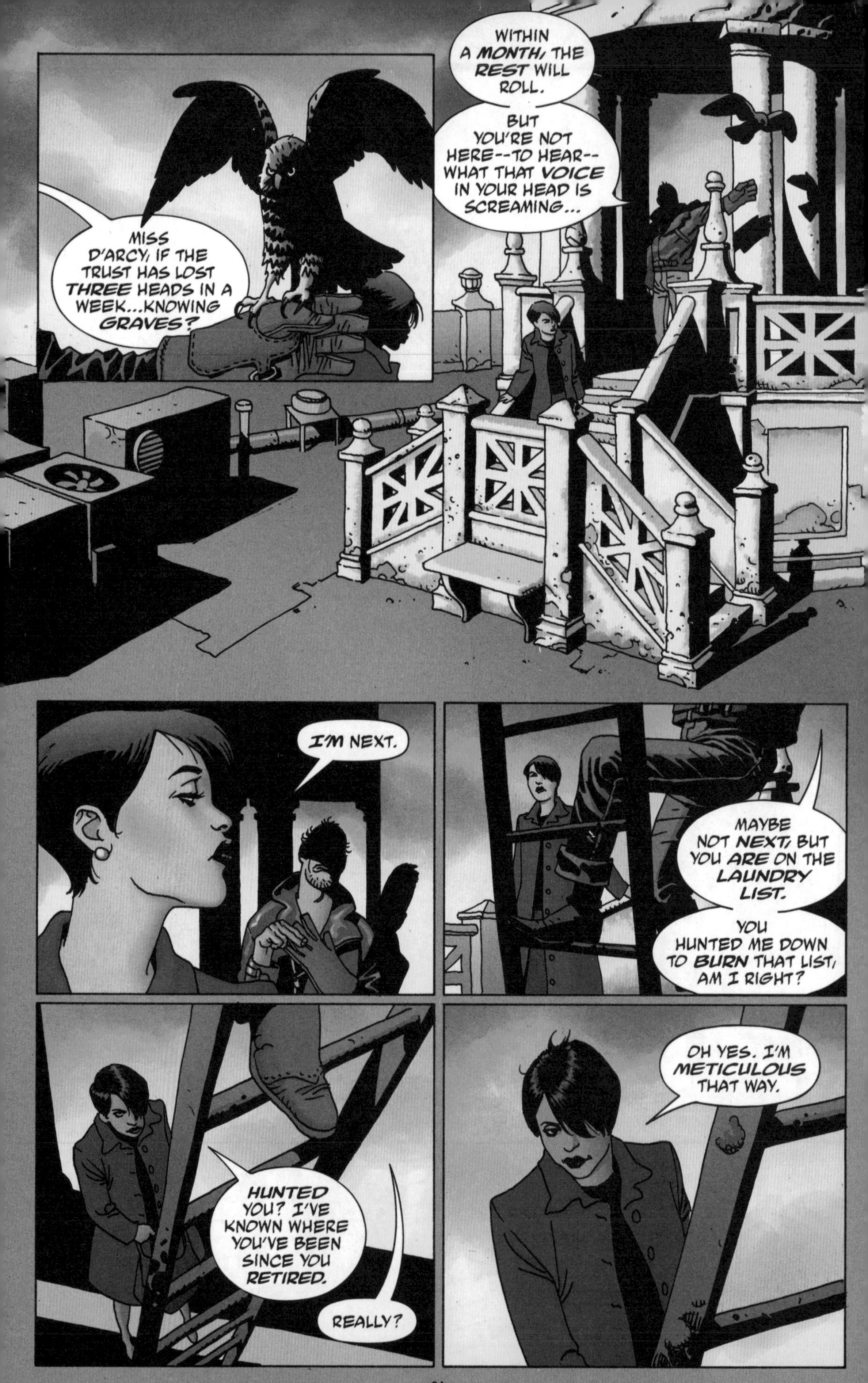
MISS D'ARCY, IF THE TRUST HAS LOST THREE HEADS IN A WEEK...KNOWING GRAVES?
WITHIN A MONTH, THE REST WILL ROLL.
BUT YOU'RE NOT HERE--TO HEAR--WHAT THAT VOICE IN YOUR HEAD IS SCREAMING...
I'M NEXT.
MAYBE NOT NEXT, BUT YOU ARE ON THE LAUNDRY LIST.
YOU HUNTED ME DOWN TO BURN THAT LIST, AM I RIGHT?
HUNTED YOU? I'VE KNOWN WHERE YOU'VE BEEN SINCE YOU RETIRED.
REALLY?
OH YES. I'M METICULOUS THAT WAY.

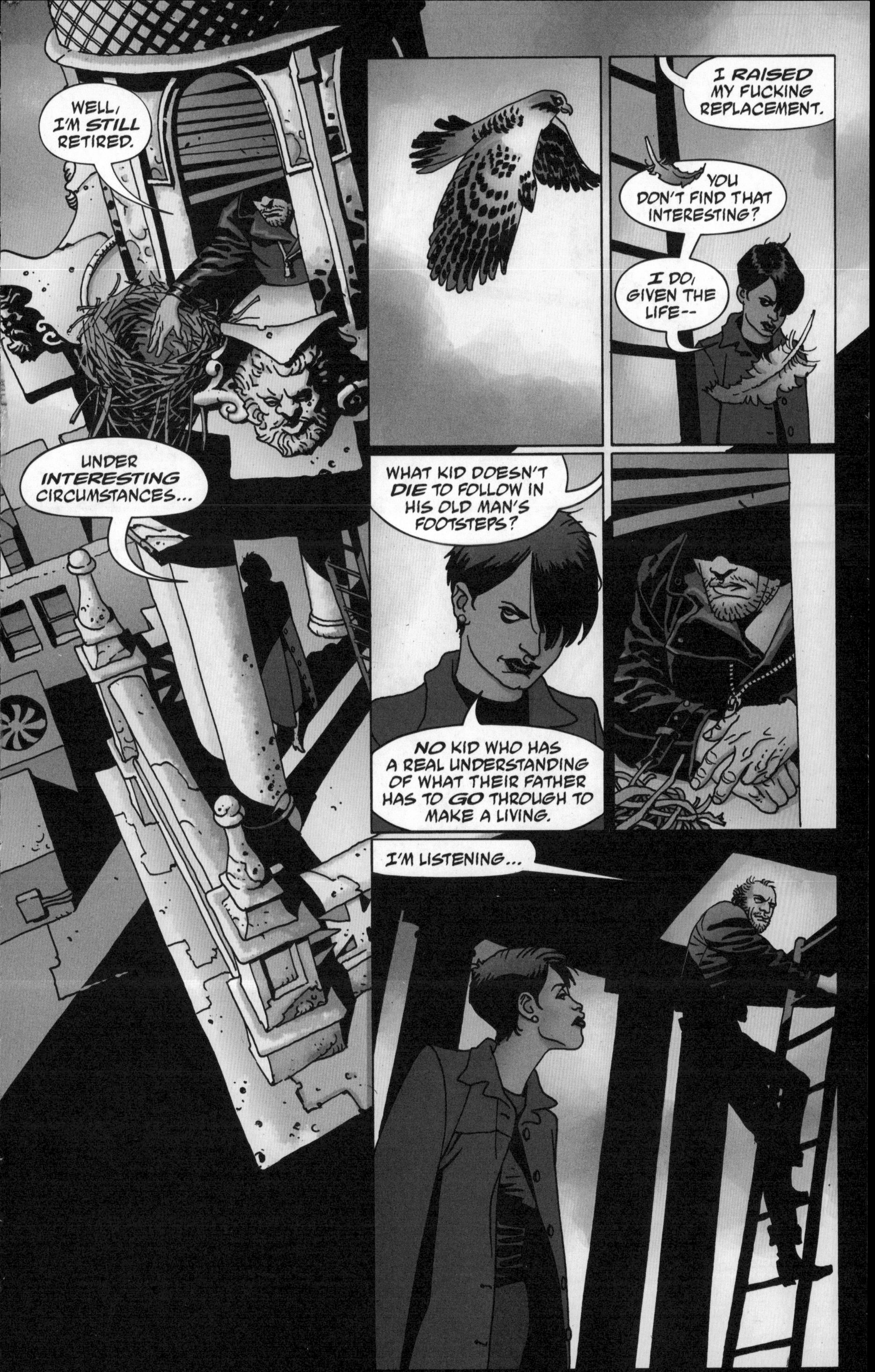
WELL, I'M STILL RETIRED.
I RAISED MY FUCKING REPLACEMENT.
YOU DON'T FIND THAT INTERESTING?
I DO, GIVEN THE LIFE--
UNDER INTERESTING CIRCUMSTANCES...
WHAT KID DOESN'T DIE TO FOLLOW IN HIS OLD MAN'S FOOTSTEPS?
NO KID WHO HAS A REAL UNDERSTANDING OF WHAT THEIR FATHER HAS TO GO THROUGH TO MAKE A LIVING.
I'M LISTENING...

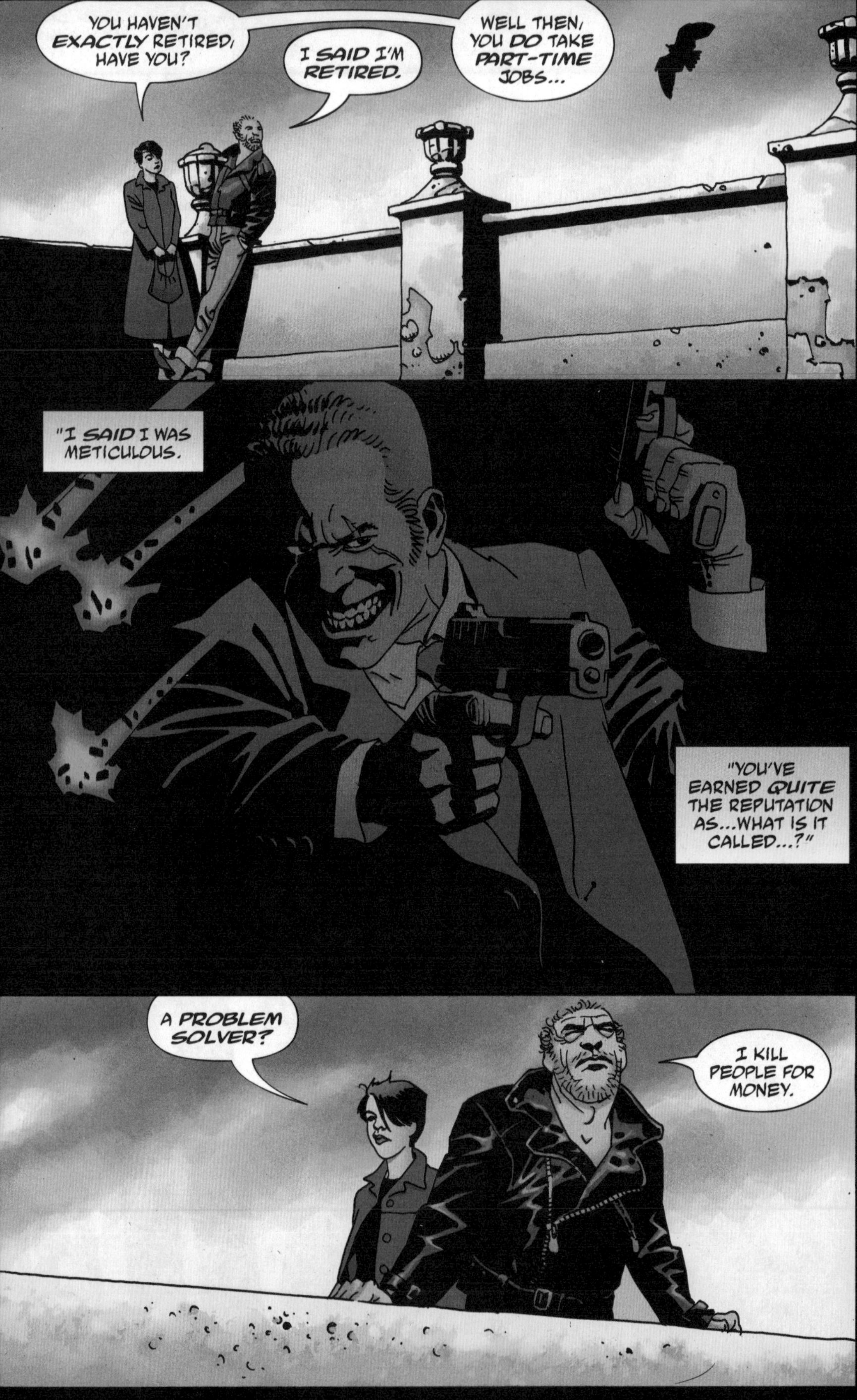
YOU HAVEN'T EXACTLY RETIRED, HAVE YOU?
I SAID I'M RETIRED.
WELL THEN, YOU DO TAKE PART-TIME JOBS...
"I SAID I WAS METICULOUS.
"YOU'VE EARNED QUITE THE REPUTATION AS...WHAT IS IT CALLED...?"
A PROBLEM SOLVER?
I KILL PEOPLE FOR MONEY.

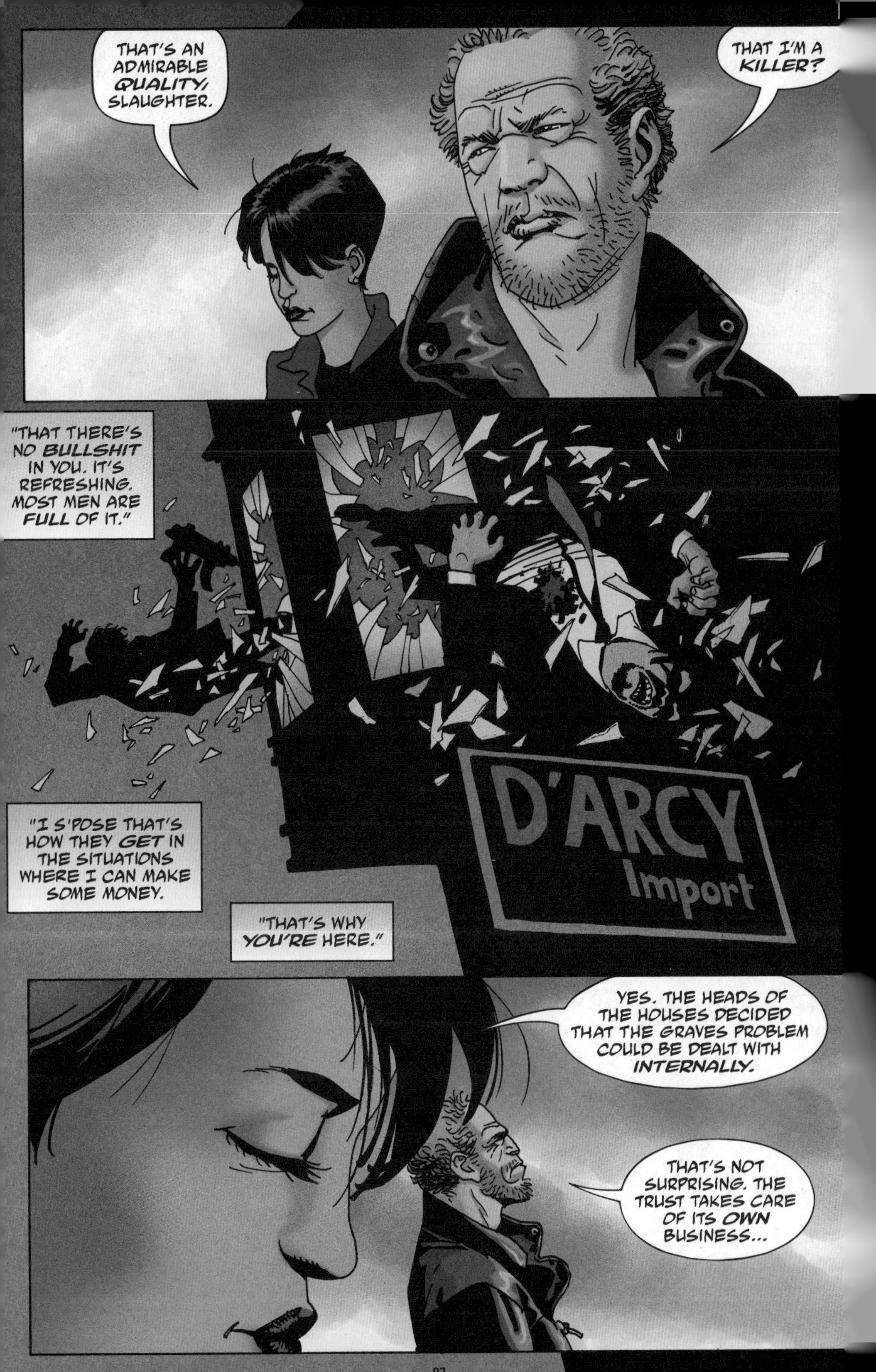
THAT'S AN ADMIRABLE QUALITY, SLAUGHTER.
THAT I'M A KILLER?
"THAT THERE'S NO BULLSHIT IN YOU. IT'S REFRESHING. MOST MEN ARE FULL OF IT."
D'ARCY Import
"I S'POSE THAT'S HOW THEY GET IN THE SITUATIONS WHERE I CAN MAKE SOME MONEY.
"THAT'S WHY YOU'RE HERE."
YES. THE HEADS OF THE HOUSES DECIDED THAT THE GRAVES PROBLEM COULD BE DEALT WITH INTERNALLY.
THAT'S NOT SURPRISING. THE TRUST TAKES CARE OF ITS OWN BUSINESS...

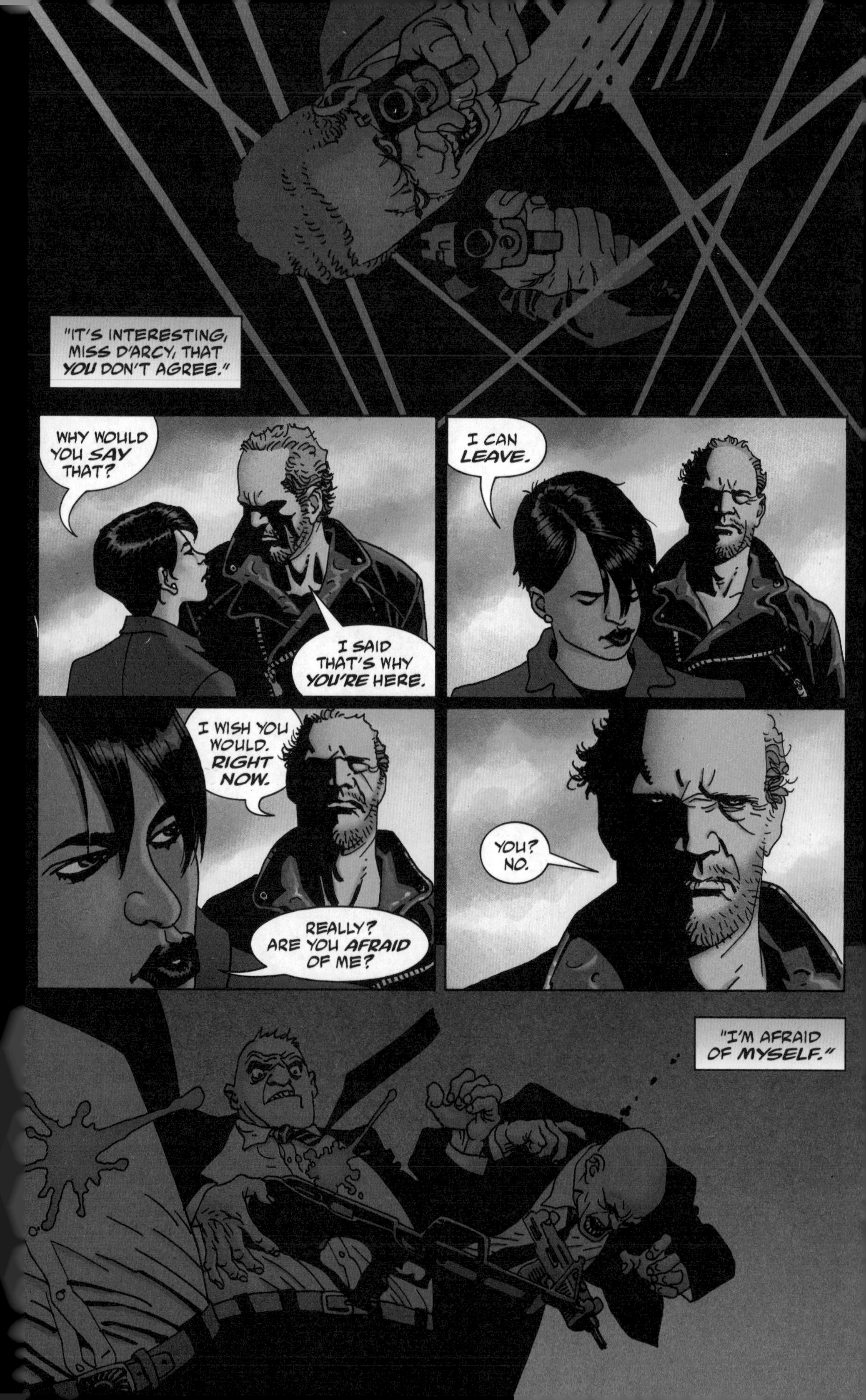
"IT'S INTERESTING, MISS D'ARCY, THAT YOU DON'T AGREE."
WHY WOULD YOU SAY THAT?
I SAID THAT'S WHY YOU'RE HERE.
I CAN LEAVE.
I WISH YOU WOULD. RIGHT NOW.
REALLY? ARE YOU AFRAID OF ME?
YOU? NO.
"I'M AFRAID OF MYSELF."

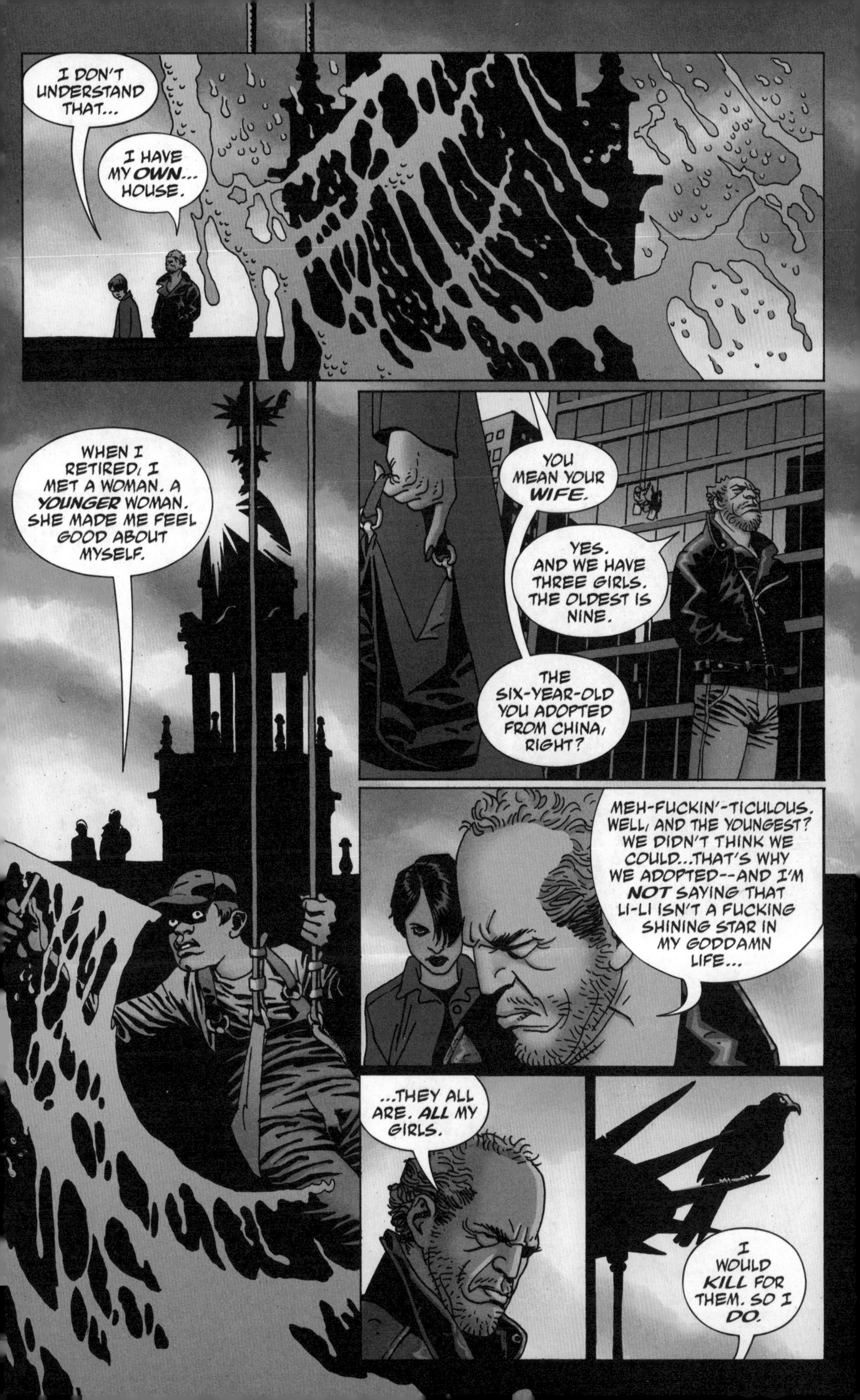
I DON'T UNDERSTAND THAT...
I HAVE MY OWN... HOUSE.
WHEN I RETIRED, I MET A WOMAN. A YOUNGER WOMAN. SHE MADE ME FEEL GOOD ABOUT MYSELF.
YOU MEAN YOUR WIFE.
YES. AND WE HAVE THREE GIRLS. THE OLDEST IS NINE.
THE SIX-YEAR-OLD YOU ADOPTED FROM CHINA, RIGHT?
MEH-FUCKIN'-TICULOUS. WELL, AND THE YOUNGEST? WE DIDN'T THINK WE COULD...THAT'S WHY WE ADOPTED--AND I'M NOT SAYING THAT LI-LI ISN'T A FUCKING SHINING STAR IN MY GODDAMN LIFE...
...THEY ALL ARE. ALL MY GIRLS.
I WOULD KILL FOR THEM. SO I DO.

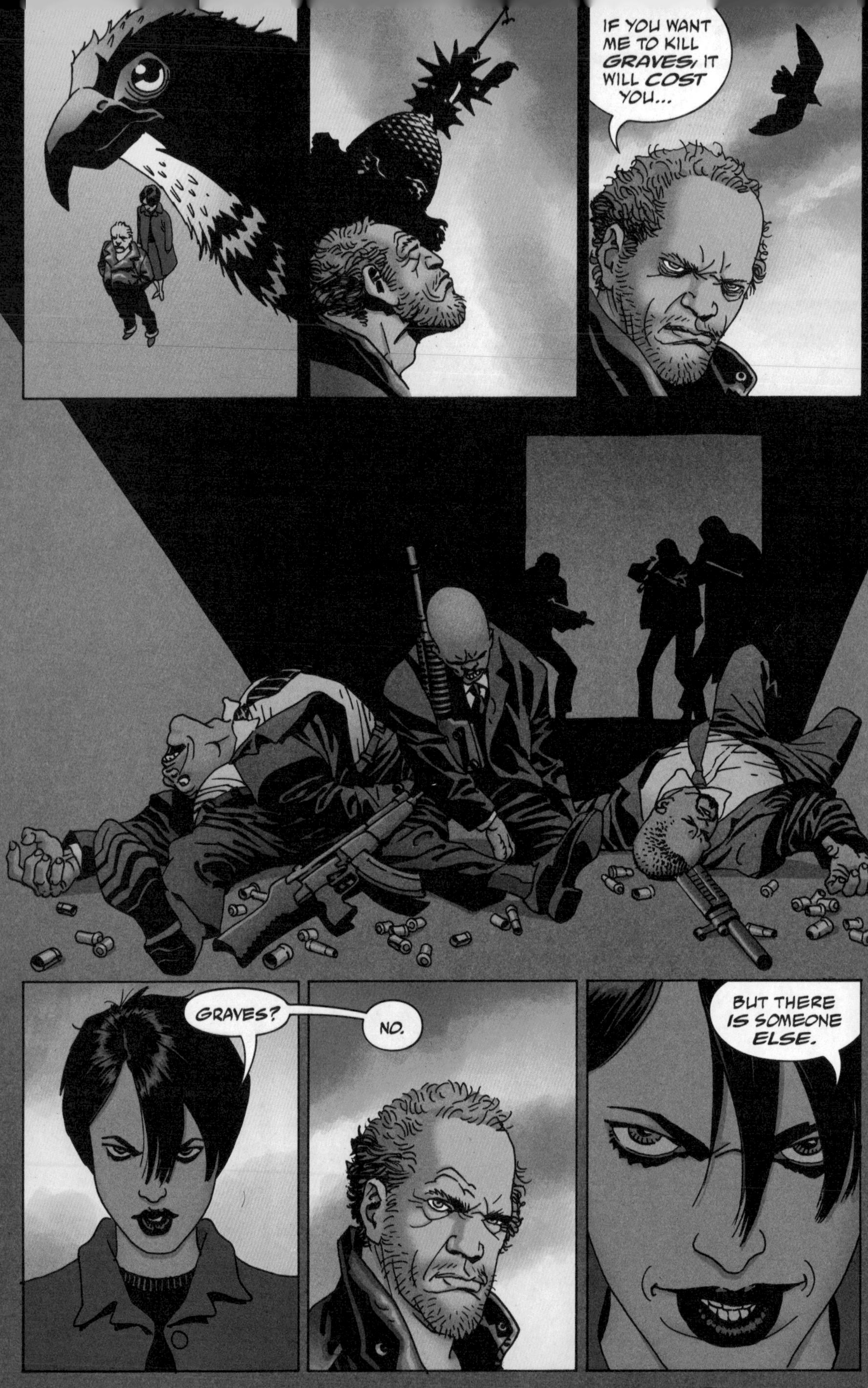
IF YOU WANT ME TO KILL GRAVES, IT WILL COST YOU...
GRAVES?
NO.
BUT THERE IS SOMEONE ELSE.

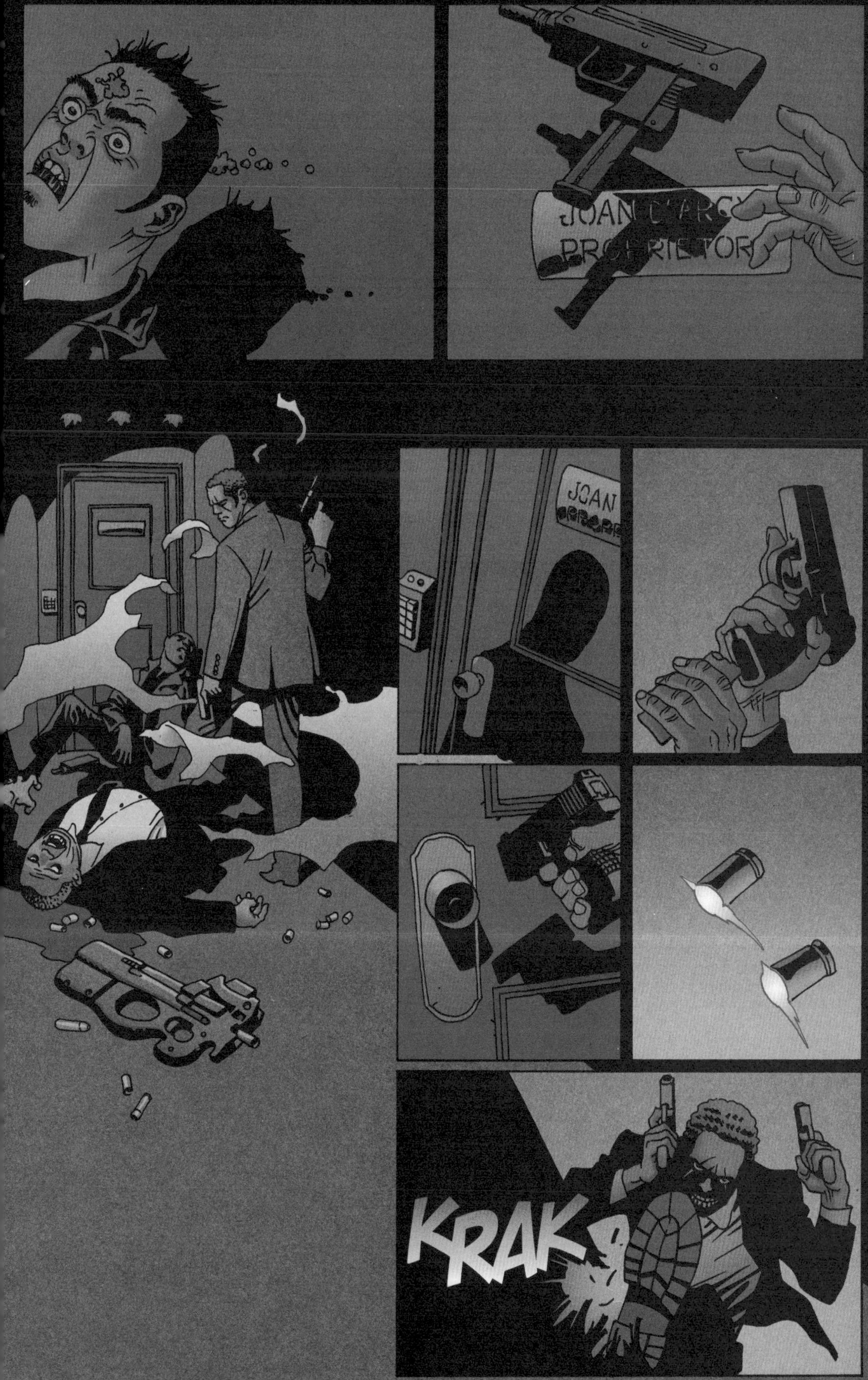
JOAN D'ARC
PROPRIETOR
JOAN
KRAK

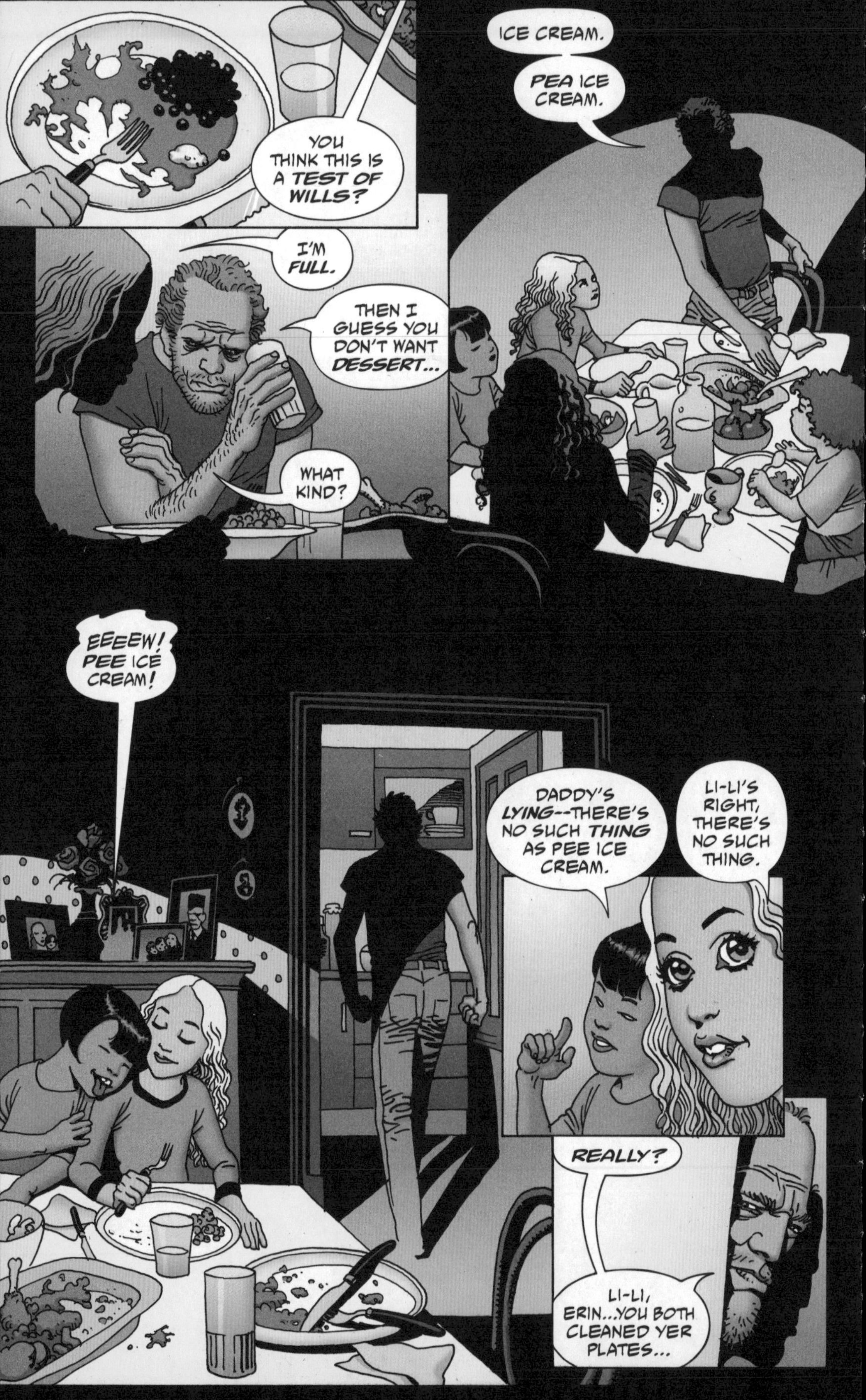
YOU THINK THIS IS A TEST OF WILLS?
ICE CREAM.
PEA ICE CREAM.
I'M FULL.
THEN I GUESS YOU DON'T WANT DESSERT...
WHAT KIND?
EEEEW! PEE ICE CREAM!
DADDY'S LYING--THERE'S NO SUCH THING AS PEE ICE CREAM.
LI-LI'S RIGHT, THERE'S NO SUCH THING.
REALLY?
LI-LI, ERIN...YOU BOTH CLEANED YER PLATES...

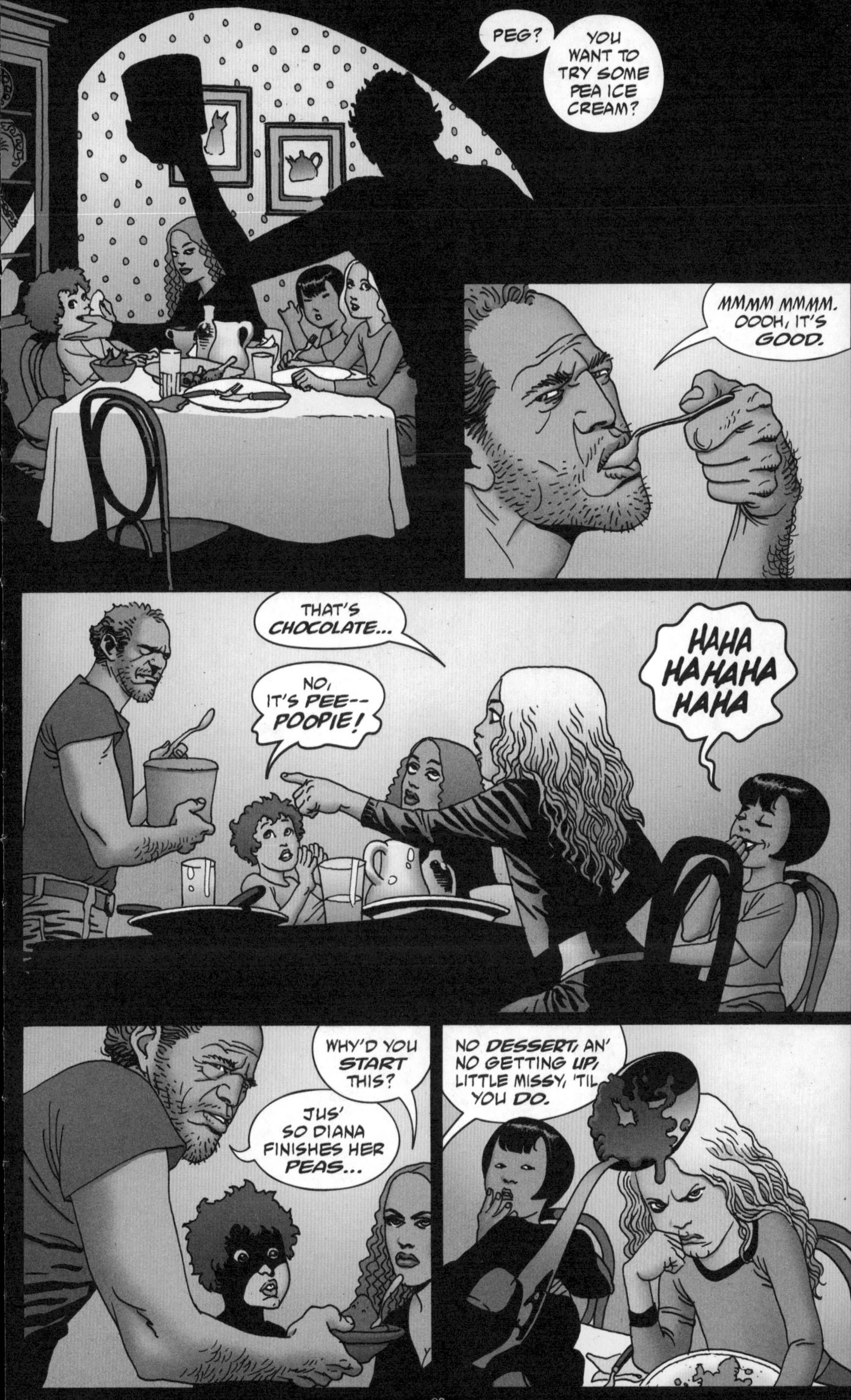
PEG?
YOU WANT TO TRY SOME PEA ICE CREAM?
MMMM MMMM. OOOH, IT'S GOOD.
THAT'S CHOCOLATE...
NO, IT'S PEE-- POOPIE!
HAHA HAHAHA HAHA
WHY'D YOU START THIS?
JUS' SO DIANA FINISHES HER PEAS...
NO DESSERT, AN' NO GETTING UP, LITTLE MISSY, 'TIL YOU DO.

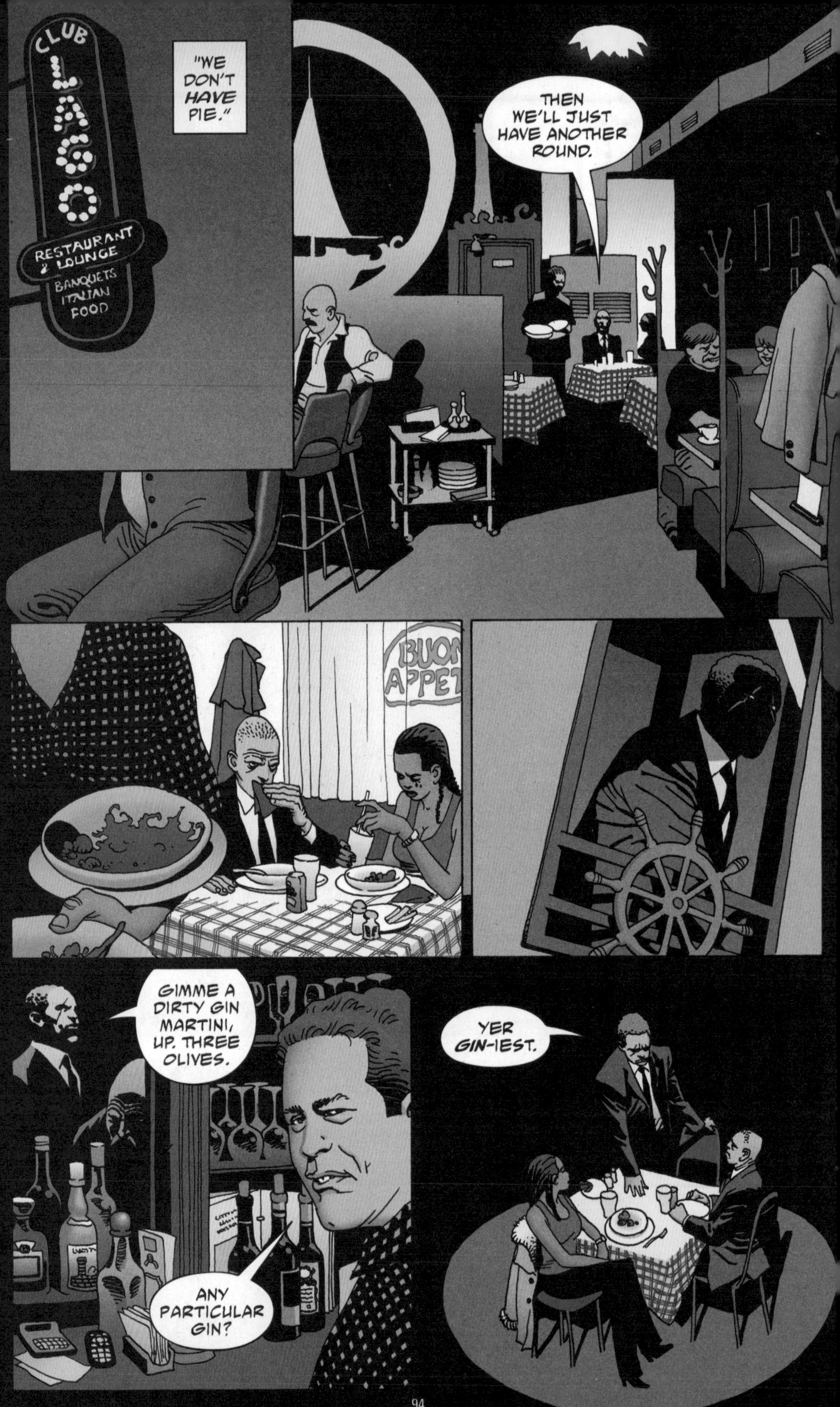
CLUB
LAGO
RESTAURANT & LOUNGE
BANQUETS ITALIAN FOOD
"WE DON'T *HAVE* PIE."
THEN WE'LL JUST HAVE ANOTHER ROUND.
GIMME A DIRTY GIN MARTINI, UP. THREE OLIVES.
ANY PARTICULAR GIN?
YER *GIN*-IEST.

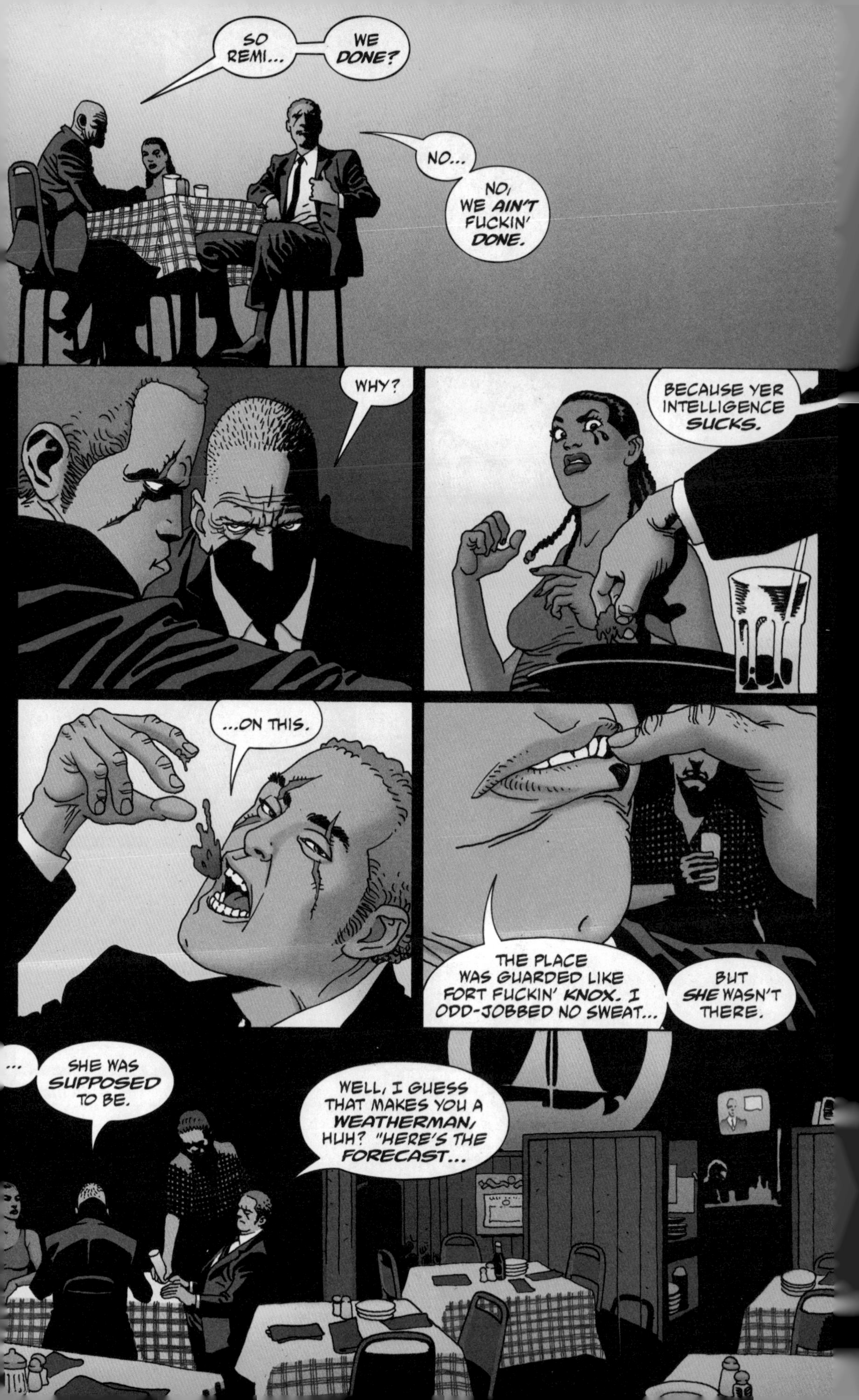
SO REMI...
WE DONE?
NO...
NO, WE AIN'T FUCKIN' DONE.
WHY?
BECAUSE YER INTELLIGENCE SUCKS.
...ON THIS.
THE PLACE WAS GUARDED LIKE FORT FUCKIN' KNOX. I ODD-JOBBED NO SWEAT...
BUT SHE WASN'T THERE.
...
SHE WAS SUPPOSED TO BE.
WELL, I GUESS THAT MAKES YOU A WEATHERMAN, HUH? "HERE'S THE FORECAST...

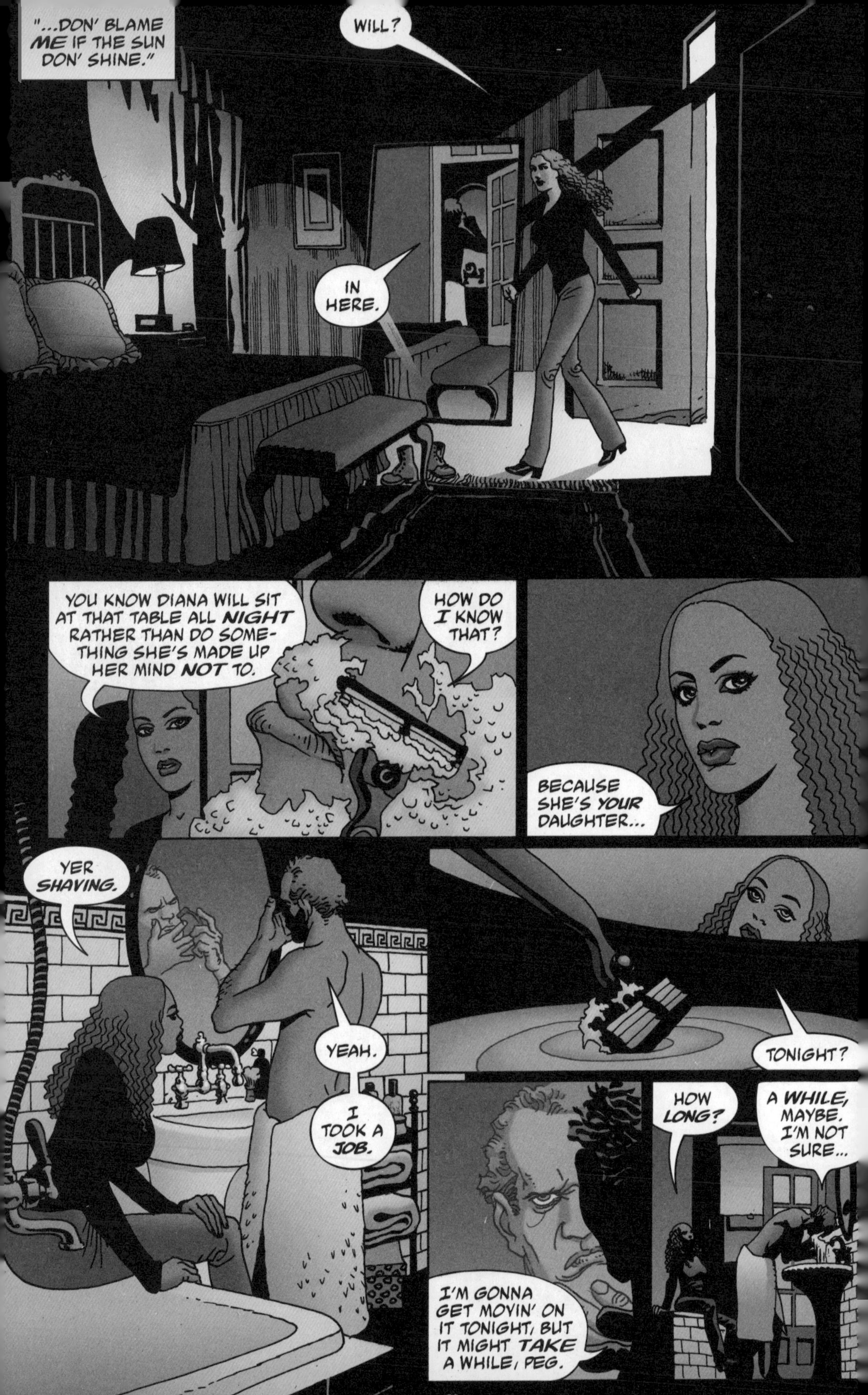

"...DON' BLAME ME IF THE SUN DON' SHINE."
WILL?
IN HERE.
YOU KNOW DIANA WILL SIT AT THAT TABLE ALL NIGHT RATHER THAN DO SOMETHING SHE'S MADE UP HER MIND NOT TO.
HOW DO I KNOW THAT?
BECAUSE SHE'S YOUR DAUGHTER...
YER SHAVING.
YEAH.
I TOOK A JOB.
TONIGHT?
I'M GONNA GET MOVIN' ON IT TONIGHT, BUT IT MIGHT TAKE A WHILE, PEG.
HOW LONG?
A WHILE, MAYBE. I'M NOT SURE...

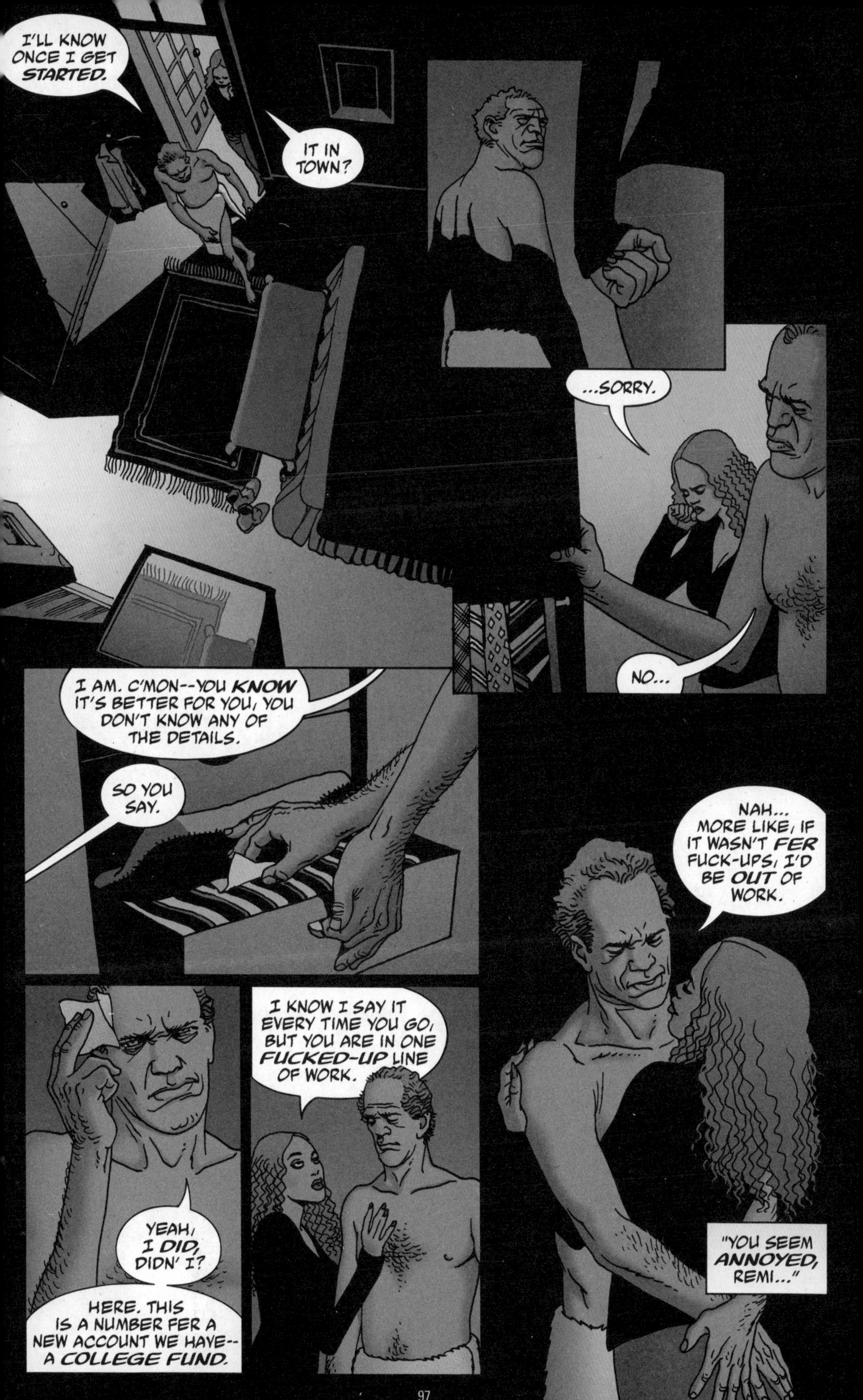

I'LL KNOW ONCE I GET STARTED.
IT IN TOWN?
...SORRY.
NO...
I AM. C'MON--YOU KNOW IT'S BETTER FOR YOU, YOU DON'T KNOW ANY OF THE DETAILS.
SO YOU SAY.
YEAH, I DID, DIDN' I?
HERE. THIS IS A NUMBER FER A NEW ACCOUNT WE HAVE-- A COLLEGE FUND.
I KNOW I SAY IT EVERY TIME YOU GO, BUT YOU ARE IN ONE FUCKED-UP LINE OF WORK.
NAH... MORE LIKE, IF IT WASN'T FER FUCK-UPS, I'D BE OUT OF WORK.
"YOU SEEM ANNOYED, REMI..."

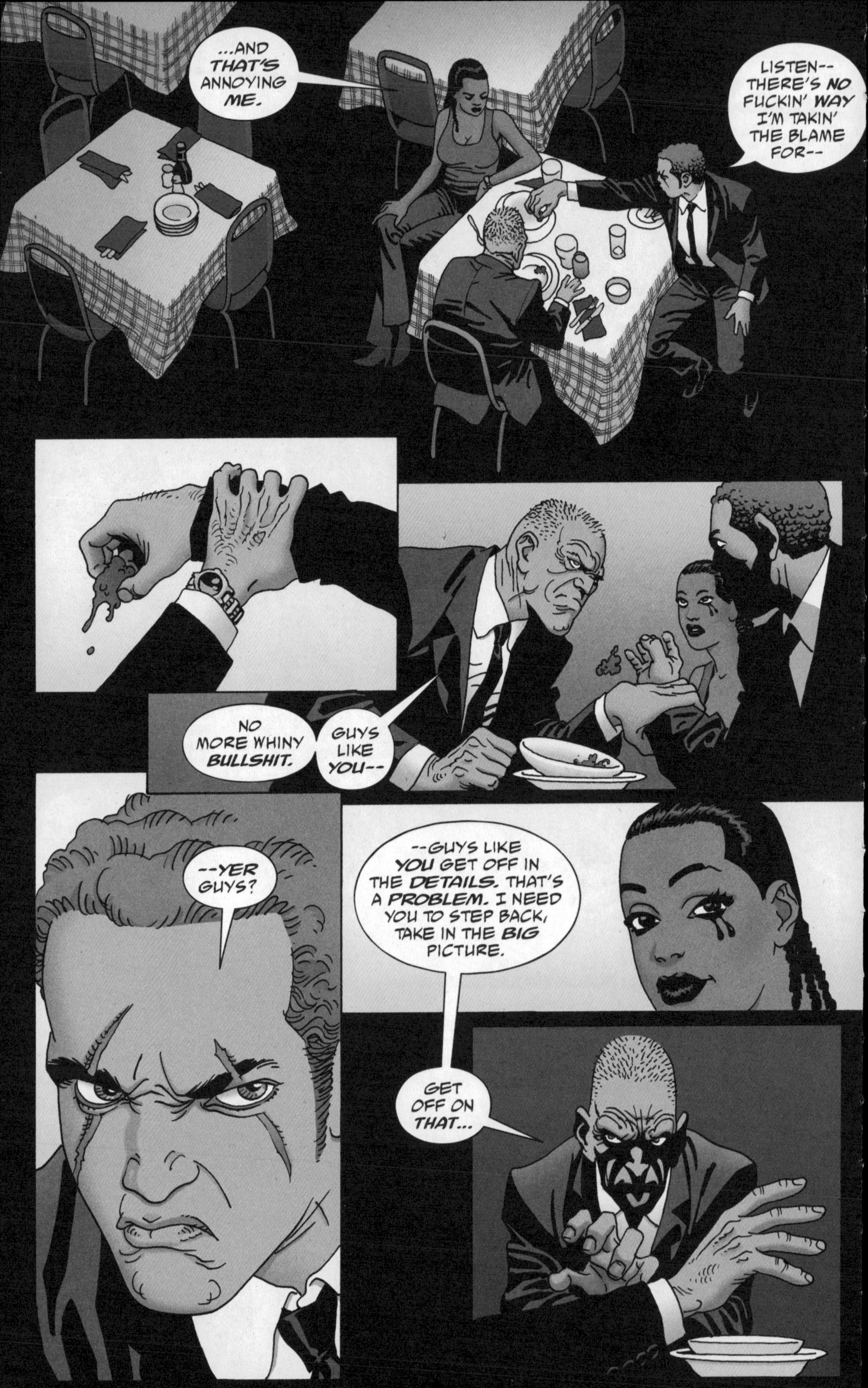
...AND THAT'S ANNOYING ME.
LISTEN-- THERE'S NO FUCKIN' WAY I'M TAKIN' THE BLAME FOR--
NO MORE WHINY BULLSHIT.
GUYS LIKE YOU--
--YER GUYS?
--GUYS LIKE YOU GET OFF IN THE DETAILS. THAT'S A PROBLEM. I NEED YOU TO STEP BACK, TAKE IN THE BIG PICTURE.
GET OFF ON THAT...

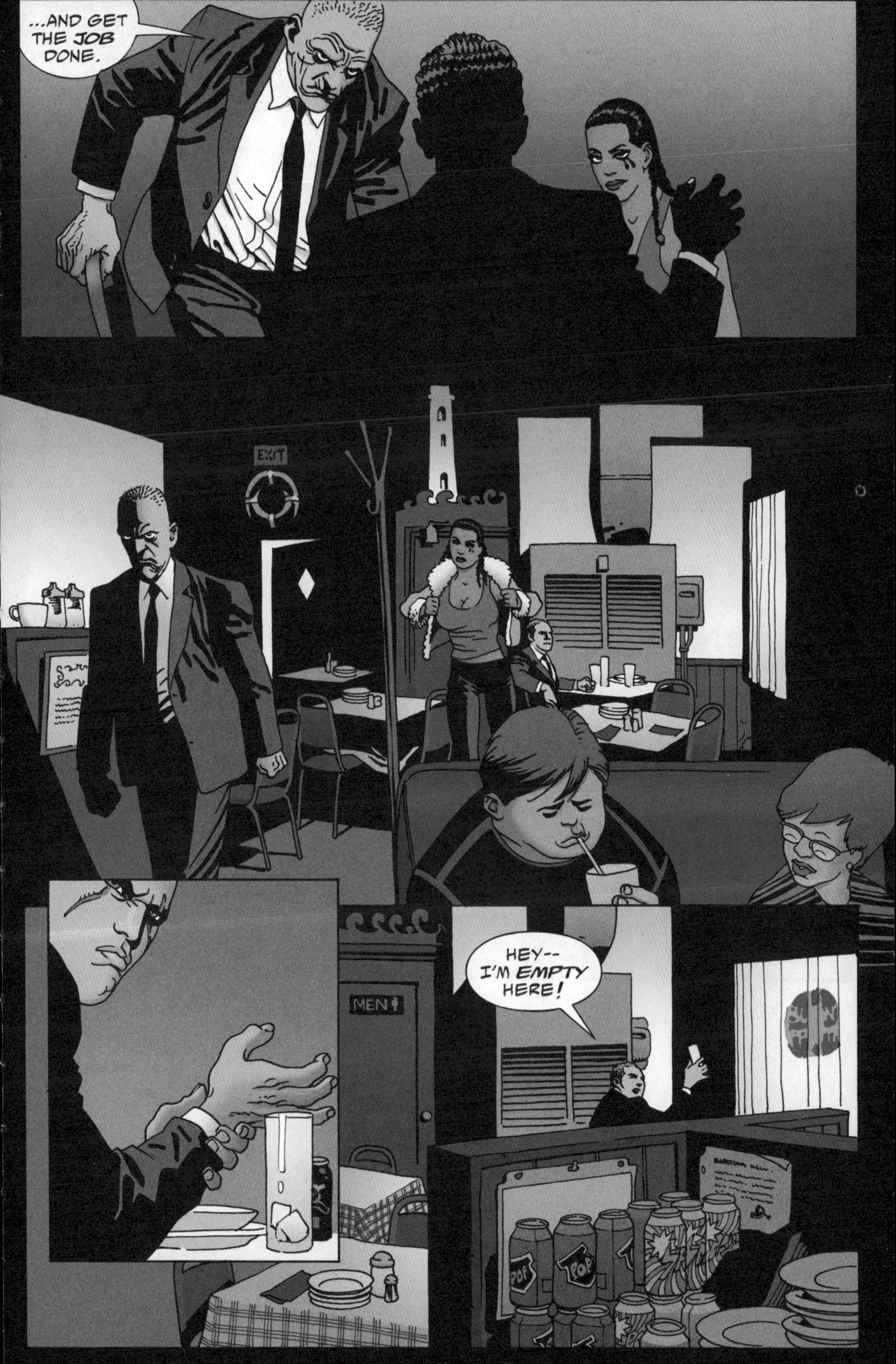
...AND GET THE JOB DONE.
EXIT
MEN
HEY-- I'M EMPTY HERE!
POP
POP

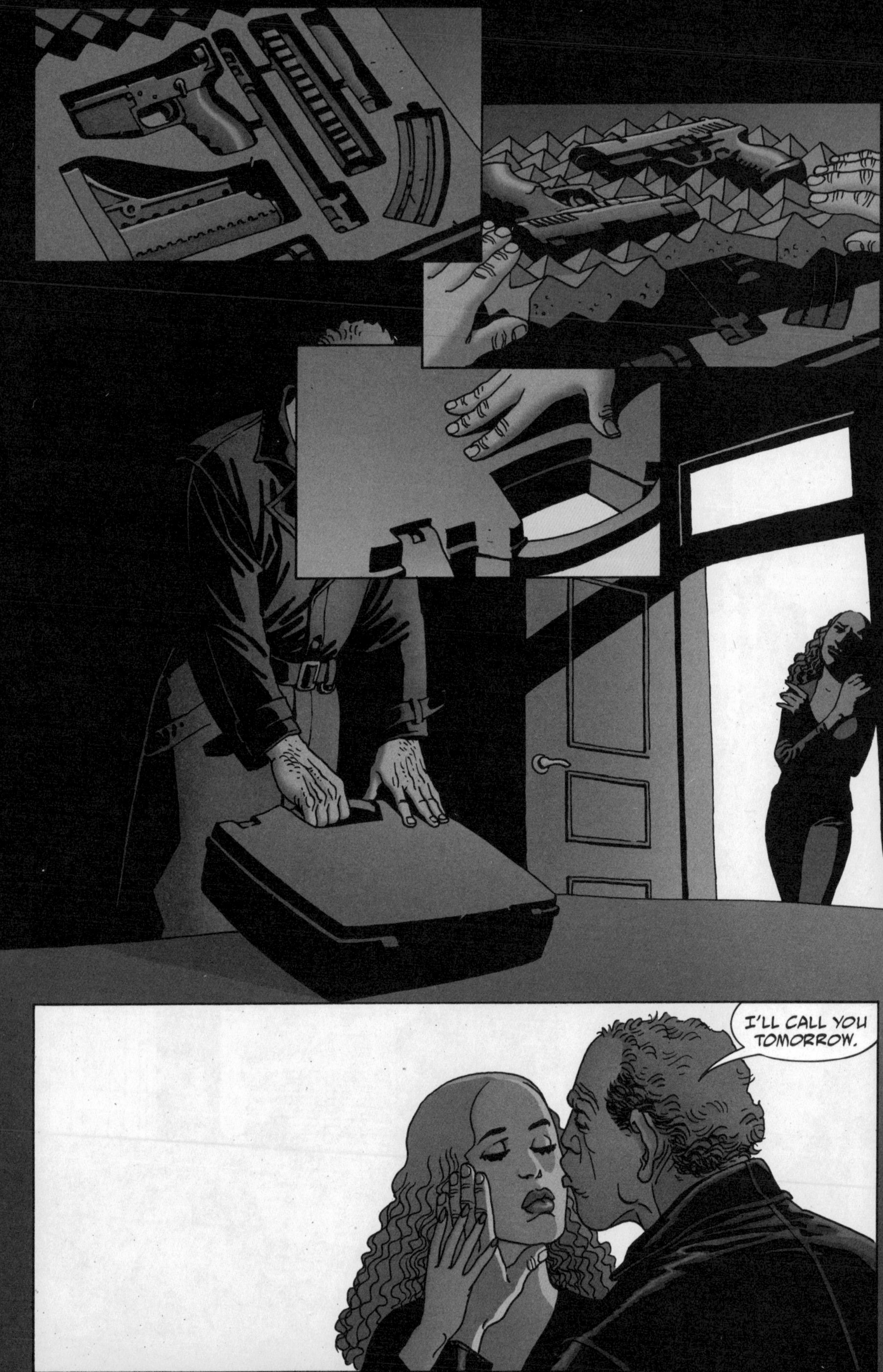
I'LL CALL YOU TOMORROW.

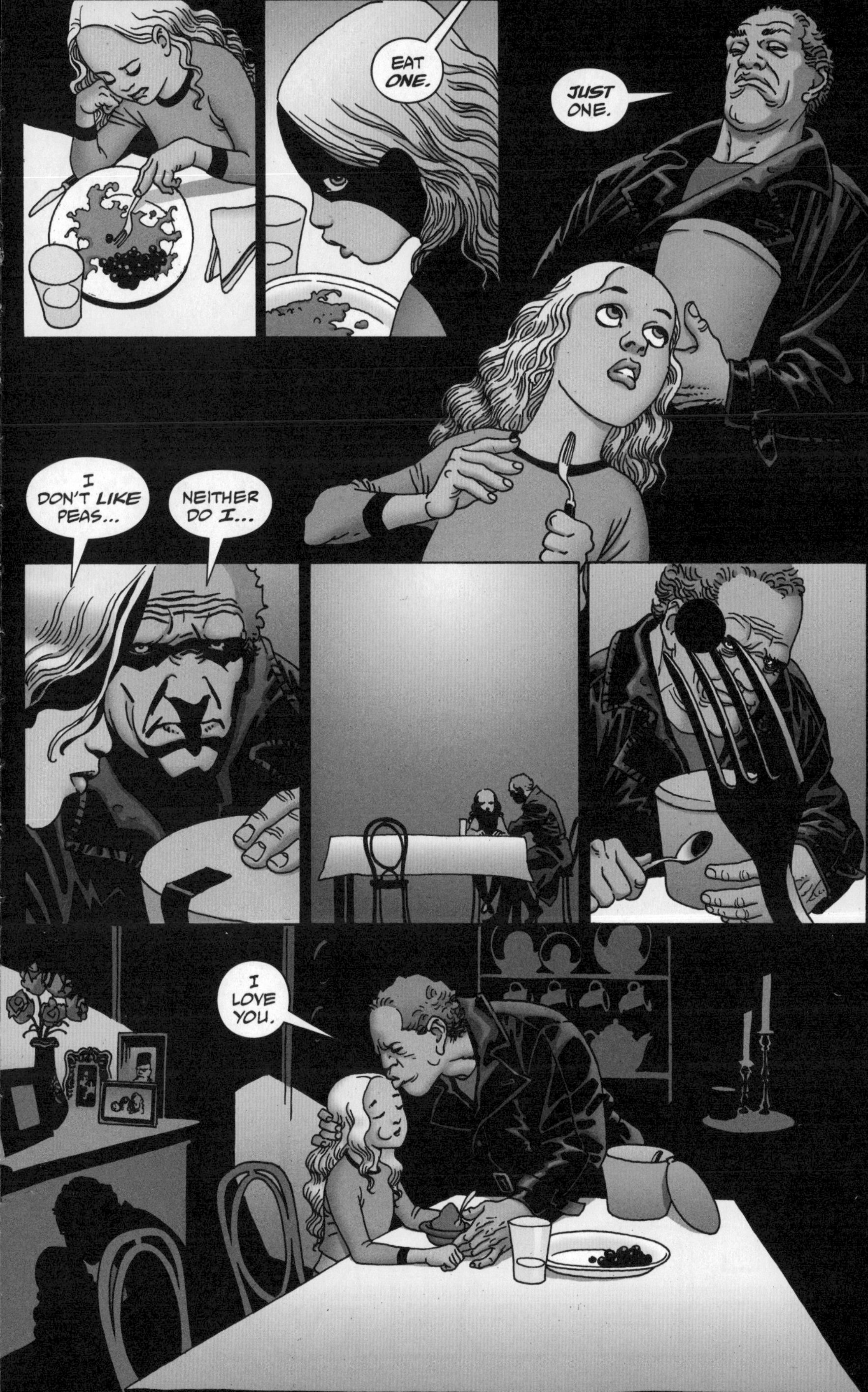
EAT ONE.
JUST ONE.
I DON'T LIKE PEAS...
NEITHER DO I...
I LOVE YOU.

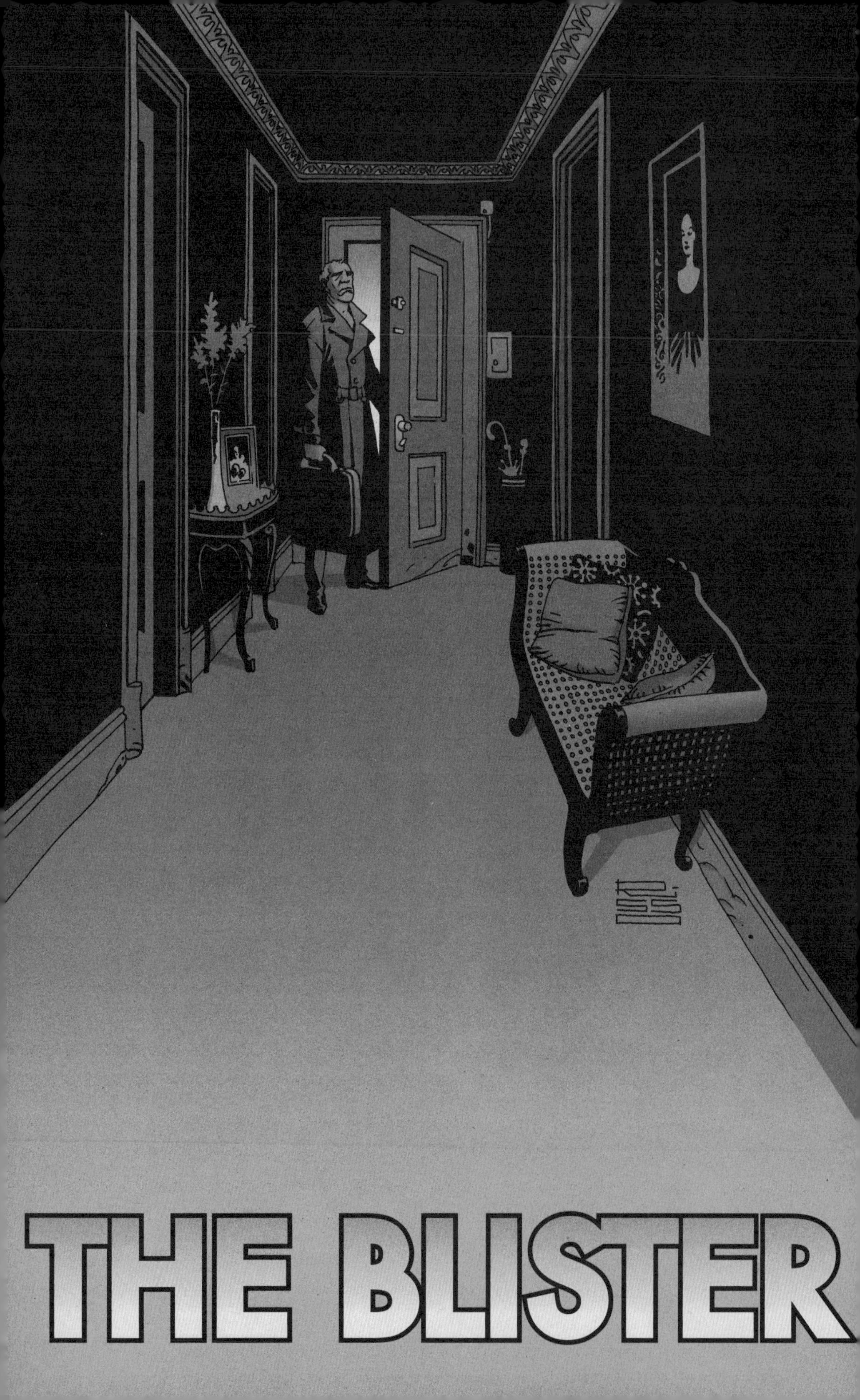
THE BLISTER

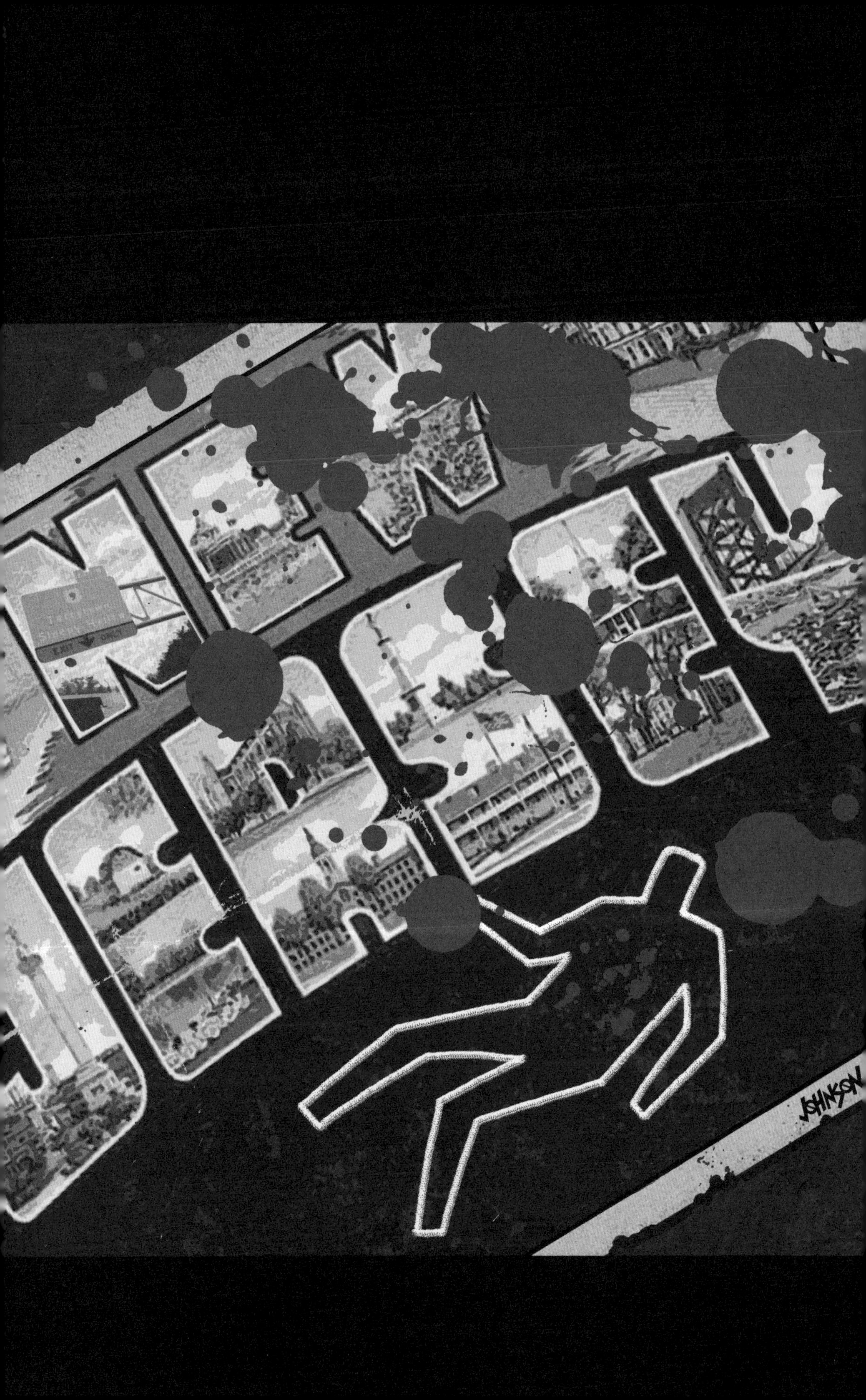
NEW JERSEY
JOHNSON

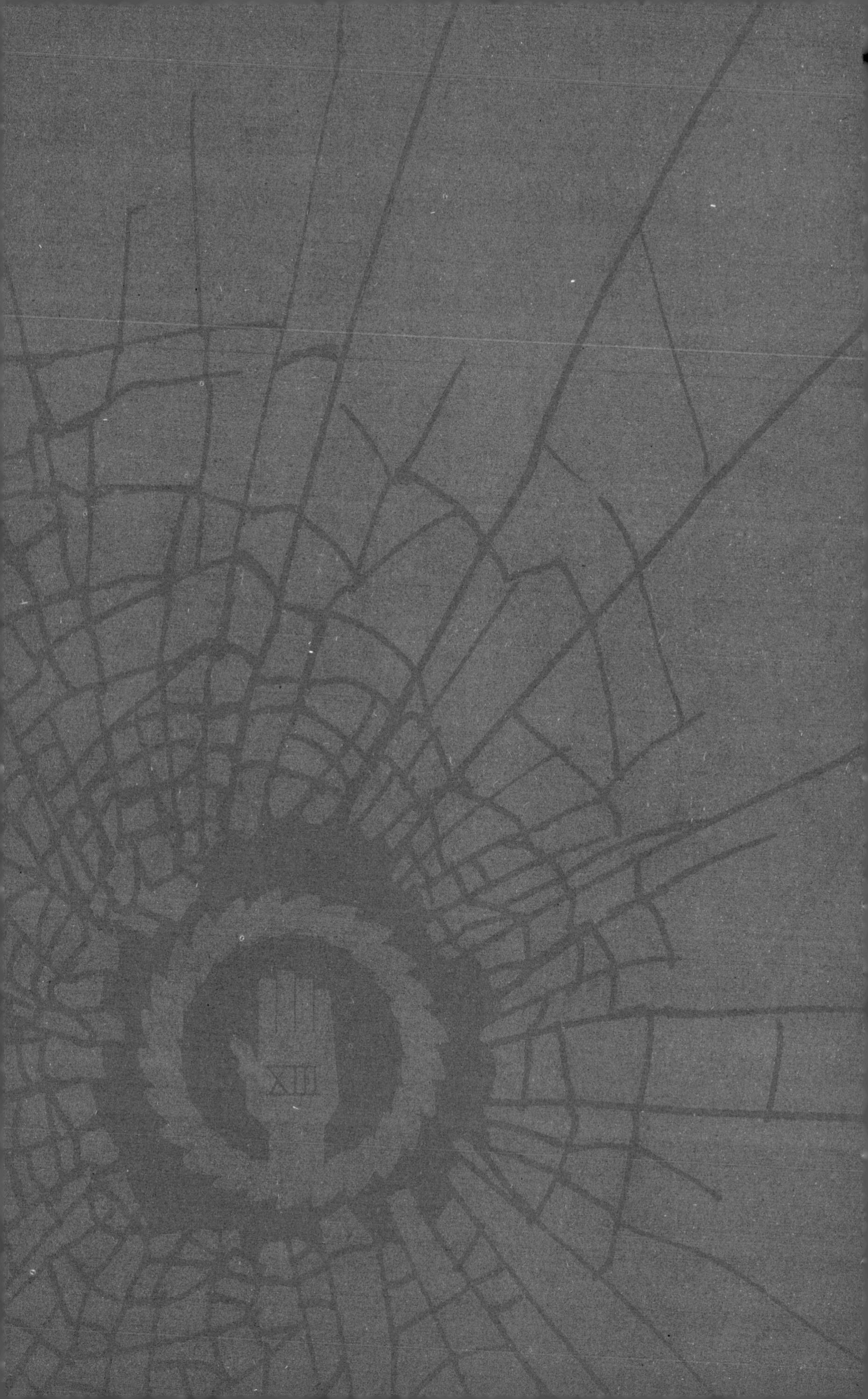
XII

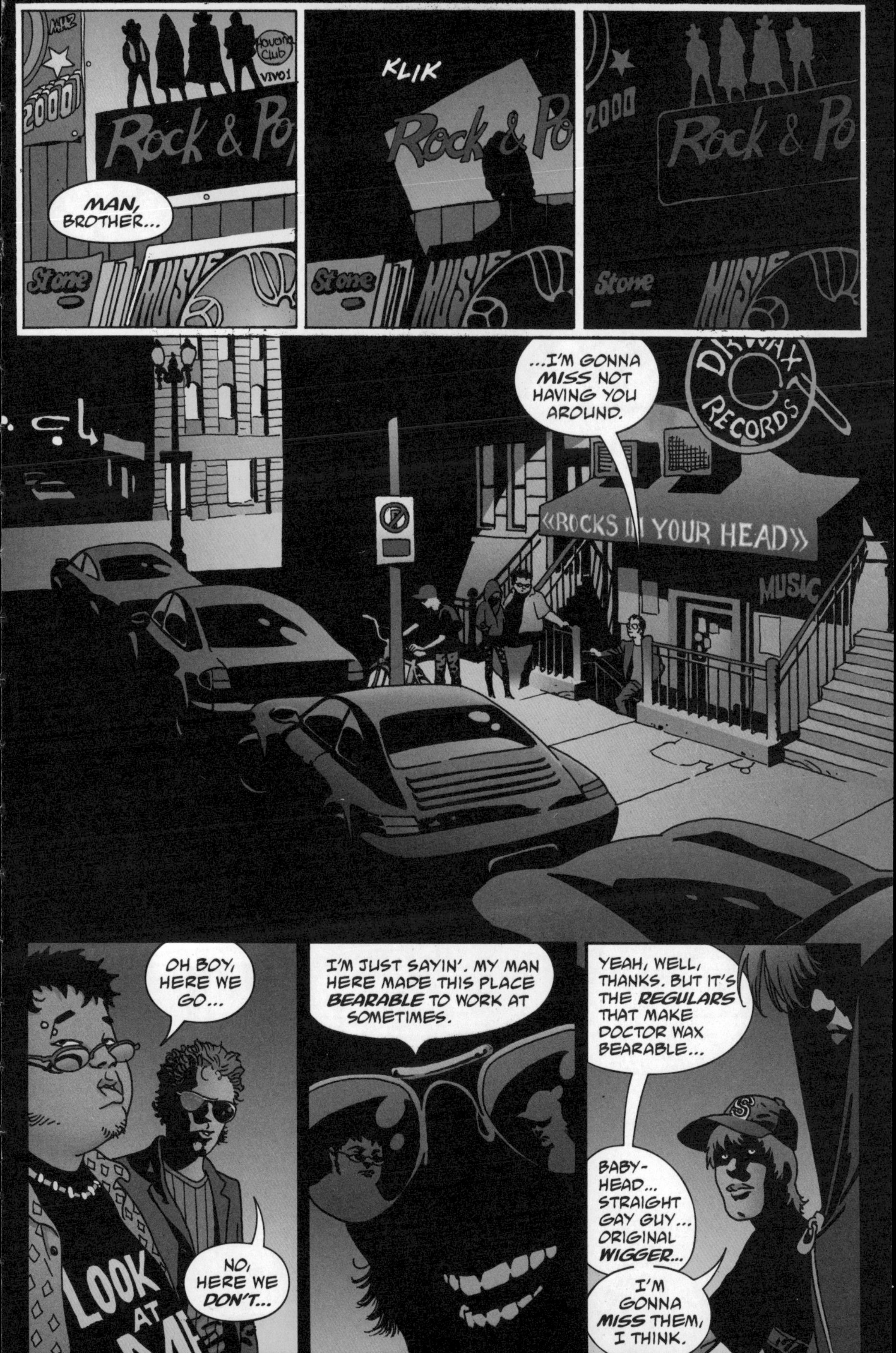
MHZ
2000
Havana Club
VIVO1
Rock & Po
MAN, BROTHER...
Stone
MUSIC
KLIK
...I'M GONNA MISS NOT HAVING YOU AROUND.
DR WAX RECORDS
«ROCKS IN YOUR HEAD»
MUSIC
OH BOY, HERE WE GO...
NO, HERE WE DON'T...
LOOK AT
I'M JUST SAYIN'. MY MAN HERE MADE THIS PLACE BEARABLE TO WORK AT SOMETIMES.
YEAH, WELL, THANKS. BUT IT'S THE REGULARS THAT MAKE DOCTOR WAX BEARABLE...
BABY-HEAD... STRAIGHT GAY GUY... ORIGINAL WIGGER...
I'M GONNA MISS THEM, I THINK.

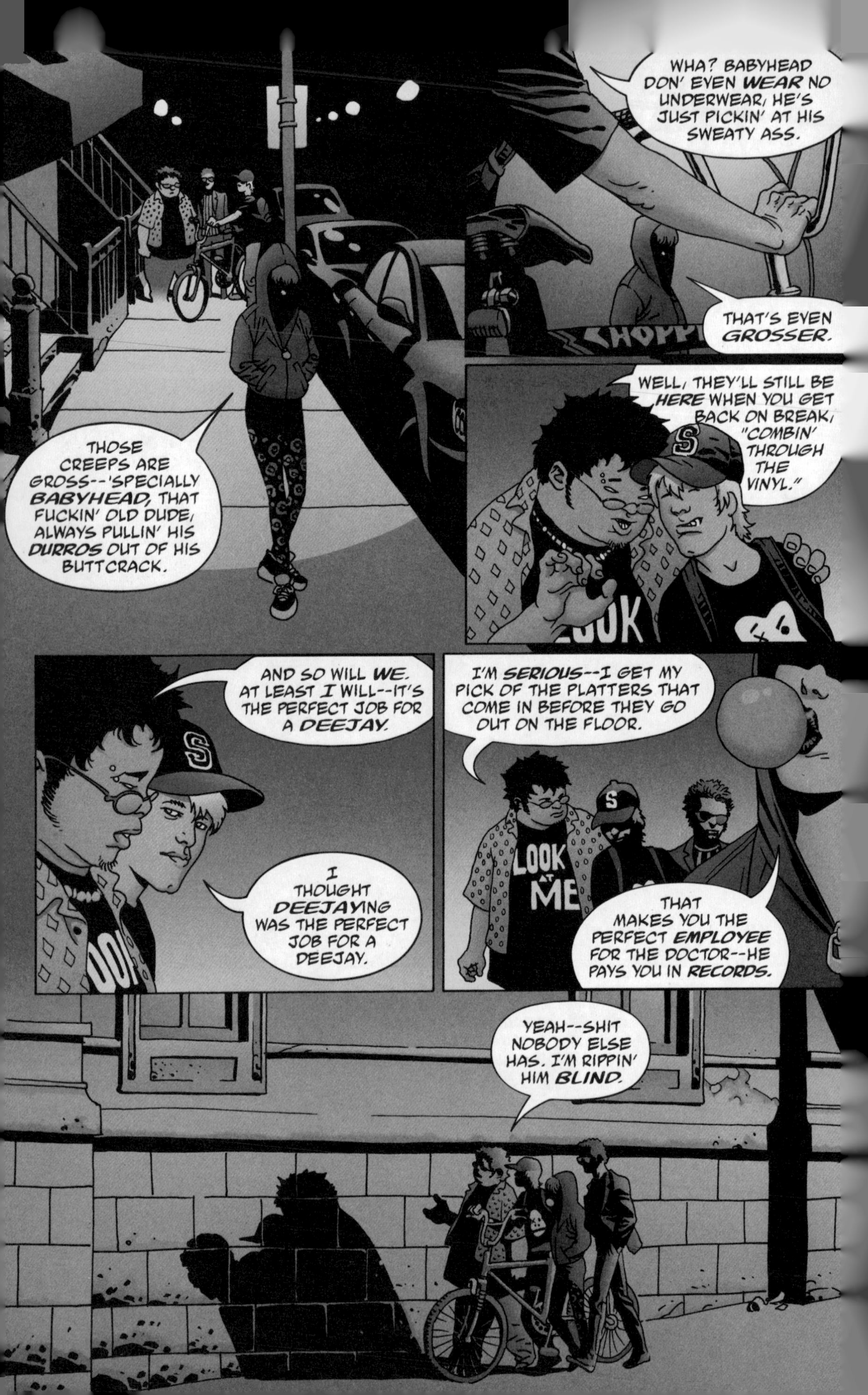
WHA? BABYHEAD DON' EVEN WEAR NO UNDERWEAR, HE'S JUST PICKIN' AT HIS SWEATY ASS.
THAT'S EVEN GROSSER.
THOSE CREEPS ARE GROSS--'SPECIALLY BABYHEAD, THAT FUCKIN' OLD DUDE, ALWAYS PULLIN' HIS DURROS OUT OF HIS BUTTCRACK.
WELL, THEY'LL STILL BE HERE WHEN YOU GET BACK ON BREAK, "COMBIN' THROUGH THE VINYL."
AND SO WILL WE. AT LEAST I WILL--IT'S THE PERFECT JOB FOR A DEEJAY.
I THOUGHT DEEJAYING WAS THE PERFECT JOB FOR A DEEJAY.
I'M SERIOUS--I GET MY PICK OF THE PLATTERS THAT COME IN BEFORE THEY GO OUT ON THE FLOOR.
THAT MAKES YOU THE PERFECT EMPLOYEE FOR THE DOCTOR--HE PAYS YOU IN RECORDS.
YEAH--SHIT NOBODY ELSE HAS. I'M RIPPIN' HIM BLIND.

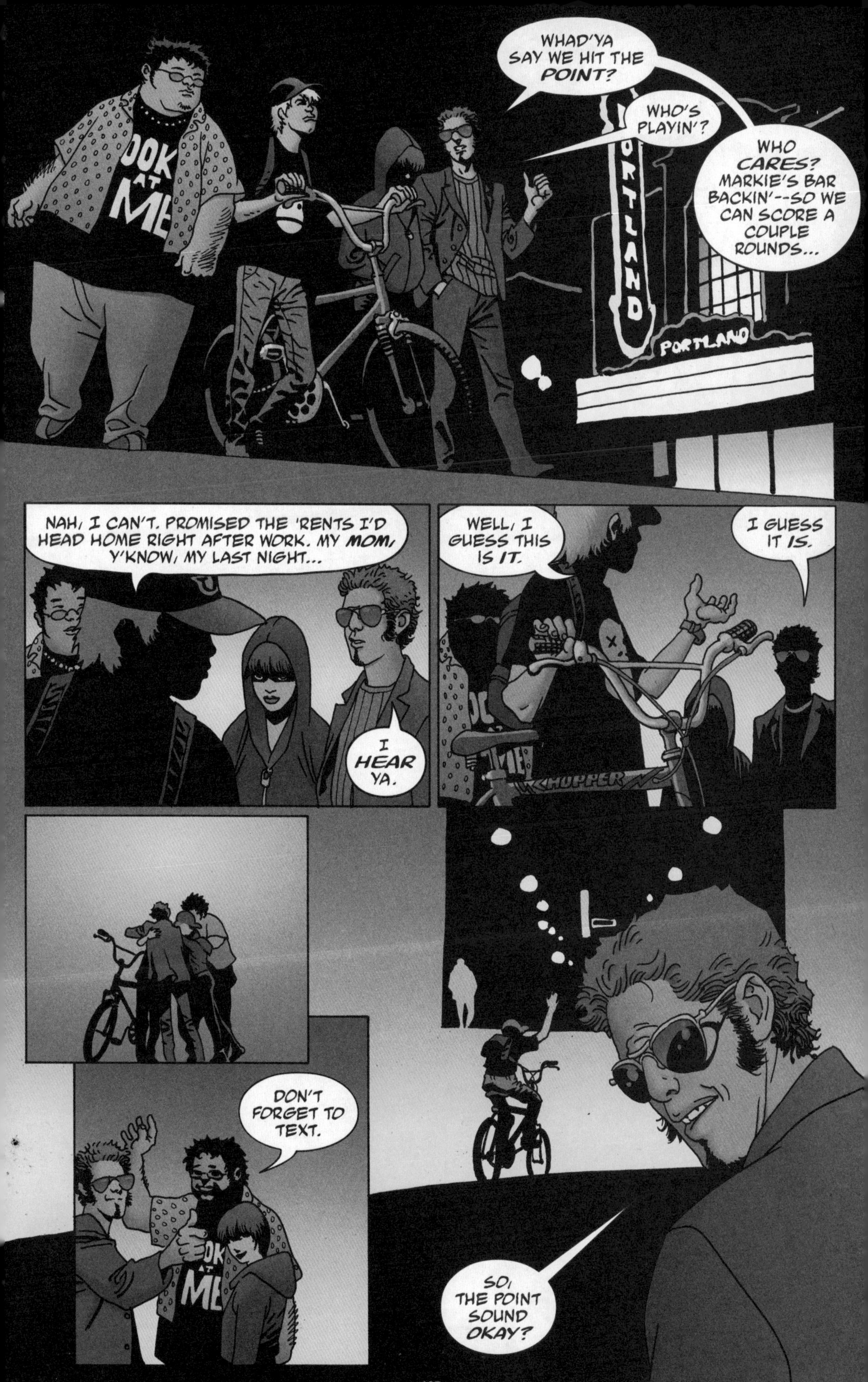
WHAD'YA SAY WE HIT THE POINT?
WHO'S PLAYIN'?
WHO CARES? MARKIE'S BAR BACKIN'--SO WE CAN SCORE A COUPLE ROUNDS...
PORTLAND
PORTLAND
NAH, I CAN'T. PROMISED THE 'RENTS I'D HEAD HOME RIGHT AFTER WORK. MY MOM, Y'KNOW, MY LAST NIGHT...
I HEAR YA.
WELL, I GUESS THIS IS IT.
I GUESS IT IS.
CHOPPER
DON'T FORGET TO TEXT.
SO, THE POINT SOUND OKAY?

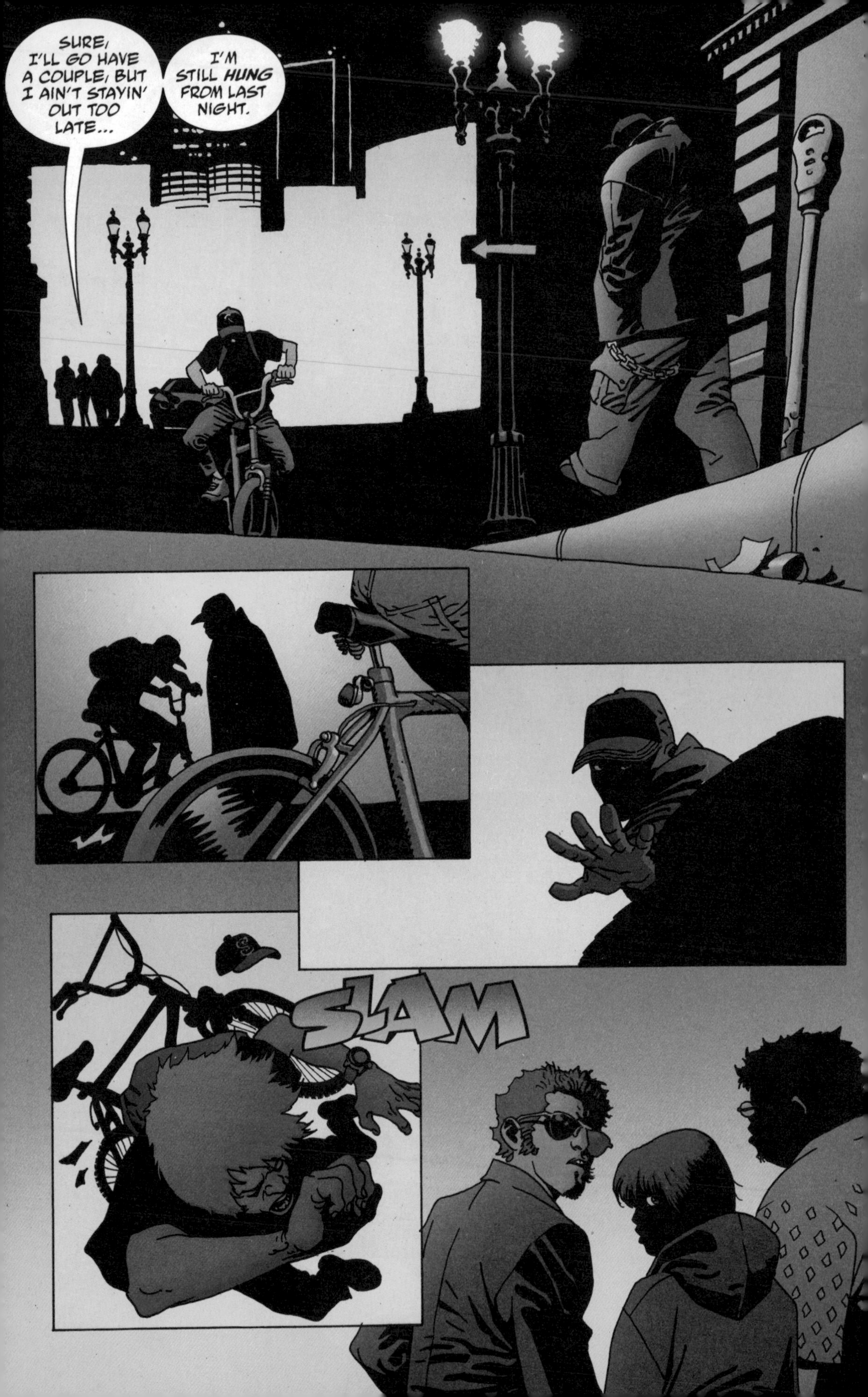
SURE, I'LL GO HAVE A COUPLE, BUT I AIN'T STAYIN' OUT TOO LATE...
I'M STILL HUNG FROM LAST NIGHT.
SLAM

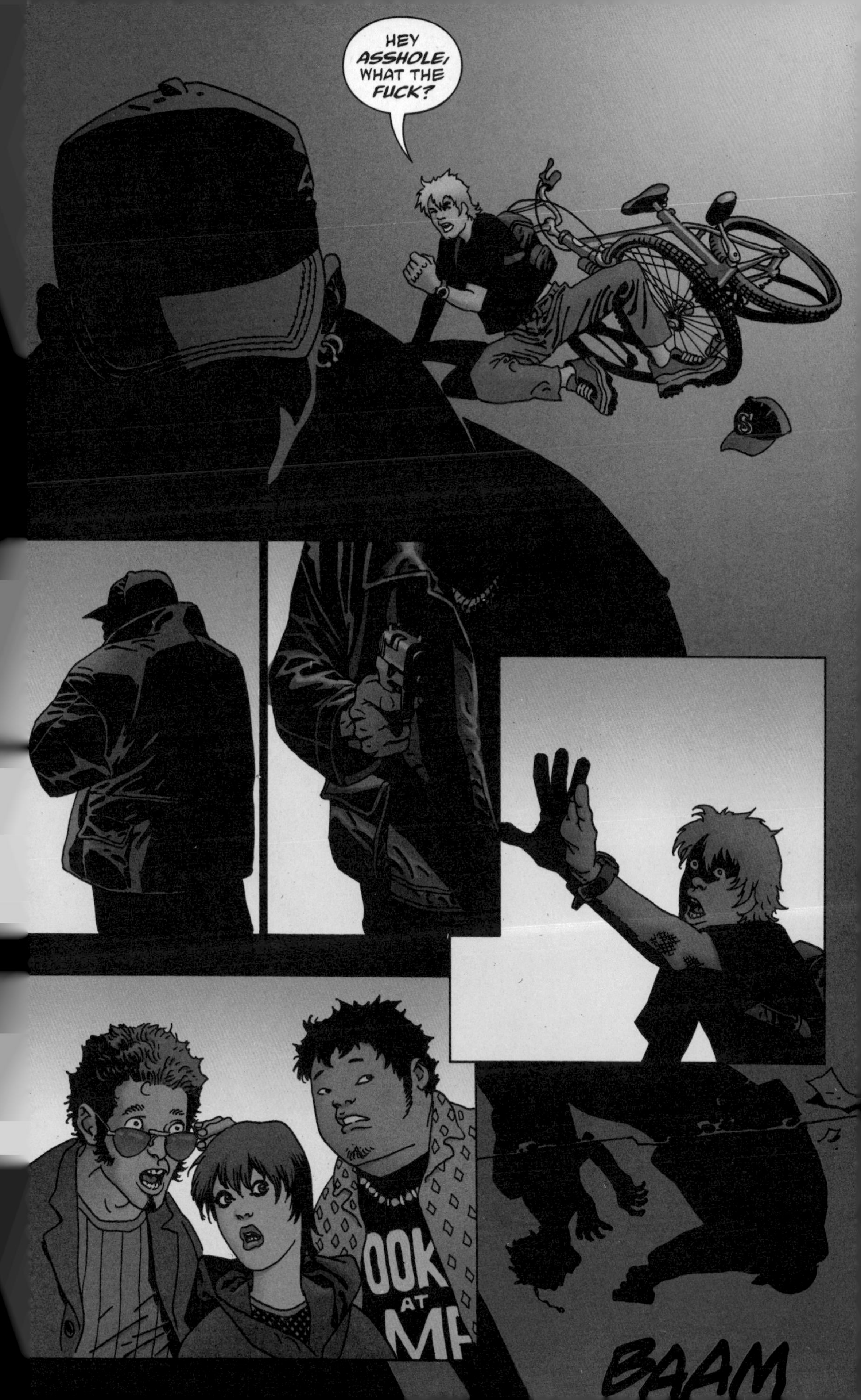
HEY ASSHOLE, WHAT THE FUCK?
OOK AT ME
BAAM

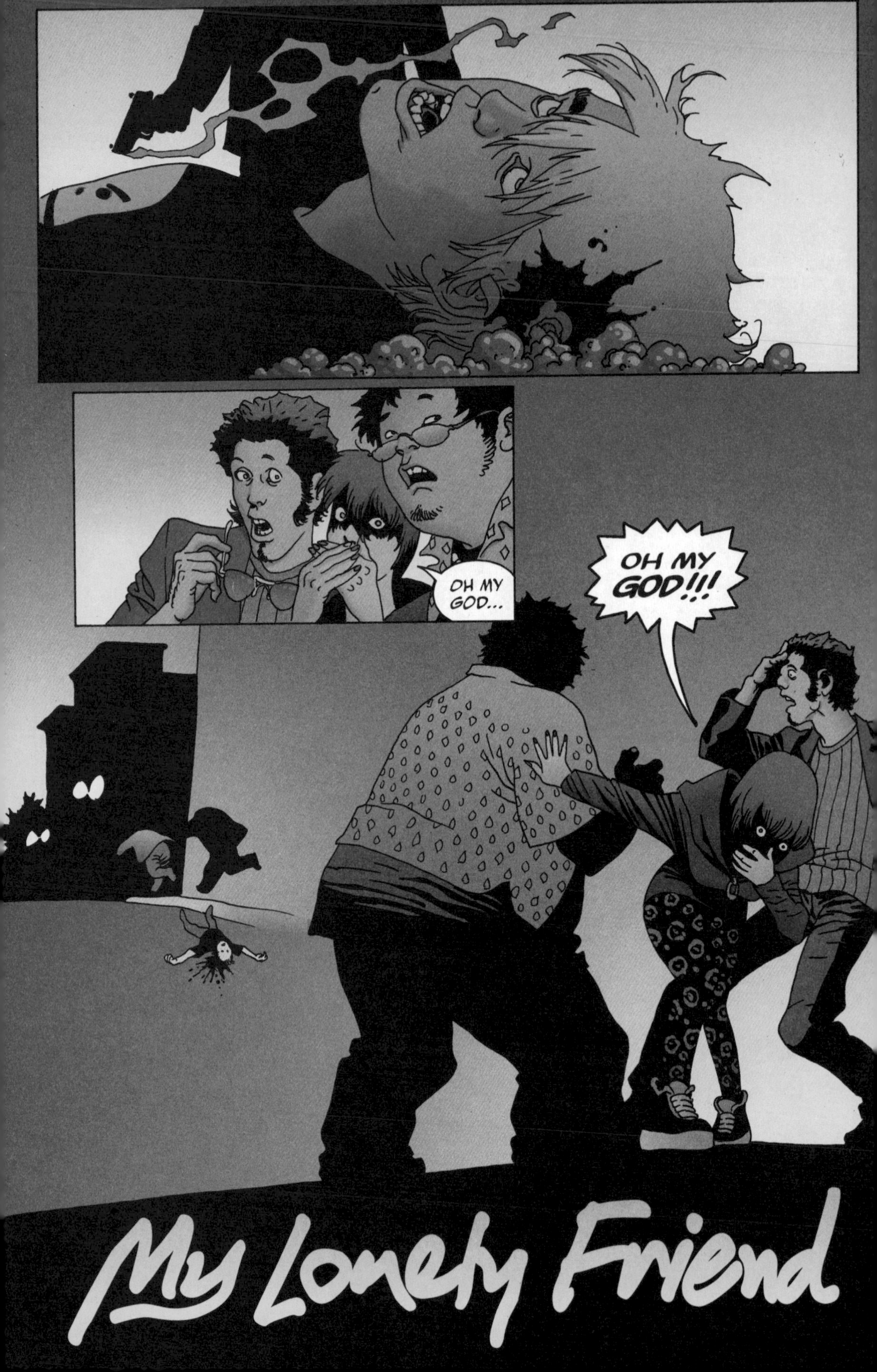
OH MY GOD...
OH MY GOD!!!
My Lonely Friend

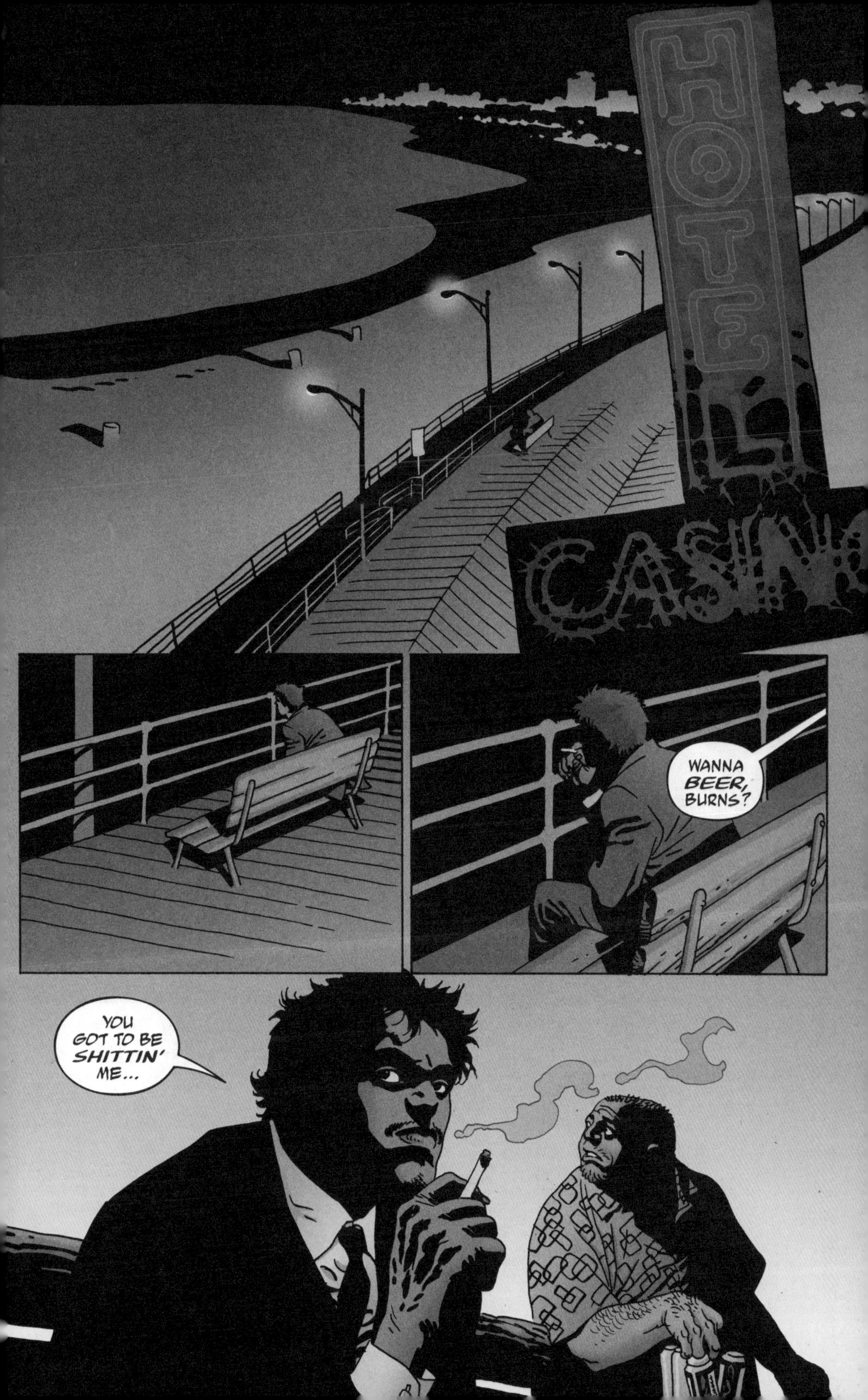
HOTEL
CASINO
WANNA BEER, BURNS?
YOU GOT TO BE SHITTIN' ME...

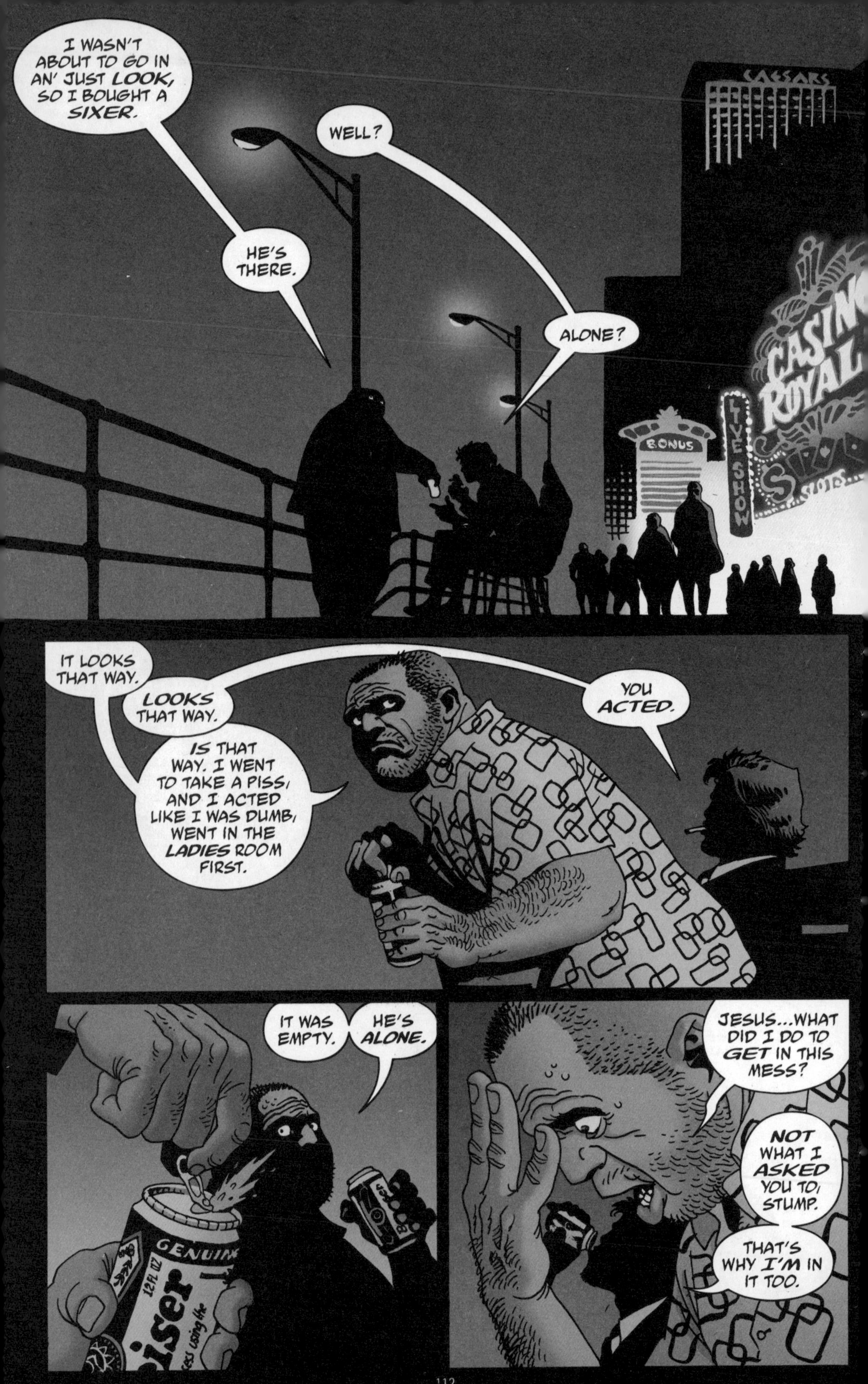
I WASN'T ABOUT TO GO IN AN' JUST LOOK, SO I BOUGHT A SIXER.
WELL?
HE'S THERE.
ALONE?
CAESARS
CASINO ROYAL
LIVE SHOW
BONUS
IT LOOKS THAT WAY.
LOOKS THAT WAY.
YOU ACTED.
IS THAT WAY. I WENT TO TAKE A PISS, AND I ACTED LIKE I WAS DUMB, WENT IN THE LADIES ROOM FIRST.
IT WAS EMPTY.
HE'S ALONE.
GENUINE
12 FL OZ
JESUS...WHAT DID I DO TO GET IN THIS MESS?
NOT WHAT I ASKED YOU TO, STUMP.
THAT'S WHY I'M IN IT TOO.

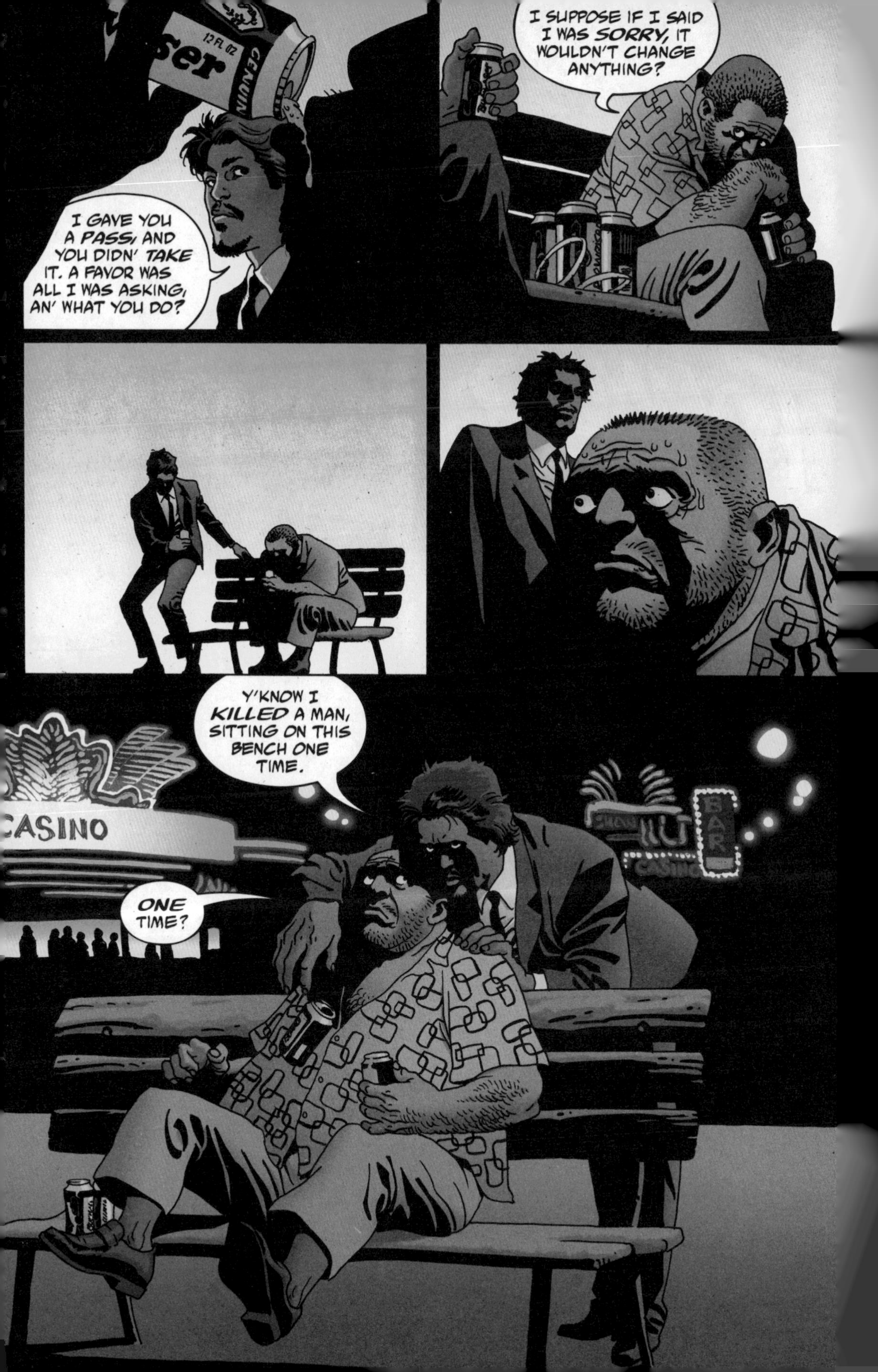
12 FL OZ
GENUINE
I GAVE YOU A *PASS*, AND YOU DIDN' *TAKE* IT. A FAVOR WAS ALL I WAS ASKING, AN' WHAT YOU DO?
I SUPPOSE IF I SAID I WAS *SORRY*, IT WOULDN'T CHANGE ANYTHING?
Y'KNOW I *KILLED* A MAN, SITTING ON THIS BENCH ONE TIME.
CASINO
BAR
ONE TIME?

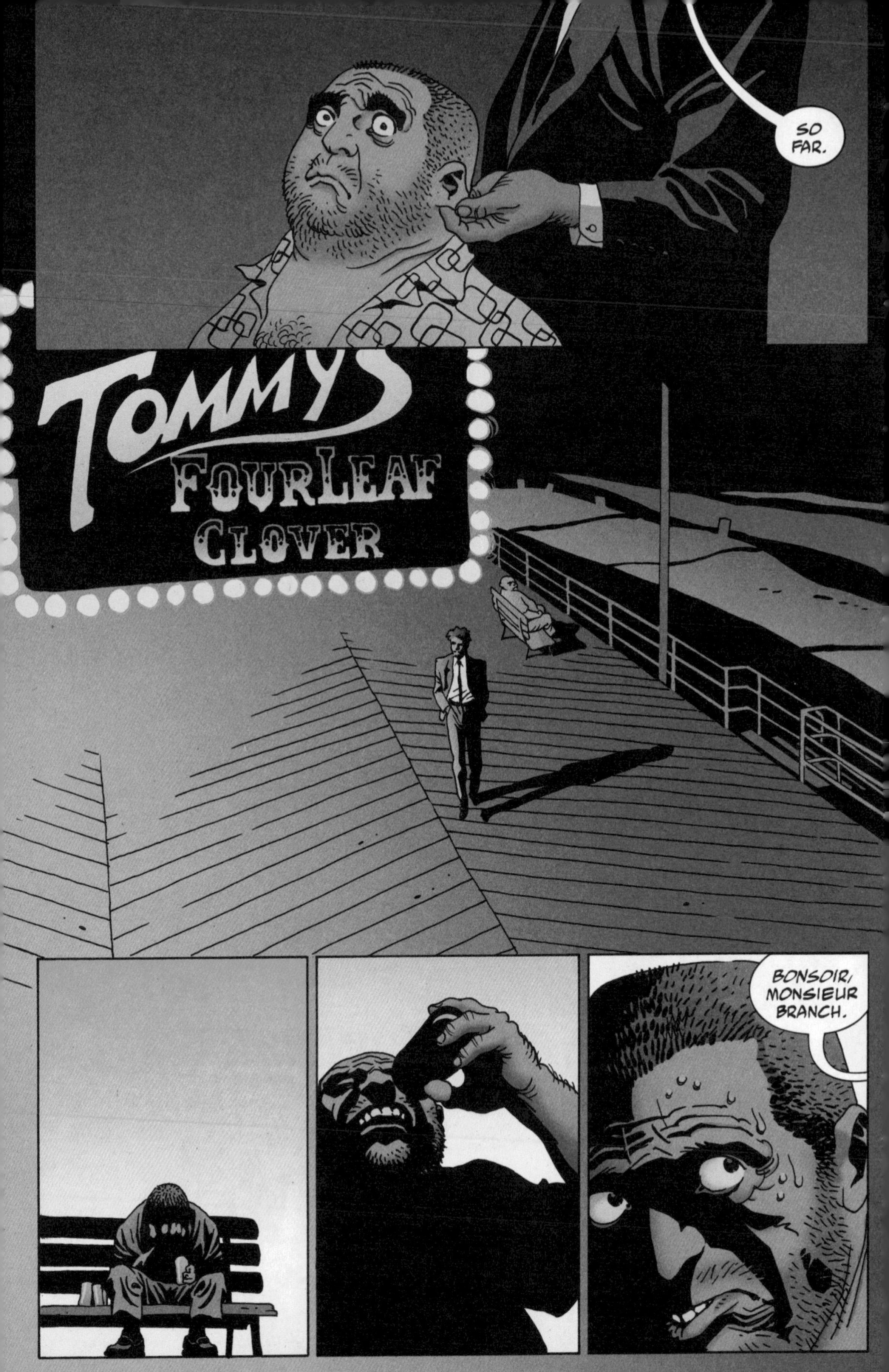
SO FAR.
TOMMYS
FOUR LEAF CLOVER
BONSOIR, MONSIEUR BRANCH.

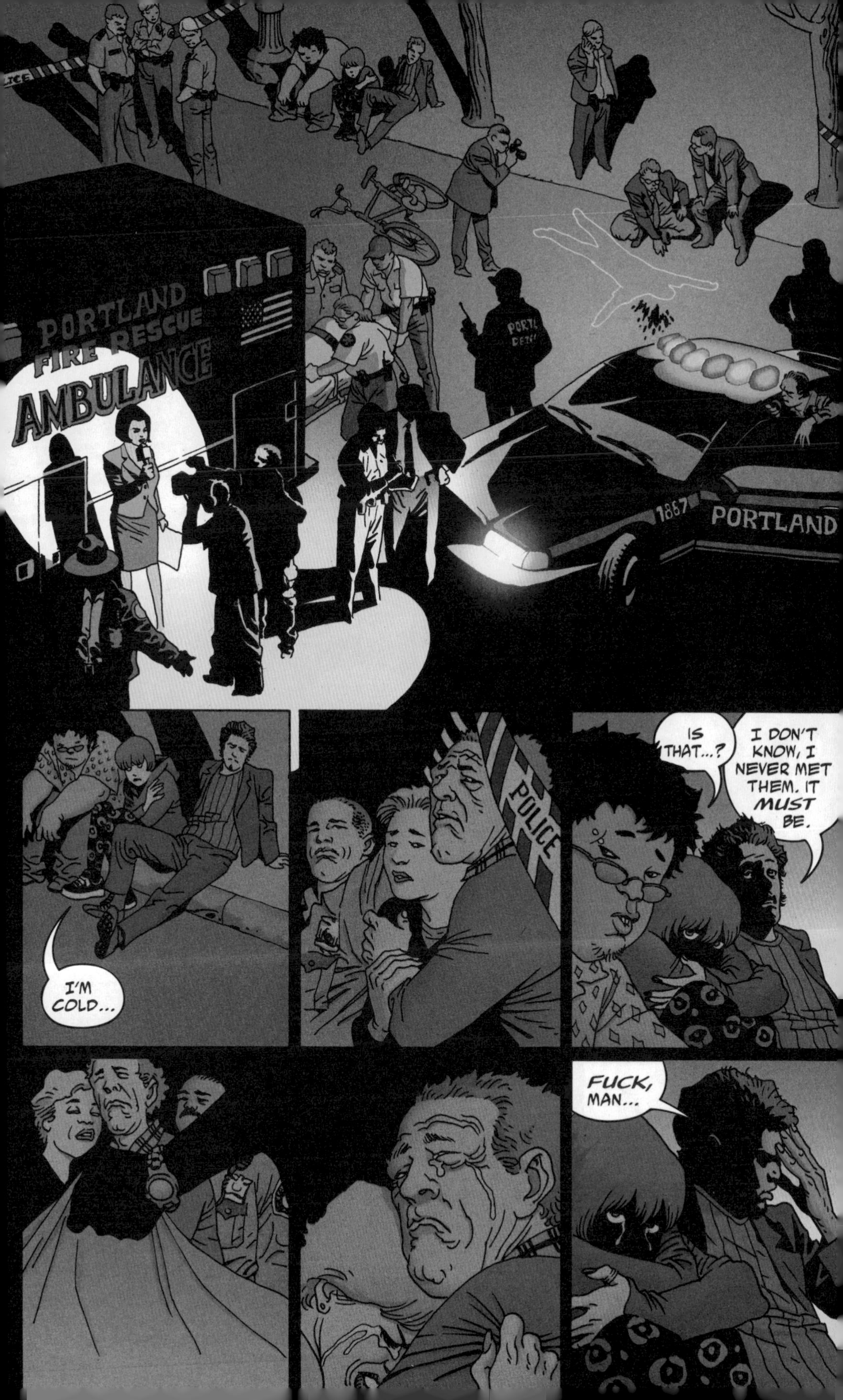
POLICE
PORTLAND FIRE RESCUE
AMBULANCE
PORTL DETEC
1887
PORTLAND
I'M COLD...
POLICE
IS THAT...?
I DON'T KNOW, I NEVER MET THEM. IT MUST BE.
FUCK, MAN...

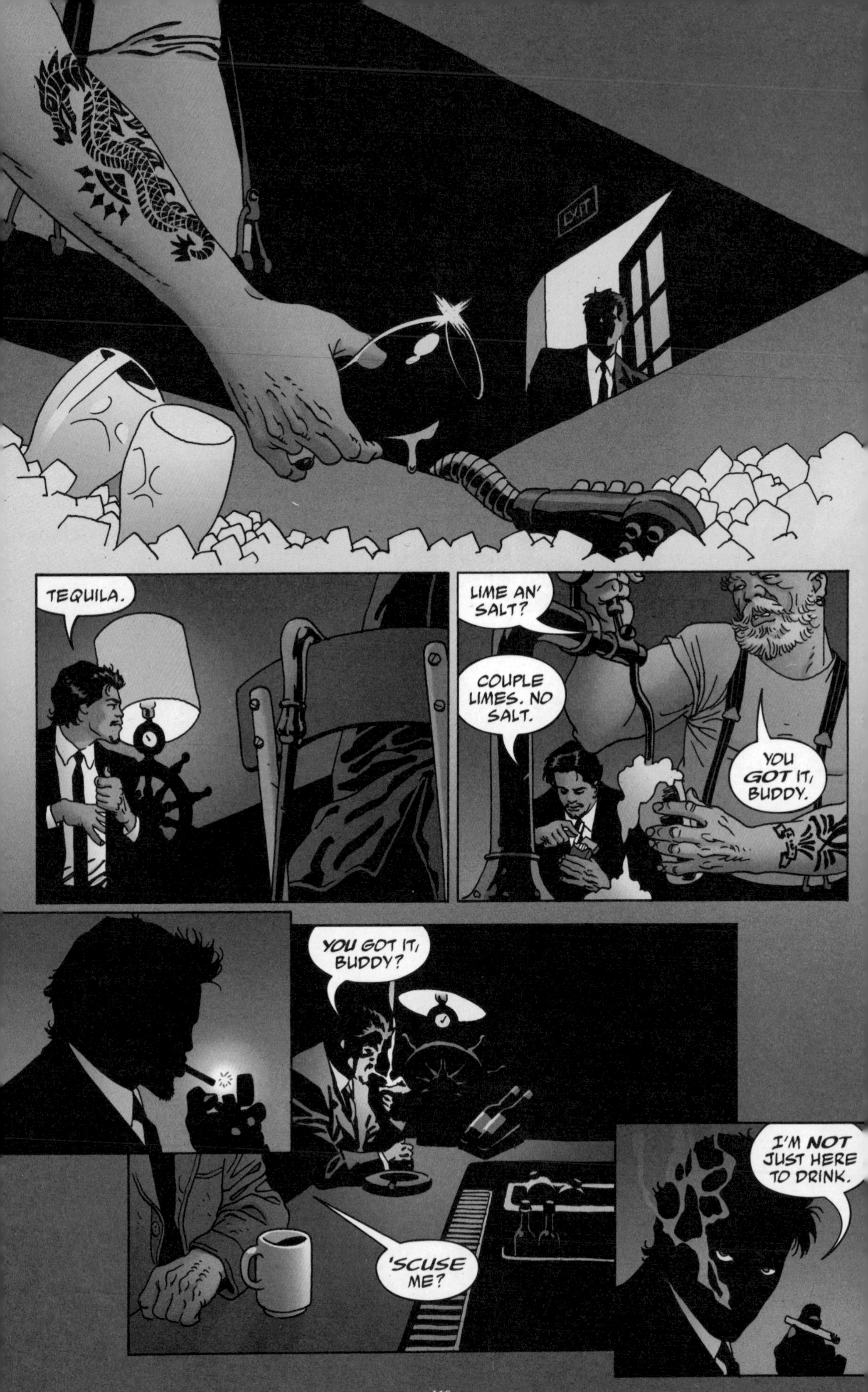
TEQUILA.
LIME AN' SALT?
COUPLE LIMES. NO SALT.
YOU GOT IT, BUDDY.
YOU GOT IT, BUDDY?
'SCUSE ME?
I'M NOT JUST HERE TO DRINK.

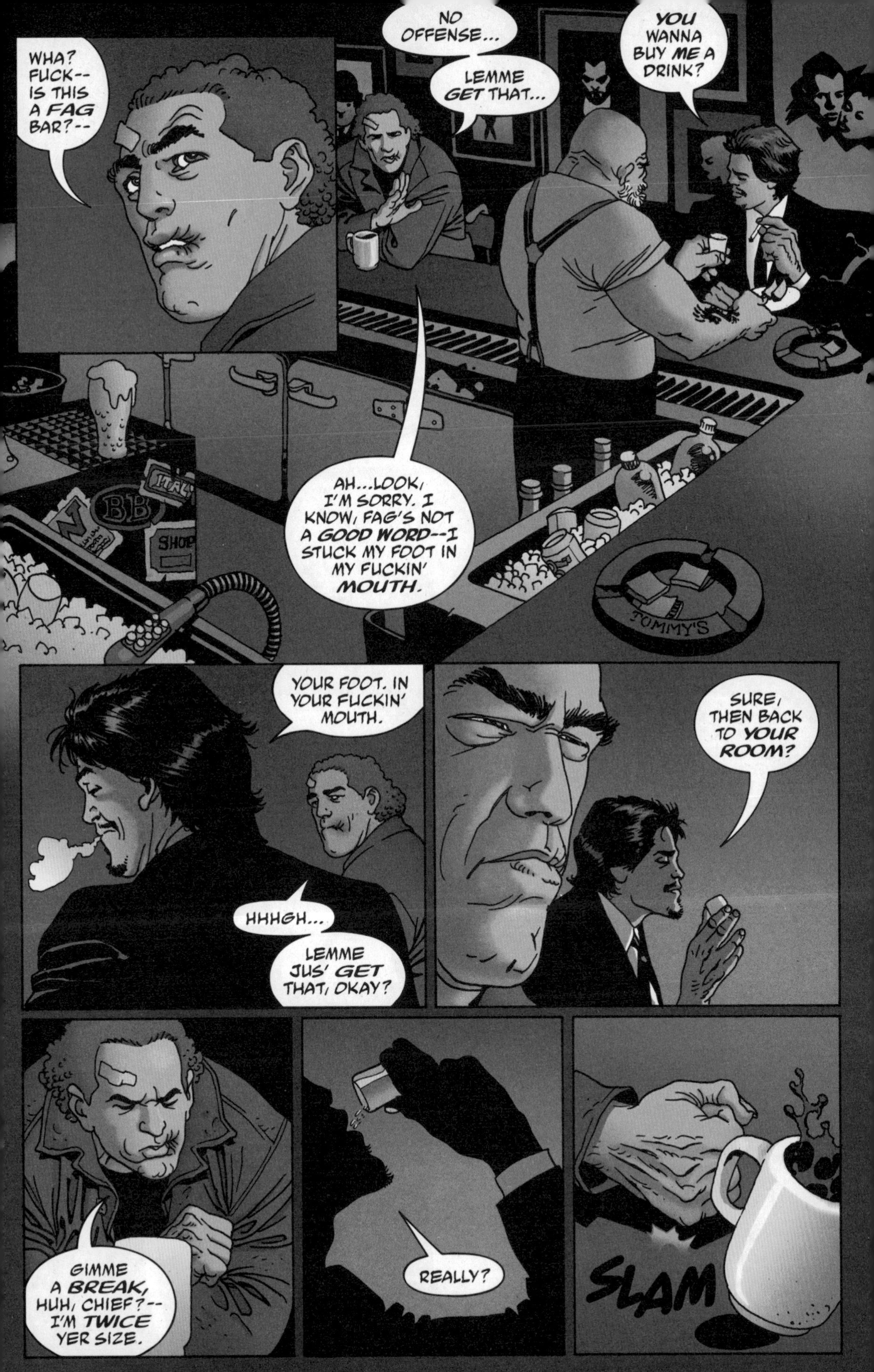
WHA? FUCK-- IS THIS A FAG BAR?--
NO OFFENSE...
LEMME GET THAT...
YOU WANNA BUY ME A DRINK?
AH...LOOK, I'M SORRY. I KNOW, FAG'S NOT A GOOD WORD--I STUCK MY FOOT IN MY FUCKIN' MOUTH.
TOMMY'S
YOUR FOOT. IN YOUR FUCKIN' MOUTH.
HHHGH...
LEMME JUS' GET THAT, OKAY?
SURE, THEN BACK TO YOUR ROOM?
GIMME A BREAK, HUH, CHIEF?-- I'M TWICE YER SIZE.
REALLY?
SLAM

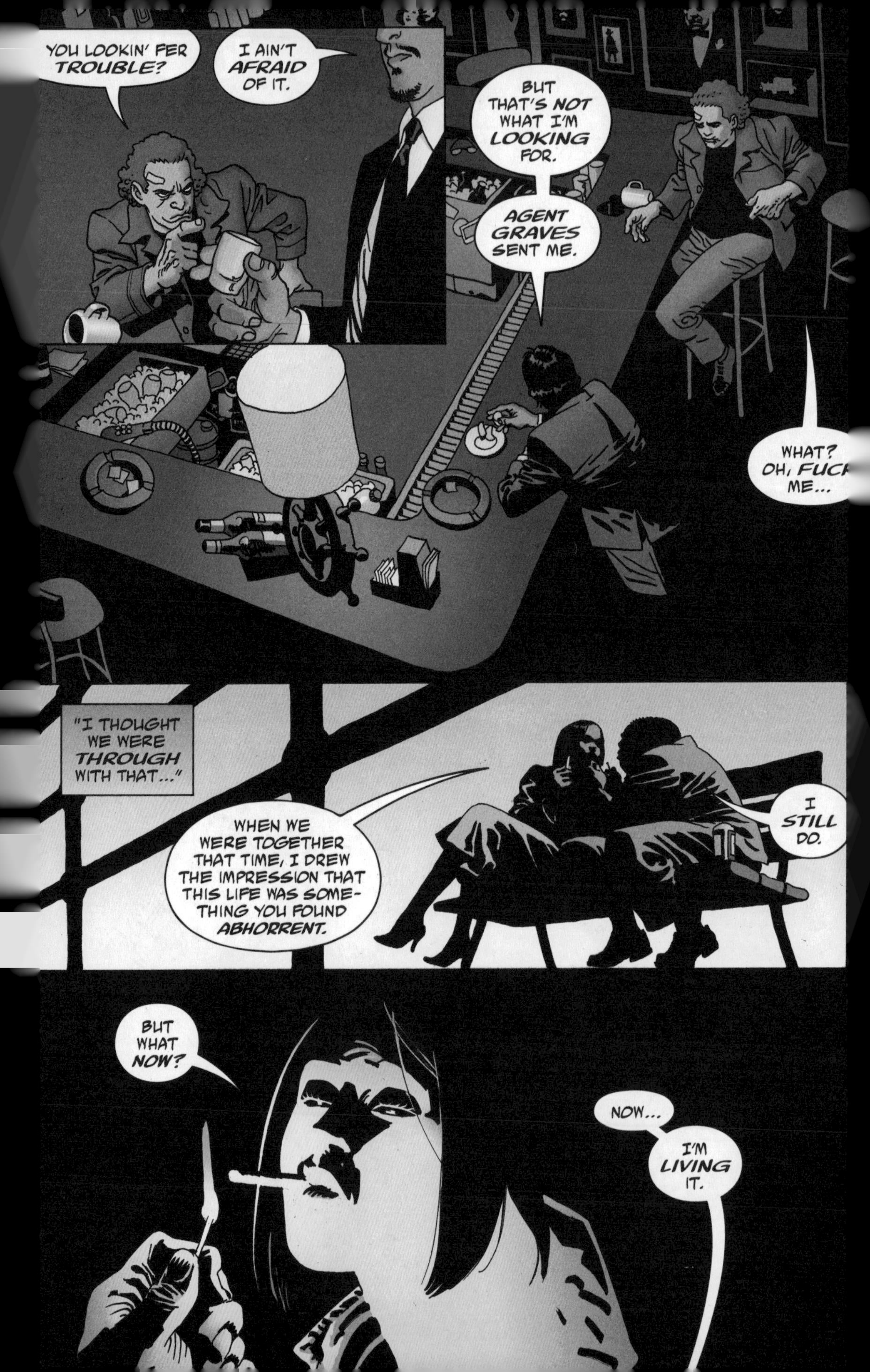
YOU LOOKIN' FER TROUBLE?
I AIN'T AFRAID OF IT.
BUT THAT'S NOT WHAT I'M LOOKING FOR.
AGENT GRAVES SENT ME.
WHAT? OH, FUCK ME...
"I THOUGHT WE WERE THROUGH WITH THAT..."
WHEN WE WERE TOGETHER THAT TIME, I DREW THE IMPRESSION THAT THIS LIFE WAS SOMETHING YOU FOUND ABHORRENT.
I STILL DO.
BUT WHAT NOW?
NOW...
I'M LIVING IT.

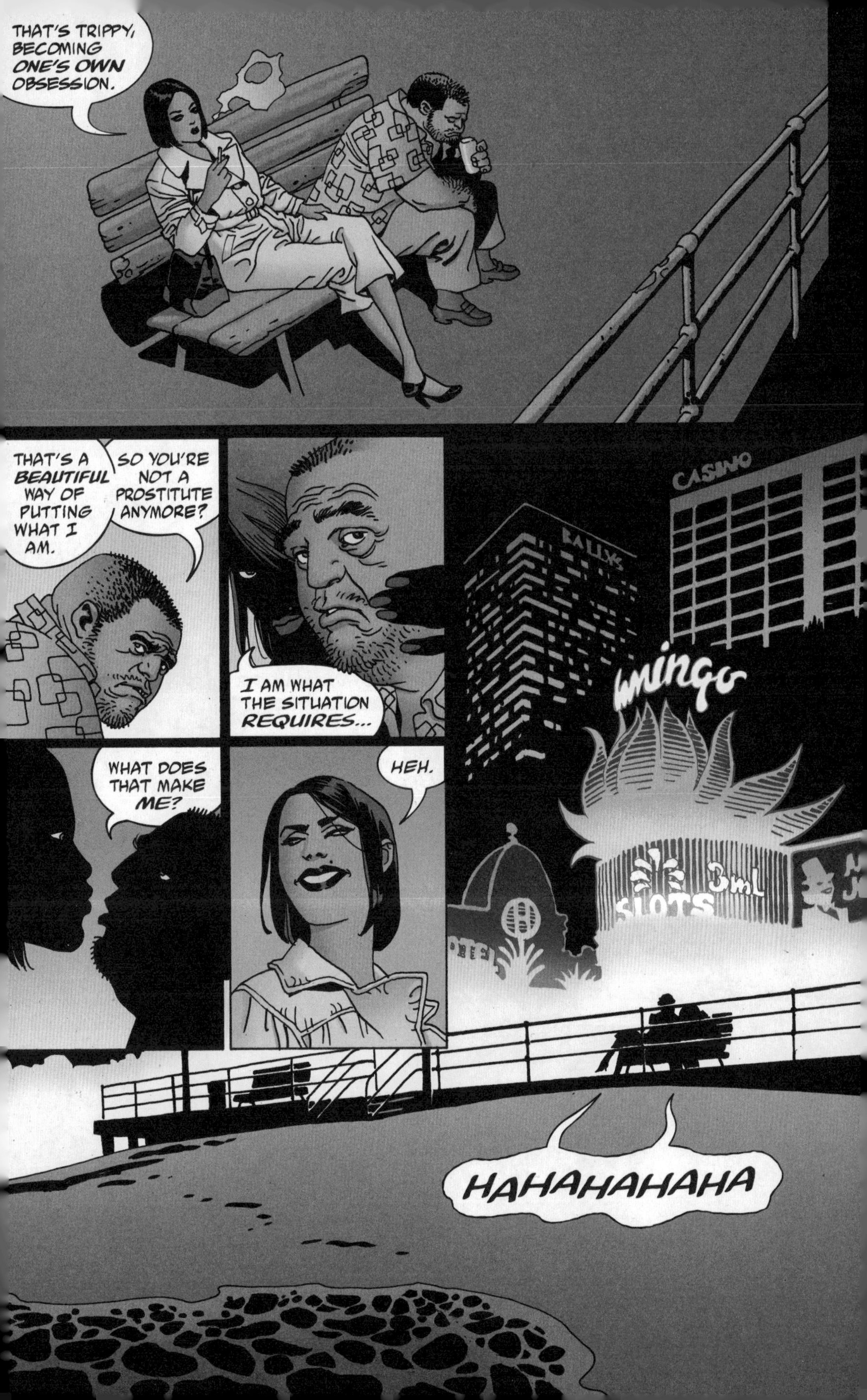
THAT'S TRIPPY, BECOMING ONE'S OWN OBSESSION.
THAT'S A BEAUTIFUL WAY OF PUTTING WHAT I AM.
SO YOU'RE NOT A PROSTITUTE ANYMORE?
I AM WHAT THE SITUATION REQUIRES...
WHAT DOES THAT MAKE ME?
HEH.
CASINO
BALLY'S
SLOTS
HAHAHAHAHA

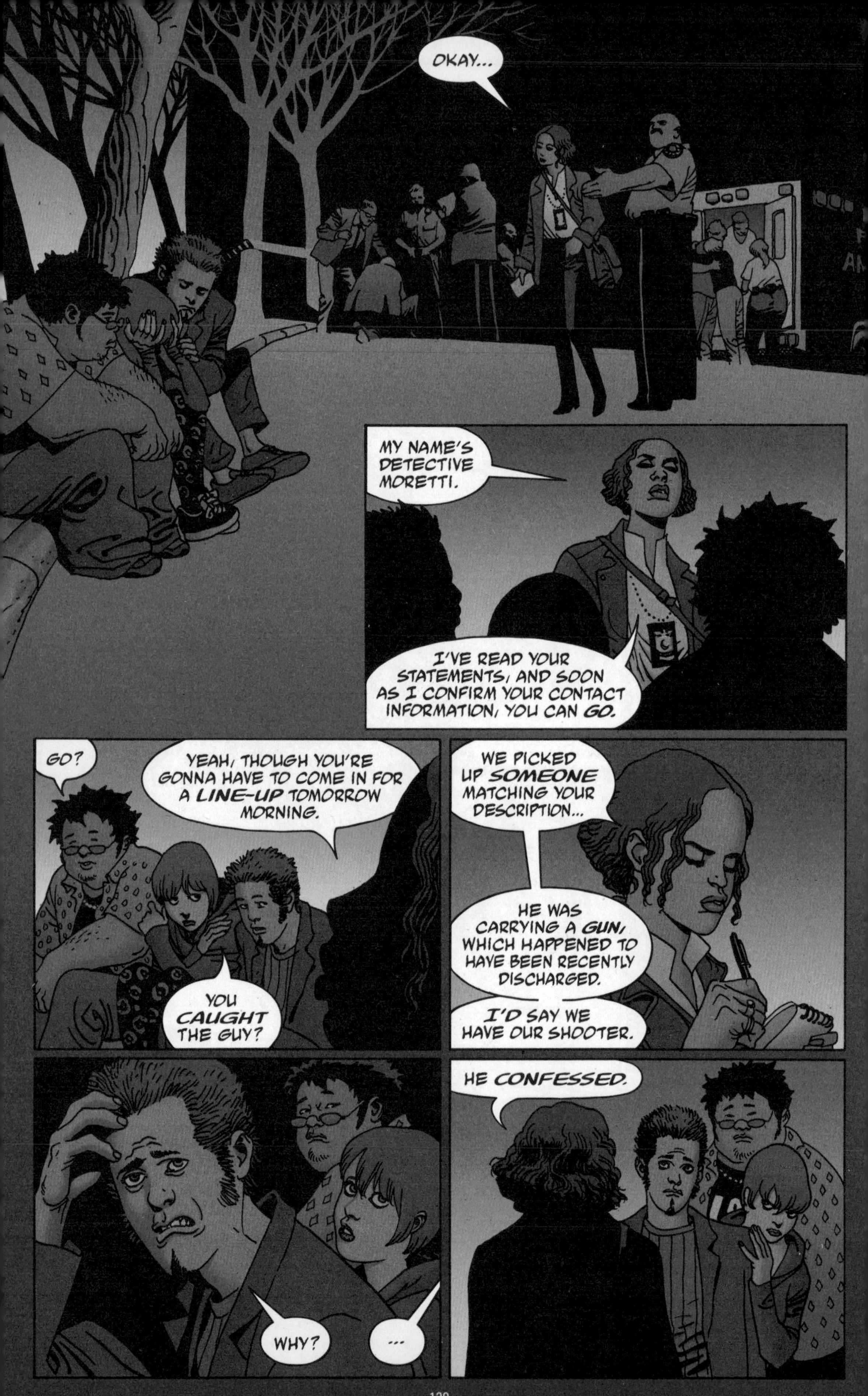
OKAY...
MY NAME'S DETECTIVE MORETTI.
I'VE READ YOUR STATEMENTS, AND SOON AS I CONFIRM YOUR CONTACT INFORMATION, YOU CAN GO.
GO?
YEAH, THOUGH YOU'RE GONNA HAVE TO COME IN FOR A LINE-UP TOMORROW MORNING.
YOU CAUGHT THE GUY?
WE PICKED UP SOMEONE MATCHING YOUR DESCRIPTION...
HE WAS CARRYING A GUN, WHICH HAPPENED TO HAVE BEEN RECENTLY DISCHARGED.
I'D SAY WE HAVE OUR SHOOTER.
WHY?
...
HE CONFESSED.

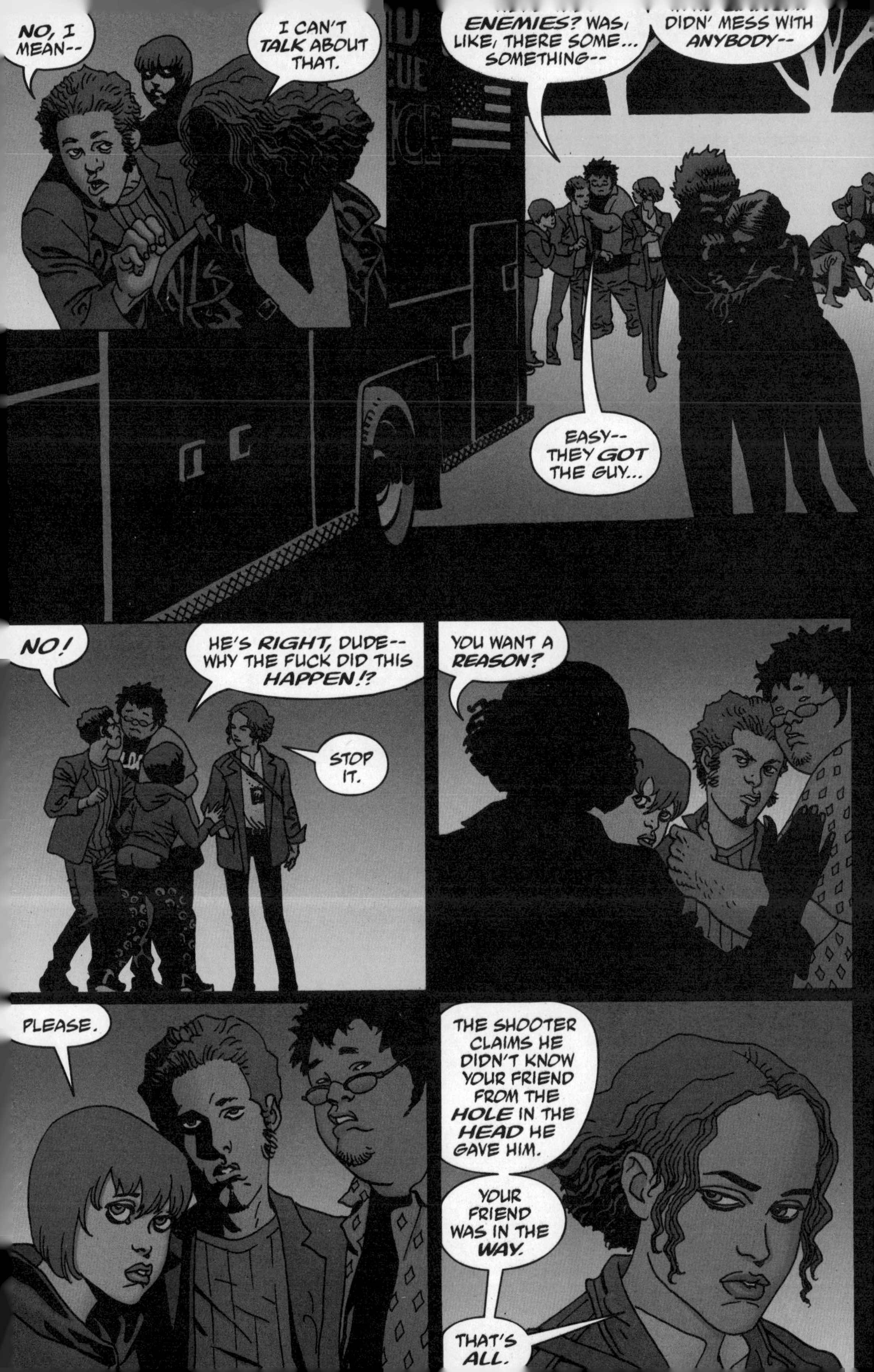
NO, I MEAN--
I CAN'T TALK ABOUT THAT.
ENEMIES? WAS, LIKE, THERE SOME... SOMETHING--
DIDN' MESS WITH ANYBODY--
EASY-- THEY GOT THE GUY...
NO!
HE'S RIGHT, DUDE-- WHY THE FUCK DID THIS HAPPEN!?
STOP IT.
YOU WANT A REASON?
PLEASE.
THE SHOOTER CLAIMS HE DIDN'T KNOW YOUR FRIEND FROM THE HOLE IN THE HEAD HE GAVE HIM.
YOUR FRIEND WAS IN THE WAY.
THAT'S ALL.

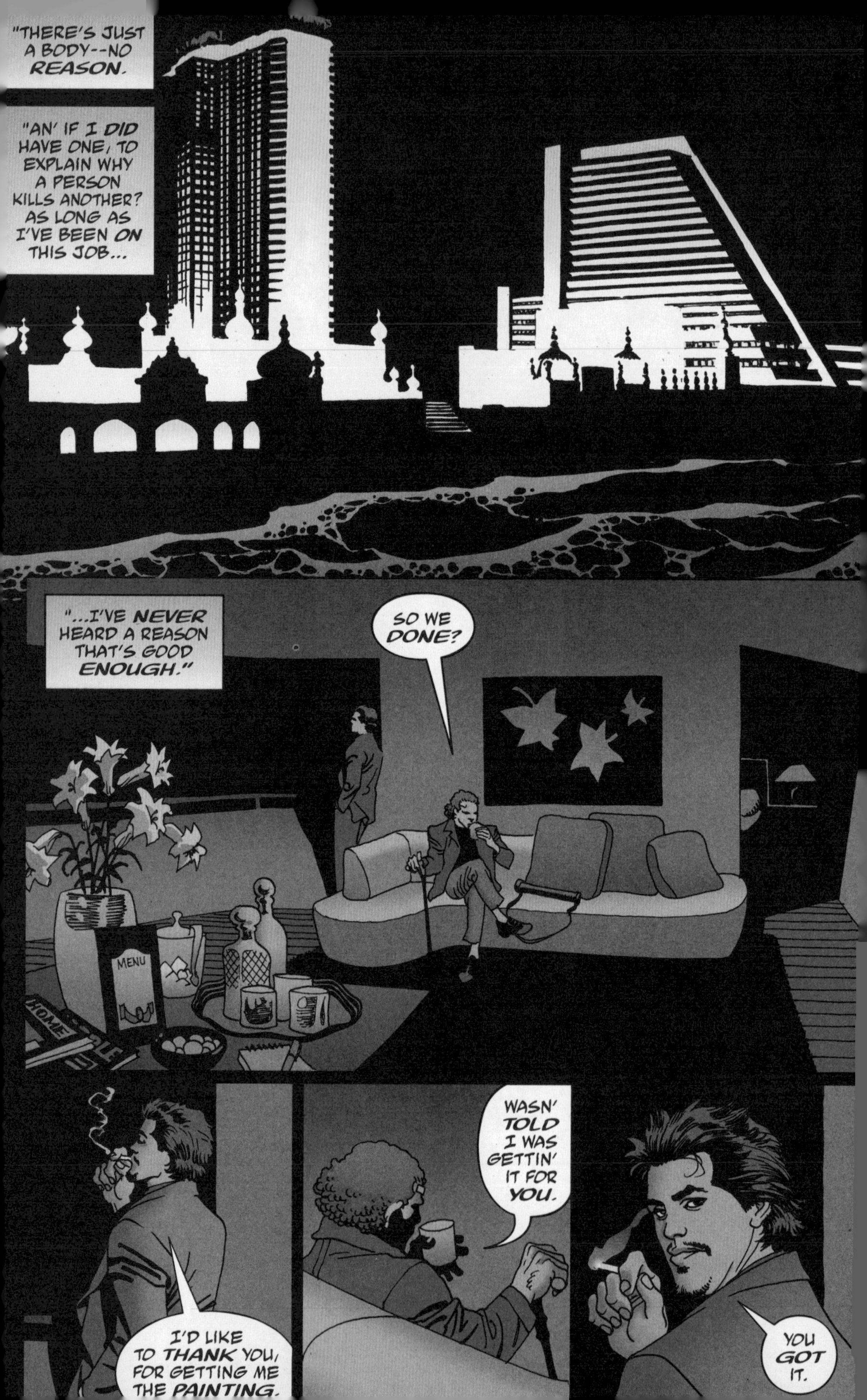
"THERE'S JUST A BODY--NO REASON.
"AN' IF I DID HAVE ONE, TO EXPLAIN WHY A PERSON KILLS ANOTHER? AS LONG AS I'VE BEEN ON THIS JOB...
"...I'VE NEVER HEARD A REASON THAT'S GOOD ENOUGH."
SO WE DONE?
MENU
HOME
I'D LIKE TO THANK YOU, FOR GETTING ME THE PAINTING.
WASN' TOLD I WAS GETTIN' IT FOR YOU.
YOU GOT IT.

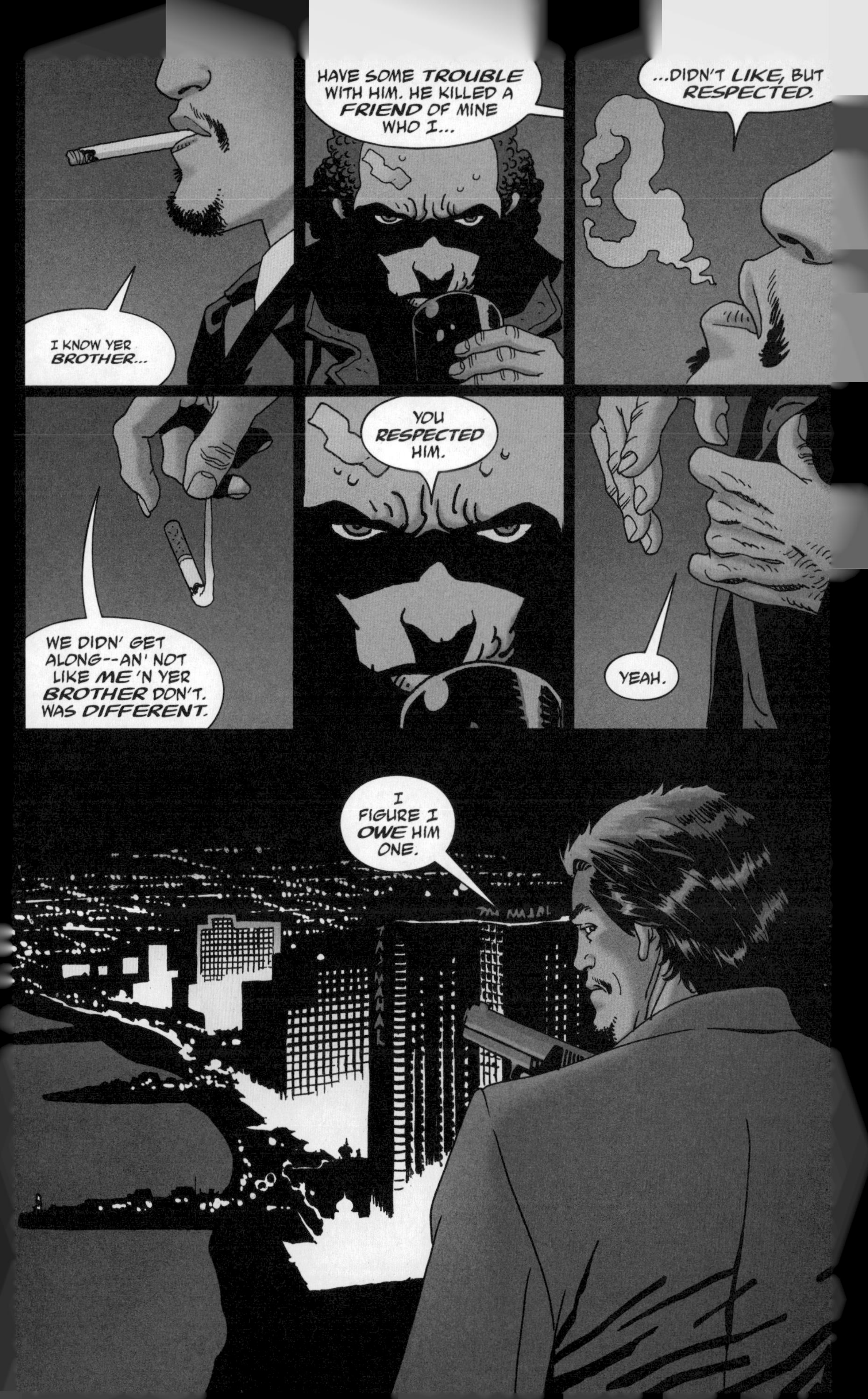
I KNOW YER BROTHER...
HAVE SOME TROUBLE WITH HIM. HE KILLED A FRIEND OF MINE WHO I...
...DIDN'T LIKE, BUT RESPECTED.
WE DIDN' GET ALONG--AN' NOT LIKE ME 'N YER BROTHER DON'T. WAS DIFFERENT.
YOU RESPECTED HIM.
YEAH.
I FIGURE I OWE HIM ONE.
TAJ MAHAL

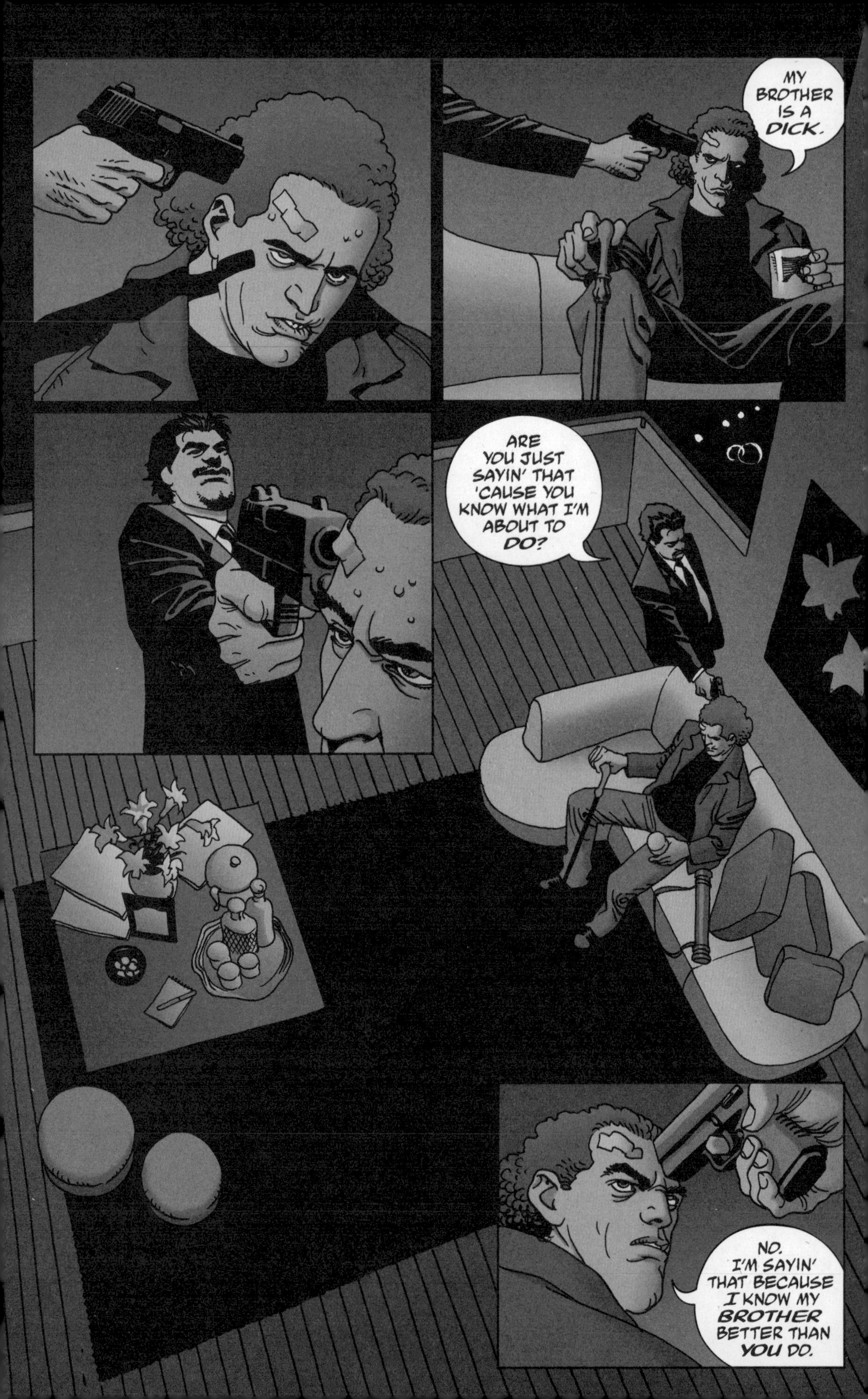
MY BROTHER IS A DICK.
ARE YOU JUST SAYIN' THAT 'CAUSE YOU KNOW WHAT I'M ABOUT TO DO?
NO. I'M SAYIN' THAT BECAUSE I KNOW MY BROTHER BETTER THAN YOU DO.

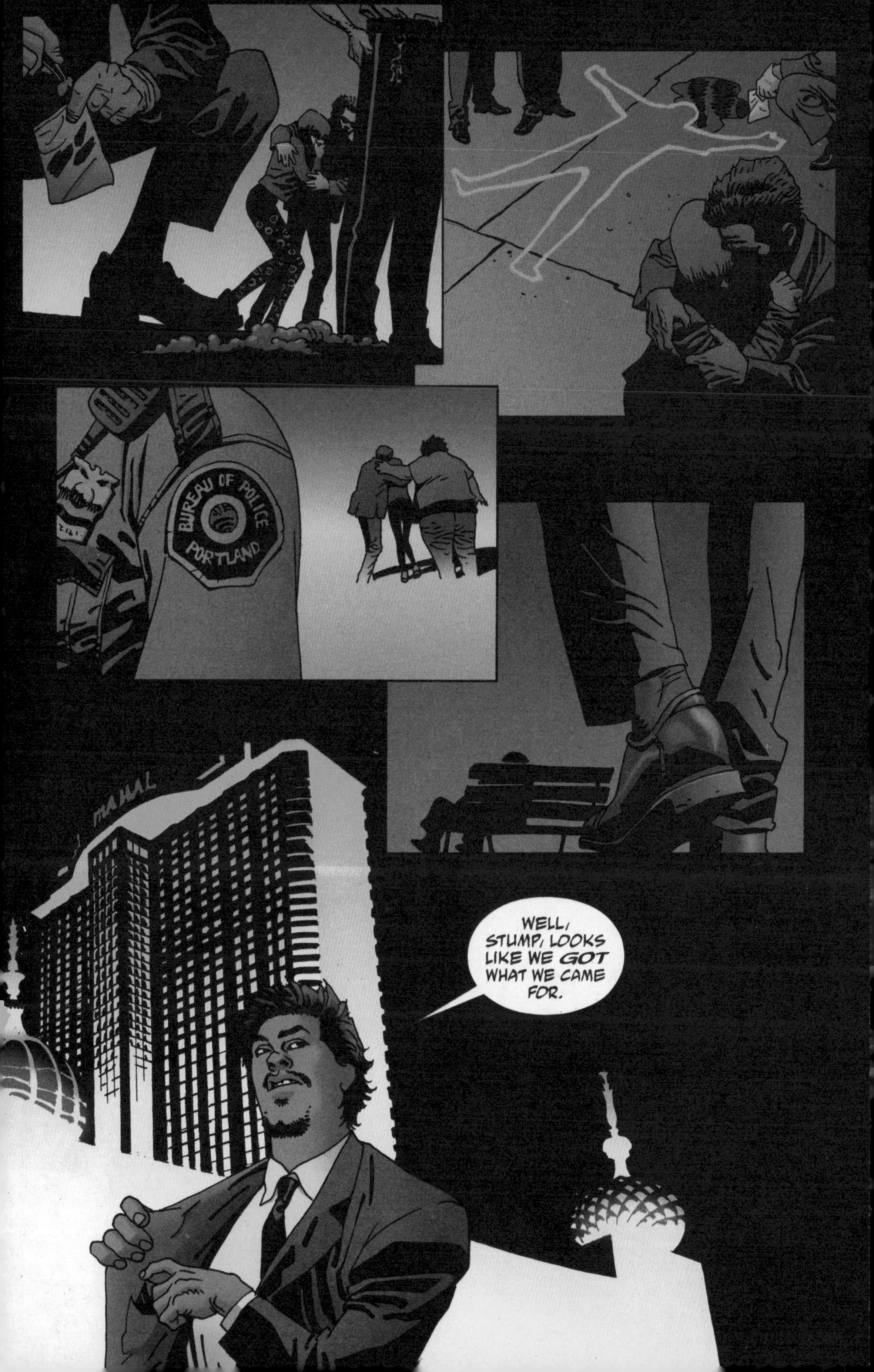
BUREAU OF POLICE
PORTLAND
MAHAL
WELL, STUMP, LOOKS LIKE WE *GOT* WHAT WE CAME FOR.

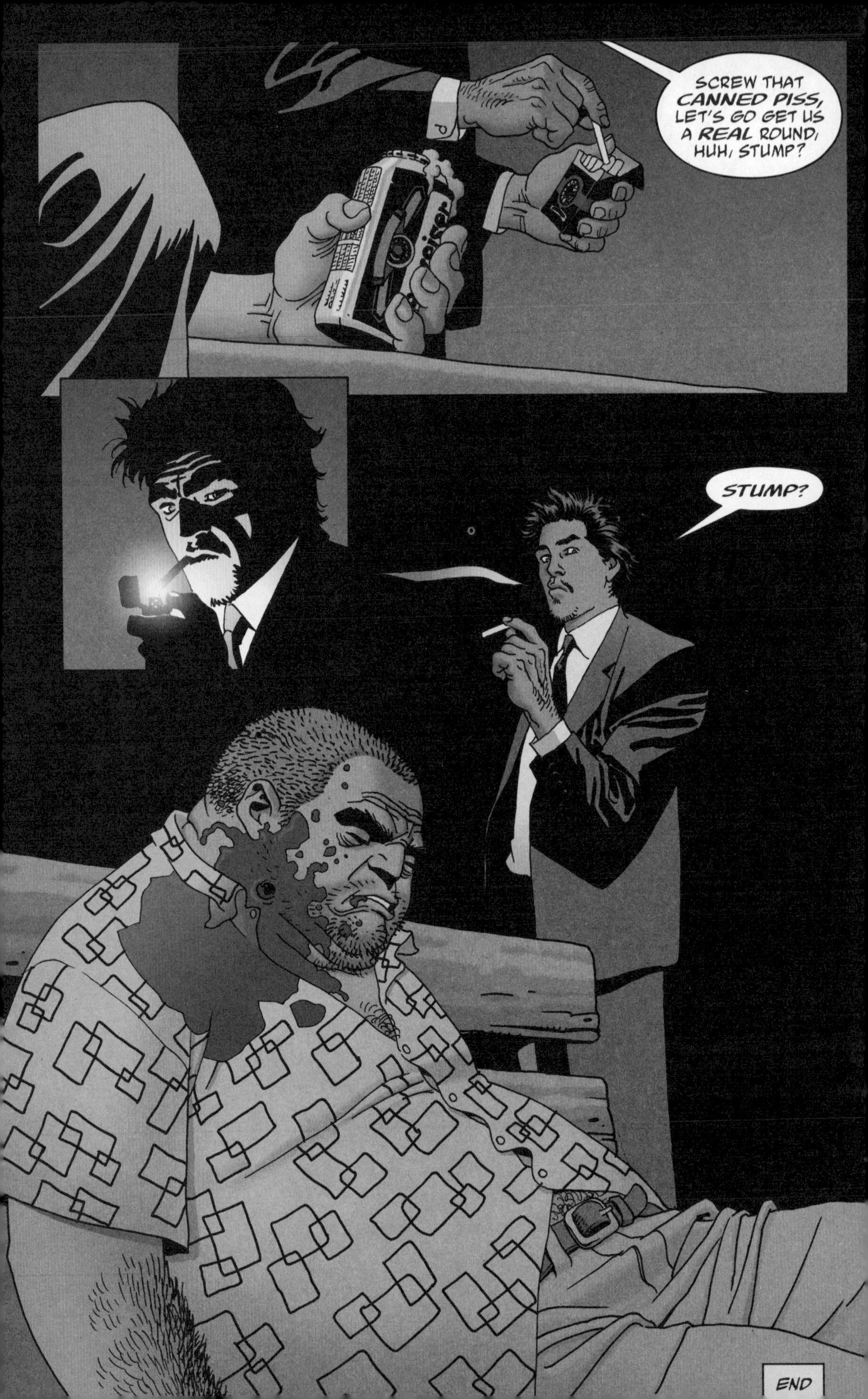

SCREW THAT CANNED PISS, LET'S GO GET US A REAL ROUND, HUH, STUMP?
STUMP?
END

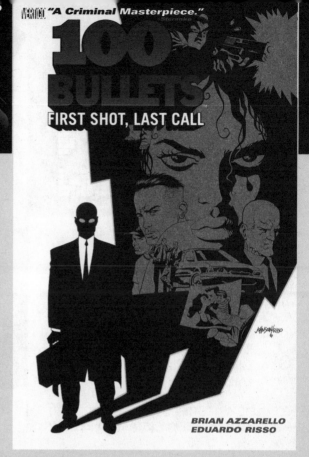

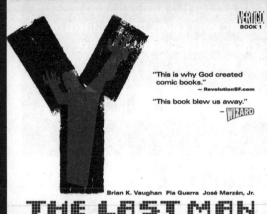

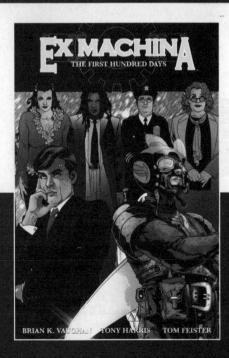

R.C.L.
JUIN 2011
A